The Aftermath

1975-85

The Vietnam Experience

The Aftermath

1975-85

by Edward Doyle, Terrence Maitland,
and the editors of Boston Publishing Company

Boston Publishing Company/Boston, MA

Boston Publishing Company

President and Publisher: Robert J. George
Vice President: Richard S. Perkins, Jr.
Editor-in-Chief: Robert Manning
Managing Editor: Paul Dreyfus
Marketing Director: Jeanne Gibson

Senior Writers:
Clark Dougan, Edward Doyle, David Ful-
ghum, Samuel Lipsman, Terrence Maitland,
Stephen Weiss
Senior Picture Editor: Julene Fischer
Staff Editor: Gordon Hardy

Researchers:
Jonathan Elwitt, Sandra W. Jacobs, Michael
Ludwig, Anthony Maybury-Lewis, Carole
Rulnick, Nicole van Ackere, Robert Yar-
brough

Picture Editors:
Wendy Johnson, Lanng Tamura
Assistant Picture Editor: Kathleen A. Reidy
Picture Researchers:
Nancy Katz Colman, Robert Ebbs, Tracey
Rogers, Nana Elisabeth Stern, Shirley L.
Green (Washington, D.C.), Kate Lewin
(Paris)
Archivist: Kathryn J. Steeves
Picture Department Assistant: Karen Bjelke

Historical Consultants:
Alan Brinkley, David P. Chandler, Lee Ewing
Picture Consultant: Ngo Vinh Long

Production Editor: Kerstin Gorham
Assistant Production Editor: Patricia Leal
Welch
Assistant Editor: Denis Kennedy
Editorial Production: Sarah Burns, Dalia Lip-
kin, Theresa M. Slomkowski

Design: Designworks, Sally Bindari
Design Assistant: Sherry Fatla

Business Staff: Amy Pelletier, Amy P. Wilson

About the editors and authors

Editor-in-Chief *Robert Manning*, a long-time
journalist, has previously been editor-in-chief
of the *Atlantic Monthly* magazine and its press.
He served as assistant secretary of state for
public affairs under Presidents John F. Kennedy and Lyndon B. Johnson. He has also
been a fellow at the Institute of Politics at the
John F. Kennedy School of Government at
Harvard University.

Authors: *Edward Doyle*, a historian, received
his masters degree at the University of Notre
Dame and his Ph.D. at Harvard University.
Terrence Maitland has written for several
publications, including *Newsweek* magazine
and the *Boston Globe*. He is a graduate of
Holy Cross College and has an M.S. from
Boston University. Messrs. Doyle and Mait-
land have coauthored other volumes in *The
Vietnam Experience*.

Historical Consultants: *Alan Brinkley* is Dun-
walke Associate Professor of History at Harvard University. *David P. Chandler*, a former
U.S. foreign service officer, is research director of the Centre of Southeast Asian Studies at
Monash University in Melbourne, Australia.
His major publications include *In Search of
Southeast Asia: A Modern History* (coauthor)
and *The Land and the People of Cambodia*.
Lee Ewing, editor of *Army Times*, served two
years in Vietnam as a combat intelligence officer with the U.S. Military Assistance Command, Vietnam (MACV) and the 101st Airborne Division.

Picture Consultant: *Ngo Vinh Long* is a social
historian specializing in China and Vietnam.
Born in Vietnam, he returned there most recently in 1980.

Cover Photo:

A decade after U.S. combat troops left Vietnam,
Americans began recovering from the trauma of
the long war. The Vietnam Veterans Memorial in
Washington, dedicated in November 1982, became
a symbol of the healing process.

Library of Congress Catalog Card Number: 85-
072839

ISBN: 0-939526-17-4

10 9 8 7 6
5 4 3 2 1

Contents

The New Vietnam

The date was April 30, 1975. The gates of Saigon's presidential palace had been left ajar, but the first North Vietnamese tank to arrive smashed through the wrought-iron fence nonetheless, as if dealing a final crushing blow to an independent South Vietnam. Four other T54 tanks quickly followed. Armored personnel carriers and pith-helmeted troops in green uniforms swarmed over the grounds; one squad of them bundled South Vietnam's president of three days, General Duong Van Minh, into a jeep and sped away. Just after noon the flag of the Provisional Revolutionary Government arose over the palace, and the capital's radio station proclaimed, "Saigon has been totally liberated." The PRG announced that Saigon was henceforth to be called Ho Chi Minh City.

At their headquarters in Ben Cat, forty kilometers north of Saigon, senior Politburo members Le Duc Tho and Pham Hung and General Van Tien Dung, architect of the final offensive, jumped

about like schoolboys, embracing each other and their aides, cheering and carrying each other around piggyback. They also wept. "Our generation had known many victorious mornings," Dung later wrote, "but there had been no morning so fresh and beautiful, so radiant, so clear and cool, so sweet-scented as this morning of total victory."

Victory brought with it responsibilities of occupation and administration, tasks for which the North Vietnamese had done little preparation. At the start of "Campaign 275," a planned two-year offensive, Hanoi had anticipated significant battlefield gains to be followed by a military stalemate in the rainy season and further negotiations. South Vietnam's collapse had come quickly and unexpectedly, and as soon as the jubilant victors caught their breath, they cast a look ahead. As Dung wrote:

Le Duc Tho, Pham Hung, and I leaned on our chairs looking at the map of Ho Chi Minh City spread out on the table. We thought of the welter of jobs ahead. Were the electricity and water in Saigon still working? Saigon's army of nearly 1 million had disbanded on the spot. How should we deal with them? What could we do to help the hungry and find ways for the millions of unemployed to make a living? Should we ask the center to send in supplies right away to keep the factories alive? How could we quickly build up a revolutionary administration at the grassroots level? What policy should we take toward the bourgeoisie? And how could we carry the South on to socialism along with the whole country? The conclusion of this struggle was the opening of another, no less complex and filled with hardship.

An equal degree of uncertainty reigned in the streets of Saigon, where, in the view of a French diplomat, a third of the people greeted the Communists with enthusiasm, a third with indifference, and a third with fear. Along with the rest of the world, the South Vietnamese had heard that upon taking Phnom Penh two weeks earlier, the Communist Khmer Rouge had proceeded with an unprecedented and brutal evacuation of the teeming Cambodian capital. Phnom Penh radio had later announced the beheadings of the leading "traitors." The frightening retributions in Cambodia, combined with dire warnings of a blood bath in the event of a Communist victory in Vietnam, raised frenzied fears among the Saigonese who had served the Americans or the South Vietnamese government.

More than 130,000 Vietnamese had fled in the chaotic final days of the Republic. Now, tens of thousands of people jammed the docks in Saigon Harbor, futilely trying to buy their way aboard the few remaining small craft that might take them out to the U.S. fleet standing offshore. A Communist tank crew, spotting one of the last boats to leave the harbor, lowered its cannon and fired a round across the ship's bow, turning the vessel back. South Vietnamese soldiers seeking anonymity peeled off their uniforms and scurried away in their underwear looking for civilian clothes. One officer from a Saigon family hurried home and burned his uniform, then searched out photographs that showed him as a soldier and dropped them into the flames.

Thousands of people looted the vacated American embassy, carrying off everything from plumbing fixtures (even the kitchen sink) to a document shredder. (What the Americans had failed to destroy were computer tapes containing the names of most U.S. and Vietnamese government employees, intelligence agents, double agents, and Communist defectors. The Americans also left behind computers and trained Vietnamese technicians to extract the information, allowing the Communists to identify and isolate former opponents.) Communist cadres who had lived double lives in Saigon now began to surface. Ky Nhan, a free-lance photographer occasionally employed by the Associated Press, arrived at the agency's office with two North Vietnamese soldiers and told bureau chief George Esper, "I guarantee the safety of everybody here." Nhan admitted to being a "revolutionary" for ten years and explained, "My job in the Vietcong was liaison with the international press."

By midafternoon on April 30, perhaps 2,000 soldiers filled the shady square in front of the presidential palace, and long convoys of Russian-made Molotova trucks carrying North Vietnamese regulars poured into the city past buildings festooned with white flags. The soldiers chatted with people on the streets, while in some cases their officers toured nearby hotels asking for accommodations. Communist soldiers carrying loudspeakers circulated in the streets, calling "Do not worry. You will be well treated."

The state radio ordered every home owner to display on his house the flag of the National Liberation Front along with that of North Vietnam, and tailor shops started a brisk business stitching and selling those flags. The radio also ordered every home to display prominently a portrait of Ho Chi Minh. For the Communists, the victory over South Vietnam had come at an appropriate time, for the following day was May 1, marking the international celebration of labor and communism.

North Vietnam's capital of Hanoi rocked with jubilation at the news from the South. Everyone in the city, it seemed, poured into the streets, setting off firecrackers, singing, and cheering. Spring blossoms from Hanoi's abundant peach and cherry trees added color and fragrance to the impromptu celebration. "It was as if a springtime of peace had suddenly replaced all the hardship and sorrow" wrote Truong Nhu Tang, the PRG minister of justice then

---

Preceding page. *Victorious troops from North Vietnam parade through Saigon (renamed Ho Chi Minh City) after the fall of South Vietnam, May 1975.*

Right. *Curious passersby in Ho Chi Minh City examine the hulk of a crashed American helicopter lying twisted like a dragon slain in battle.*

present in Hanoi, who with his colleagues had followed the war's final days in a round-the-clock radio vigil. "We were celebrating the advent of a new world."

Deliverance into a debate

Rejoicing over the Communist victories in Indochina marked May Day celebrations throughout the world. Peking, Moscow, and Havana sent congratulations for what Fidel Castro called "one of humanity's greatest feats," and demonstrations also took place in capitalist countries such as West Germany, where 30,000 people gathered in West Berlin's John F. Kennedy Square, chanting "Ho, Ho, Ho Chi Minh" and "The first of May and Vietnam is free."

On a Sunday ten days later in New York, some 50,000 veterans of the antiwar movement flocked to Central Park for a daylong carnival of songs by Peter Yarrow, Paul Simon, and Phil Ochs and speeches by Representatives Elizabeth Holtzman and Bella Abzug. People hugged each other in the spring sunshine and reminisced about the years of protest. "There's lots of lumps in lots of throats," a participant named Pamela Chapman said to a reporter. "It's unbelievable . . . the war is over."

But for most Americans the events of April 30 were an anticlimax. They had made a separate, emotional peace with Vietnam more than two years earlier when the United States signed the Paris peace accords, withdrew the last U.S. soldiers, and repatriated prisoners of war. For all but a handful of Americans who remained, the war had ended in 1973; the reports of Hanoi's final offensive now came from distant, hazily remembered battlefields. President Gerald R. Ford set the tone for the American reaction when he said, as soon as the last Americans had left Saigon, that the fall of South Vietnam "closes a chapter on the American experience." Although Ford did not use the word "defeat," commentators introduced it as self-evident. In the *Washington Post*, William Greider posed "the monumental question which six American Presidents tried to duck: How would the American voters respond to defeat?"

The answer was, rather wearily. Perhaps this was because few targets remained against which to direct anger. The policymakers who had brought the United States into the war had already been turned out of office, and of their successors, the only prominent holdover was Secretary of State Henry Kissinger. His superior, President Richard Nixon, had resigned only eight months prior to the fall of Saigon because of Watergate.

While Hanoi's victory put an end to the Republic of South Vietnam's twenty years of existence, the United States had only days before celebrated the 200th anniversary of the April 19, 1775, battles at Lexington and Concord, Massachusetts, that touched off the American Revolution. The years 1975 and 1976 were to see countless displays of American pride and nostalgia for an epoch

when Americans had doubtlessly been in the right in throwing off an oppressor. Some people affected revolutionary war themes in comments to the media. "What happened is what happened to us 200 years ago: a revolution for independence," said actress Jane Fonda, who was to remain a symbolic bête noire of conservatives and veterans for her pro-Communist, antiwar activism. "To say Saigon has 'fallen' is to say that the 13 colonies 'fell' two centuries ago." Daniel Ellsberg, the ex-marine and government official who had pilfered and made public the Pentagon Papers, reacted similarly. "It was the will of the American people, expressed to Congress, that ended this war now," he said, referring to the Congressional denial of President Ford's request for last-minute emergency aid to Saigon. "That's the best possible celebration of the Bicentennial of the American Revolution that I can imagine."

Others, however, interpreted that Congressional inaction as shameful abandonment of an ally. Speaking at Georgia Tech, former California Governor Ronald Reagan, seen as a rival to President Ford for the 1976 Republican nomination, won a standing ovation when he blamed "the most irresponsible Congress in our history" for the loss of South Vietnam, adding that members of Congress now had "blood on their hands." President Ford found an opportunity four days later to reassure America's allies. At a May 4 ceremony to commission the nuclear-powered aircraft carrier U.S.S. *Nimitz* at Norfolk, Virginia, Ford said, "This great ship is visible evidence of our commitment to friends and allies and our capability to maintain those commitments." The evacuation of Americans and South Vietnamese from Saigon, said Ford, demonstrated the "readiness and flexibility" of aircraft carriers "in the successful execution of national policy." Five U.S. aircraft carriers had participated in the evacuation of Saigon.

In the wake of those chaotic final days, the press seemed to be caught in unusually tongue-tied ambiguity, pleased by the end of the war yet incapable certainly of saluting the Communists on their victory. In its lead editorial the *Washington Post* forgave the country its trespasses: "The fundamental 'lesson' of Vietnam surely is not that we as a people are intrinsically bad but rather that we are capable of error—and on a gigantic scale. . . . The country will fare better if it regards what has finally happened in Vietnam as bearing, for Americans, the potential for deliverance as well as disaster." The *New York Times* recognized that an end to the war did not mean an end to the national debate over Vietnam. Its editorial predicted:

Untangling the meaning of the rapid events that have flashed past the American and South Vietnamese people these last few days will be an arduous task for the historians. Too many questions are unanswered in the heat of defeat; too many others will be deliberately obscured in the days—and years—to come, for the protection of reputations and ideals that will not easily be given up.

Amerasians

Products of wartime liaisons between American fathers and Vietnamese mothers, Amerasian children are a living legacy of U.S. involvement in Vietnam. Some 8,000 to 15,000 Amerasians remain in the country; many, rejected by their mothers and ostracized by other Vietnamese, have been forced onto the streets. In 1982 the U.S. began to accept Amerasians and by 1985, 2,400 of these orphans had been resettled in America.

Above. Rumors that a Westerner was in town attracted this crowd of Amerasians posing in front of the Hotel Majestic in Ho Chi Minh City. Left. An Amerasian boy's white skin and blond hair stand out on this Ho Chi Minh City street.

Establishing order

In the days following the fall of South Vietnam, Saigon was like a body without a head. The Communists had brought with them no uniformed police or military police, and a mild form of anarchy reigned, as the normal functions of the city packed with 3.5 million people came to a halt. Garbage had not been collected for two weeks prior to the end and was piled up around the city. "Saigon used to be known as the Pearl of the Orient," said one official. "What we found was one great heap of garbage."

By the count of the new government, Saigon contained 130,000 drug addicts, perhaps 200,000 prostitutes and bar girls, and an equal number of thieves, pickpockets, and orphans. During the last years of the war, thousands of peasants had flocked to the cities to flee the ravages of war, and as many as 8 million Vietnamese—one-third the population of essentially rural South Vietnam—were living in cities. In addition, as many as 1 million members of the Republic of Vietnam Armed Forces (RVNAF)—comprising the armed services, Regional Forces, and national police—as well as the entire civil government of South Vietnam were now unemployed.

Thieves came out in force. Prison guards had walked off the job, and as many as 7,000 Saigon convicts broke out of jail and helped themselves to weapons abandoned by ARVN soldiers. The thieves often worked in pairs on motor scooters, snatching money or goods and then weaving their way through thick traffic. According to one official, the troops developed a technique when a theft occurred of firing a warning shot in the air to stop traffic. Pedestrians had to lie down on the sidewalks. The thieves escaping on their motor scooters were thus isolated and arrested. The crime wave was so bad that in order to discourage other thieves the Communists publicly executed several criminals after hasty "People's Court" sessions.

Despite such draconian incidents, the Party leadership imposed no martial law and, in fact, moved somewhat slowly to restore order without alarming a public that had been primed to expect a wholesale slaughter of anti-Communists. Within a week, a daily newspaper appeared in two languages—Vietnamese and Chinese—to alert Saigonese to developments. One of the earliest announcements was that the regime would make no physical retaliation against people who had served the Saigon administration. Another came when the North Vietnamese dong began to be traded on the black market, in expectation that the dong would soon become the currency of the South. The authorities quickly announced that South Vietnamese piasters remained the only legal tender in the South. Still, the people realized that the piaster would soon be worthless.

Banks were closed in May and remained so until June, and then a withdrawal limit of the equivalent of $50 per family member was imposed so that only families that had mistrusted banks and hoarded piasters or, even better, gold, had much money to buy food. (A currency conversion in September established a new South Vietnamese dong—distinguished from the northern dong—convertible at a rate of 500 piasters for one new dong. The conversion and the relative scarcity of the new dong had the practical effect of hiking—some said by three times—the cost of living.) The government called on merchants to open their shops and even guaranteed their profits. But the greatest activity was taking place at the expanding free markets.

Southerners short of cash, or those wishing to look less prosperous to the Communist victors, took their possessions, which they called "dry food," to the sidewalk flea markets. The markets offered everything from gasoline to refrigerators to ball-point pens. After the revolution, one Saigonese later wrote, "such worthless bric-a-brac as a ream of paper used only on one side, an old magazine, or a few rusty bolts would be sold for the equivalent of a worker's salary for one day." Women discarded their Western-style clothes and cosmetics, and men dug out their old clothes. People also threw away books and music of the bourgeois culture, which the new regime condemned as "false music" and "false culture" of the "false authorities." The regime substituted "revolutionary music," martial tunes played over and over on radio and television networks, in restaurants, and at public functions.

PRG edged aside

As the revelry and celebration receded in the streets of Hanoi after the surrender of South Vietnam, PRG Justice Minister Truong Nhu Tang and his colleagues prepared for an immediate, and triumphant, return to the South after fourteen years of revolution. But their enthusiasm turned to impatience when their departure was blocked by Politburo members. The situation in the South remained unclear, they said, and the PRG leaders should not return until security had been assured. Yet Hanoi dispatched its own cadres to the South to aid in restoring order and establishing government. As he sent them off, North Vietnamese Premier Pham Van Dong sounded a warning that was to resonate for years, urging them to "strictly maintain the morality of revolutionaries and of the working class" and to beware in the dissolute South of material temptations that he characterized as "poison pills encased in sugar."

The Provisional Revolutionary Government, founded in the South in June 1969 as the political arm of the National Liberation Front, and made up of South Vietnamese Communists and some non-Communists who had cast their lot with the North, appeared to step into the vacuum after the fall of Saigon. On Liberation Day, Dinh Ba Thi, its spokesman in Paris, where the PRG had participated as one of four parties to the peace talks, saluted the People's Liberation Armed Forces (the Vietcong) who, "supported and staunchly helped by their brothers in the North, [had] brought the uprising and attacks" against South Vietnam to a successful end. Thi emphasized that the PRG's policy of "union and national concord" was aimed at reconciling "hatred and divisions and offering a place and a role to all inhabitants irrespective of their past."

Indeed the PRG's all-encompassing twelve-point "Action Program," promulgated at the birth of the PRG in 1969, promised pardons and "equal treatment" to Saigon's soldiers and civil servants who "are now repentant and sincerely return to the people." The program also guaranteed elections "to build a truly democratic and free republican regime," freedom of thought, speech, and the press, and a neutralist foreign policy. As for North Vietnam, the PRG, once in power, intended first to reestablish normal relations and then move toward peaceful reunification. The program stated: "The unification of the country will be achieved step by step through peaceful methods and on the basis of discussions and agreement between both zones, without coercion by either side." From inception the PRG had spoken for the South and was, as Hanoi termed it, "the sole genuine representative of the Southern people."

But the reality unfolding was starkly different from the idealism of the Action Program. On May 3, Saigon radio, citing the authority of the PRG, announced formation of a Military Management Committee to take charge of the Saigon region. Its head was Colonel General Tran Van Tra, PRG defense minister and a member of the North's ruling Lao Dong party Central Committee who had served as military commander of COSVN, Hanoi's political and military headquarters in the South. None of the other ten members of the Military Management Committee were figures in the PRG. Tra's deputy, Vo Van Kiet, was a southerner but a Lao Dong Central Committee member who was to become a Politburo member. (His wife and children had been killed by a U.S. B-52 raid as they traveled to visit him in his jungle headquarters.) The absence of PRG members, like Hanoi's stalling the return of PRG officials, signaled North Vietnam's intention to control events in the South.

"Throw away the peel"

That intention became clear to Truong Nhu Tang on May 15. Two days earlier, Tang and his colleagues had finally won permission to return to the South, and they flew home

Soldiers carry out a People's Court death sentence against Vo Van Ngoc, described as a thief. The picture was published in the newspaper Saigon Giai Phong ("Liberated Saigon") as a deterrent to others.

to a jubilant welcome, replete with cheering crowds and banners. The celebrations culminated in a May 15 "Victory Day" ceremony, which drew half a million people to Independence Palace Square. Dignitaries from Hanoi, such as Le Duc Tho and Van Tien Dung, and PRG leaders, including President Huynh Tan Phat and Nguyen Huu Tho, presided over the parades from the reviewing stand.

The civilians came first. Groups such as students, laborers, and Catholics who had worked for the revolution paraded past, carrying banners and portraits of Ho Chi Minh and two flags—those of North Vietnam and the South's Provisional Revolutionary Government. Then came the People's Army of Vietnam, victors over South Vietnam's army in the fifty-five-day final offensive. The soldiers wore crisp uniforms and new pith helmets, and, in the din created by marching bands and air force planes that passed overhead, PAVN presented an impressive array of conventional military might—infantry units, tanks, artillery and antiaircraft batteries, Soviet-made surface-to-air missiles. Tang and his PRG colleagues waited impatiently for the Vietcong, which during the war had expanded from peasant guerrilla groups to Main Force divisions. As the war progressed, Vietcong units, ground down in battle, had been increasingly filled out by northern soldiers, yet they had maintained their identities as NLF units.

At last the Vietcong appeared, several ragged companies trailing the northerners, and for their standard they carried North Vietnam's flag—a yellow star on a red background. The PRG flag—red and blue with a yellow star—was nowhere in evidence. A shocked Tang turned to General Van Tien Dung, standing next to him on the dais. "Where are the famous First, Fifth, Seventh, and Ninth Divisions?" Tang asked the chief of staff and Politburo member. "The army has already been unified," Dung coldly answered, his lip, Tang reported, curling in a slight smile. A bitter Tang later reflected:

At that moment I began to understand my fate and that of the NLF. In Vietnam we often said "Take the juice of the lemon and throw away the peel." On that dais the years of Communist promises and assurances revealed themselves for the propaganda they were. Victory day celebrated no victory for the NLF, or for the South. . . .
The North Vietnamese Communists had engaged in a deliberate deception to achieve what had been their true goal from the start, the destruction of South Vietnam as a political or social entity in any way separate from the North.

But rather than seizing power outright as conquerers, the northerners insinuated themselves into the structure of the new government, taking over gradually. Cadres from the North continued to arrive in the South to assume political and administrative tasks. In many cases they joined ministries of the PRG, took more and more responsibility, and opened direct pipelines to their northern counterparts. Tang remarked on "the emerging arrogance and disdain

of our Party staff cadres—almost as if they believed they were the conquerers and we the vanquished." Top PRG leaders were even assigned northerners to serve as "bodyguards"; in effect, they were security guards. Disputes between the northern cadres and PRG ministers were often settled by northern officials acting as arbiters; they naturally overruled the PRG.

Some ministers slowly relinquished their functions, simply failing to show up for work that became increasingly frustrating and, ultimately, meaningless. Health Minister Dr. Duong Quynh Hoa, a jungle resident since 1968 who had given premature birth while fleeing a 1970 ARVN attack on PRG headquarters, walked out of her ministry in disgust. "Let the Northern cadres make the wind and the weather," she said. The voice of the "sole genuine representative of the Southern people" was effectively being stilled.

Throughout 1975 and into 1976 the PRG remained in name the government of South Vietnam, but the accent was on "provisional." Key members conducted themselves as leaders of an emerging nation and seemed intent on putting the PRG Action Program into practice. PRG President Huynh Tan Phat was known as the president of South Vietnam. Foreign Minister Madame Nguyen Thi Binh, prominent from her visible role in the Paris peace talks, courted foreign countries on behalf of the PRG. South Vietnam even sought individual membership in the United Nations, an application soon to be denied. Yet privately some of these leaders faithfully hewed to the Party line. According to Tang, Phat and NLF President Tho began to expound the North's program of forced reunification of North and South and rapid socialization of South Vietnam.

The question of formal reunification posed political problems. Hanoi had to make it seem as if reunification was the choice of the Vietnamese people, freely arrived at after negotiations and elections, the approach advocated and long fought for by the PRG. To do otherwise risked isolating Hanoi from whatever non-Communist international support it had tenuously won. The PRG had to be maintained as at least the façade of a legitimate government.

In a real sense, the PRG had never been more than that. In a 1978 interview, North Vietnam historian and publicist Nguyen Khac Vien provided an epitaph for the PRG that addressed the naiveté of its members as well as Hanoi's original intentions, so perfectly concealed during the war and so effectively implemented afterward. "The PRG was always simply a team emanating from the government of [North] Vietnam," Vien said. "If for a long time we pretended otherwise, that's because in war one doesn't have to show all his cards."

As its first action in remaking southern society, the Military Management Committee moved to isolate any potential resistance to the new regime. The committee's Order Number One promulgated early in May required all who had served in the Army of the Republic of Vietnam to register throughout the month and to turn in any weapons. The soldiers were destined for reeducation, a process of "productive labor" and "political study" that the Communist leaders viewed as a form of rehabilitation. While confined, people forfeited their rights as citizens until deemed ready to return to society. The magnitude of the program was staggering: By Hanoi's count, 1.3 million people who had served military or political functions in the South Vietnamese government required reeducation. Overall the regime believed some 6.5 million South Vietnamese—the typical family had five members—had been compromised by their service or relationship to someone who had served.

Reeducation camps had existed in North Vietnam since

ment, underwent a three-day period of "reform study" from June 11 to 13, going home each night. The leniency accorded these minor participants in the military or political prosecution of the war created a positive impression for those higher officials whose turn was to come.

Later in June, the committee instructed lieutenants, captains, and warrant officers to report for reeducation and to "bring enough paper, pens, clothes, mosquito nets, food or money for use in 10 days beginning from the day of gathering." Higher-ranking officers and senior government officials, civil servants, and legislators received similar instructions to bring enough personal articles and food for a thirty-day period.

On the appointed days, tens of thousands of men carry-

1961 as a means of dealing with "counter-revolutionary elements" and "professional scoundrels." A writer named Nguyen Ngoc Giao explained in the army newspaper *Quan Doi Nhan Dan*, "Reeducation is a meticulous and long-range process. Management must be tight, continuous, comprehensive, and specific. We must manage each person. We must manage their thoughts and actions, words and deeds, philosophy of life and ways of livelihood and travel. . . . We must closely combine management and education with interrogation." As to the management of thought, the newspaper *Saigon Giai Phong* published this definition on June 13: "Thought reform is a process enabling the mind to part with what is bad and to assimilate what is good."

Noncommissioned officers and privates—with the significant exception of those who had served in intelligence or in the Marine, Airborne, or Ranger corps—along with rank-and-file workers of the South Vietnamese govern-

Victory Day celebration. Dignitaries reviewing the May 15, 1975, parade include (left to right) NLF President Nguyen Huu Tho, PRG Justice Minister Truong Nhu Tang, Politburo member Le Duc Tho, NLF official Tran Buu Kiem, future Ho Chi Minh City Mayor Mai Chi Tho, and Senior General Van Tien Dung.

ing their allotted provisions voluntarily reported to the designated centers. To curry favor, many of them dressed shabbily. "The people I saw gathered outside the school more resembled beggars than the recent ARVN officers I knew most of them were," wrote former ARVN Lieutenant Nguyen Ngoc Ngan. "Knowing the Communists' bias in favor of the poor, many were deliberately affecting the role." The cadres displayed no favoritism, however. Surrounded by armed guards, those in Ngan's group filled out questionnaires of personal data and service and then were locked up in the school for the night. "With a vague

Reeducation

An indefinite period of internment undergone by more than 1 million people, "reeducation" at over 150 remote camps throughout Vietnam combined intensive political instruction with strenuous physical labor as a means of inculcating in former soldiers and civil servants of the South Vietnamese government the principles of the new Communist regime.

Above. At Camp Number 2 in Ben Tre, holding 220 "former spies and policemen of the Thieu regime," the men prepare a meal. Left. Former military officers listen to a political cadre at a Tay Ninh camp. Right. Under the gaze of local peasants, former South Vietnamese soldiers till the fields.

sense of unease," Ngan later wrote, "it occurred to me that we were now prisoners." The following night the men were packed into enclosed Russian-built Molotova trucks. As the trucks pulled out of Saigon, one guard shouted, "Anyone who attempts to escape or to look out will be shot!" Perhaps 250,000 men, the large majority of them ARVN officers, left Saigon in this first deportation. More than 1 million people from throughout the country were to undergo such forced reeducation over the next decade.

The trucks brought the men to any of more than 150 reeducation camps, subcamps, and prisons throughout Vietnam in military bases or abandoned firebases; other prisoners were set down in remote areas and had to construct their own camps. Their sole "productive labor" often consisted of building up the camps, repairing existing structures, and planting rice for their own food. In some cases prisoners without experience, using sticks or bare hands, had to clear away mines, booby traps, dud mortar rounds, and grenades from fields around the base. Inevitably some of the explosives were accidentally detonated, killing and wounding the prisoners. The Geneva Convention expressly forbade such activity.

The political phase of reeducation meant intensive indoctrination on such topics as the evils of American imperialism, the inevitability of the Communist victory, the glory of labor, and the benevolence of the new government toward the "rebels" (the current prisoners who had fought against them). Each course began with lectures over one or two days from a political cadre, followed by closely supervised discussion groups that might last a week. Inmates had to write essays summarizing and evaluating the lectures. The success of their reeducation was based on their professed "understanding" of the political lesson, hence the prisoners tended to exaggerate the benefits of communism. In concert with political indoctrination, inmates had to write "confessions" of alleged past transgressions against the Communists or their countrymen. Naturally the former South Vietnamese officers minimized their own roles in the war effort, since the consequence of admitting to "crimes against the people" was a longer term of reeducation.

When ten days and then thirty days and another thirty passed and none of the men returned home, their families agitated for information. But Military Management Committee member Mai Chi Tho said, "The government's communique said they were asked to bring food for only a month. The communique did not say that the reeducation period is one month." President Phat told an angered Truong Nhu Tang, two of whose brothers were interned, "You've got to distinguish between the criminals and the ones who were just cannon fodder. Those who were in on decisions, they need a lot more [reeducation]." In response to public pressure the government announced in *Saigon Giai Phong* that detainees who fit several categories would be released: for example, draftees who did

Laos: The Last Domino

During the spring of 1975, with world attention riveted on the blindingly rapid climaxes in Vietnam and Cambodia, the "Gentle Revolution" of the Laotian Communists was heading languidly toward its own dénouement in December. Throughout the spring and summer, the Pathet Lao struggled steadily, more or less peacefully, but ultimately successfully against its partners in the coalition government. When Kaysone Phoumvihan became prime minister of a new Lao People's Democratic Republic on December 2, 1975, the Communists had knocked over Indochina's third and last domino.

Laos had played a key strategic role for North Vietnam in its prosecution of the war. The Ho Chi Minh Trail, running through Laos's southern panhandle, served as the main North Vietnamese logistical pipeline into South Vietnam. To preserve it, Hanoi fostered an insurgency against the Laotian royal government and stationed thousands of NVA regulars in the country.

While President John F. Kennedy had shared his predecessor's profound apprehension that Vientiane was indeed a vulnerable domino, he confined his response to modest economic aid and clandestine military support. Hanoi then took advantage of the 1962 Geneva accords supposedly guaranteeing Laotian neutrality. While the U.S. withdrew its 666 advisers, North Vietnam left some 7,000 troops. The fundamental imbalance thus established paved the way for the Communist victory thirteen years later.

Hamstrung by Geneva, the U.S. waged throughout the 1960s a so-called secret war against the Pathet Lao and its backers. The CIA financed and led Meo tribesmen as irregular troops, fighting behind Communist lines. U.S. aid funneled cash support to the royal government.

Presidents Johnson and Nixon unleashed tremendous unpublicized bombing strikes against the Ho Chi Minh Trail. LBJ's Operation Steel Tiger, which peaked at 1,000 sorties per month, paled in comparison to Nixon's efforts, which in 1969 averaged 650 sorties *per day.* The Pathet Lao and the Vietcong outlasted the barrages.

The Laotian Communists lay the groundwork for their takeover in June 1974, when—with the U.S. on its way out of Indochina—they forced creation of a coalition government in which they would wield disproportionate authority. Unwilling as the royal government may have been, it had little choice. By taking and holding 80 percent of the countryside, the Communists had achieved the whip hand.

The Pathet Lao consolidated its control during the summer and fall of 1975. It orchestrated intimidating demonstrations against rightist members of the national cabinet, many of whom, along with much of the Laotian middle class, fled to Thailand. Following a Communist-instigated eight-day takeover of USAID's Vientiane headquarters by Laotian students on May 20, the U.S. withdrew its ambassador, reduced American personnel in Laos from 800 to 30, and, on June 26, terminated the Laotian USAID program. An American commitment of twenty years and an estimated $1 billion was down the drain. So too was any non-Communist military resistance.

The stage was set for complete Communist control, and on December 2 the 650-year-old Lao monarchy was abruptly discarded by the Pathet Lao in favor of a new forty-five-member "Supreme People's Council." Kaysone Phoumvihan, the new premier, was the most powerful figure in the new Laotian leadership. His four deputy prime ministers similarly came from the Politburo of the Pathet Lao. Rounding out the new regime was Laos's legendary "Red Prince," the half-brother of the deposed neutralist premier Souvanna Phouma, Souphanouvong, a protégé of Ho Chi Minh and the public figure most closely associated with the Pathet Lao.

Laos's new government faced several intertwined problems during its first months in power. Following a shooting incident in which a Thai soldier was killed,

an enraged Thai government closed the borders to Laos on November 18, 1975, and kept them closed until January 1, 1976. The Thai action triggered an economic crisis—the extent of which made it abundantly clear that, at least in the short term, the Americans and their annual $30 million dole would be missed in Laos. As gasoline, vegetables, and other foodstuffs customarily imported across the Mekong became scarce, the country's national currency, the kip, lost more than half its black-market value in only two weeks.

Kaysone's new regime, to be sure, may have started out as its own worst enemy. The 1976 tax it placed on agricultural production, for example, backfired because the tax bite went up as harvests increased. So peasants either scaled back or eliminated what they might otherwise have produced. Another tack the Communists took was to relegalize opium production, an act meant to benefit the Meo tribesmen, who depended on opium for their livelihood. But despite that move, the Meo, opponents of the Pathet Lao during the civil war, were of all Laotians perhaps the least favorably disposed toward the new government.

General Vang Pao, who had led the CIA's mercenary army, was himself one of the first Meo to depart, flitting during 1975 from Laos to Thailand to France and eventually landing on a ranch in Montana. Twenty-five thousand Meo followed him to Thailand in 1975, with about half of them going within a year to the United States.

The extent to which Laos's new rulers would be able to control their country's destiny was in doubt from the beginning. Within a year the Soviet Union, according to press reports, had more than 500 diplomats and technicians in their country, and Vietnam had stationed roughly 30,000 troops in Laos's southern panhandle. The three nations, pressured by an increasingly hostile China, grew much closer as the decade wore on—but with Laos clearly the junior partner. Only three years after Kaysone and his allies had won their three-decade battle to drive out, successively, the Japanese, the French, and the American-backed Royal Lao Government, 75 percent of the country's outlays were coming from two sources: Hanoi and Moscow.

not commit crimes against the people, close relatives of revolutionary cadres, and people whose families had "a good political attitude toward the Revolution."

The regime released a great many detainees after three months. In one estimate, as many as 500,000 prisoners returned to their families in 1975, but 200,000 were destined to serve an average of three years and an additional 240,000 five years in the "Bamboo Gulag." By 1983, as many as 60,000 were estimated to remain incarcerated.

For eight hours a day, six days a week, prisoners labored for the revolution at tasks that included cutting trees and clearing jungle, digging wells, constructing camps, and erecting fences. Prisoners had to fulfill a quota for a day's work or be deemed lazy and ordered to do "compensation work" on Sunday. Uncooperative prisoners or those attempting escape were shackled in crippling positions, sent into solitary confinement, or subjected to severe torture. One prisoner who berated a guard for using the South Vietnamese flag as a dust cloth was sentenced to be tied upright to a wooden stake outdoors for three months. Lashed to the pole with telephone wire, the prisoner wilted under the brutal sun during the day and endured clouds of mosquitoes at night. By the second week, he had contracted malaria and slumped, seriously ill, but the punishment continued. At the end of a month he was given an opportunity to repent, but the man remained defiant. The guards removed him from camp and he was never seen again.

The food supply was barely above survival level, and some inmates believed that the government intended deliberately to weaken them and their resistance to camp policies. The normal diet provided no protein, only about 300 grams a day of rice, corn, and manioc, a starchy root crop. Said a letter smuggled out of one camp:

In our conversation we only talk about eating and how to find things to eat. When we do not talk about eating, we silently *think* about eating. As soon as we finish lunch, we begin to imagine the supper awaiting us when we return from the field. The food put into the mouth is like one breath of air blown into a vast empty house. What little food is given is chewed very slowly. Still, it makes no difference—we feel even more hungry after eating. Even in our sleep, our dreams are haunted by food. There are those who chew noisily in their dreams. ... Such food as mice, rats, birds, snakes, grasshoppers, must be caught and eaten secretly. It is forbidden, and if the camp guards learn about it, the prisoners will be punished.

Because of malnutrition many contracted malaria, dysentery, and beriberi. Death became a commonplace.

Social reconstruction

While the reeducation camp system dealt with RVNAF officers and civil servants, the Party faced a monumental task in remaking the individualistic and intensely capitalist southern society according to the Marxist principles of socialism and class struggle. By emphasizing class conflict and class consciousness—those who do not support the ruling class of "the people" are therefore its enemies—the regime intended to ostracize the middle and upper classes. Such a system immediately isolated any nonconformist, branding him and his family "class enemies," and hence pariahs. Such a person might be hounded out of a job, his children expelled from school, and his family denied food and the benefits of society.

The Communists engendered this class struggle by dividing workers from managers, teachers from students, employees from employers, and requiring the upper classes to "confess" to their crimes in having exploited their subordinates and in having supported the "false authorities" of the former government of South Vietnam. Subordinates meanwhile were encouraged to denounce superiors. To maintain the benefits of society, many who did not actively embrace the socialist principles at least tried to present the appearance of doing so.

The regime established tight control over the people by means of overlapping district, ward, and cluster committees (a ward comprising about 1,000 people and a cluster being about one city block). The ward people's committee, closely attended by political and military cadres, attended to every societal function, from administration to entertainment to food distribution. Each ward also had a security office whose cadres provided police protection and also conducted surveillance and registered anyone wishing to spend the night away from his home.

Economically and militarily, North Vietnam reaped a bonanza in its conquest of the South, capturing a huge arsenal of American-made weapons and a complex of U.S.-built military installations, ports, airfields, and highways. When the U.S. withdrew its troops in 1973, the Pentagon had valued the military supplies left behind at $5 billion. Some of that had obviously been consumed by South Vietnamese forces, and many of the larger weapons such as planes and tanks would not prove serviceable for long without spare parts. Still, the military spoils of war catapulted the 615,000-man People's Army of Vietnam into a major regional force. Hanoi stationed sixteen PAVN divisions in the South to aid in reconstruction and to quell any potential dissent. Some of those troops moved to the Cambodian border, where flare-ups with Cambodian soldiers had arisen within days after the end of the war.

In conquering the South, North Vietnam, whose small industrial capacity had been heavily damaged by American bombers, acquired some 500 factories capable of employing perhaps 300,000 workers. Among the modern facilities were textile mills, including a polyester fiber plant, a pork-processing plant, fish-processing plants with enormous refrigeration storage, and chemical and paper plants. Although most of the trained workers remained in Vietnam, the factory owners and top managers had fled. The Americans "scared them into running away," said

Huynh Van Tam, head of the NLF trade union organization. "Ford with his prediction of 'blood baths,' Schlesinger with 'a million to be massacred,' Kissinger on the same line. . . . We ought to send a vote of thanks to Ford, Schlesinger, and Kissinger for their services to the Revolution!"

Hanoi also inherited an agricultural system worth an estimated $12 billion in South Vietnam, with a potential for helping to feed the North where nonarable mountainous land and lagging productivity resulted in a perennial shortfall of rice. Years of attempts at land reform by the South Vietnamese government, culminating in President Nguyen Van Thieu's "Land to the Tiller" program, had brought belated results, easing peasants' grievances. American-provided mechanization, irrigation water pumps, and chemical fertilizers, not to mention the so-called miracle rice seed, had boosted productivity. It required five times more man-hours to produce a pound of rice in North Vietnam than in the South. Even so, South Vietnam itself experienced shortages of rice.

To bring more land into production, and to alleviate the crowding in the cities, the regime instituted "New Economic Zones," by which it meant to recover acreage abandoned during the war and to clear and farm jungle lands. The regime strongly encouraged—and in some cases forced—the unemployed and underemployed, refugees, or any "socially undesirable" people to move to the NEZs. In many instances groups were deposited in a remote area with only the bare necessities of tools, food, and supplies and were forced to build shelters and scratch out an existence. "The NEZ is an opportunity of struggle, by all to transform nature, by each to reform himself," said Vo Van Kiet, a member of the Military Management Committee who was to become head of State Planning. In the first five years of the regime, some 5 million people were to move to about 500 NEZ locations, although many of them gravitated back to the cities.

A clash of cultures

Hanoi had ample social and cultural reasons to hasten reunification. At the cessation of hostilities, communication opened between people in North and South as northern soldiers made acquaintances, families sought out surviving relatives from the other side of the seventeenth parallel, and northern cadres flowed into the South. After years of warfare, sacrifice, and deprivation, many northerners were quite easily seduced by the standard of living and personal freedom they found in the South. One newsman characterized the phenomenon as Sparta meeting Byzantium. Despite an official drive against prostitution, for example, which the government referred to as "decadent American slave culture," some troops from the North discretely visited cafés in the Khanh Hoi waterfront sector and along Truong Minh Giang Street near Tan Son Nhut Airport. The prostitutes called the long-deprived liberation troops "my luong," or yellow Americans. Northern soldiers and cadres crowded the expanding sidewalk markets, buying, as one observer wryly noted, "the same kind of watches that fall apart and the same self-destructing radios purchased in previous years by their foreign counterparts." The northerners spent freely for consumer goods they could not find or afford in the North—bicycles, clocks, new and used clothing, fabric, tape recorders, sunglasses, neon light bulbs. They also made more sentimental purchases. The North's centrally planned economy had produced few nonessential items since 1954, and the northerners bought plastic children's toys—which they themselves had never had—to bring home to their children and relatives. Anyone fortunate enough to travel to the South could bring back consumer items and sell them at a substantial profit.

Those returning from the South also smuggled the southern pop culture back into the North: music and books that contrasted starkly with the droning, ideological Party songs and poetry were passed from hand to hand. This insinuation of southern values threatened authoritarianism in North Vietnam, and the Party vigorously condemned the decadent culture that had "poisoned" the South. Hanoi seemed to realize that the longer reunification was put off, the more difficult it would become to control the increasingly "contaminated" people in the North, as well as to subdue the resistant South.

Southerners were learning about the northern system they were about to inherit from the cadres and the bo doi, or northern soldiers, whose peasant simplicity made them the butt of jokes among more sophisticated Saigonese. Sample: A bo doi who has never experienced the conveniences of modern life washes his rice in the hotel toilet bowl, then complains that his dinner disappeared down the drain of the "rice washing machine." Another: A bo doi boasts that the weather and food are better, the stores bigger, and the cars more numerous in the North. He is asked if there are big refrigerators in Hanoi. "Sure," he replies, "you can see them driving all over the streets!"

While the southerners were amused by the peasant soldiers, they built up immediate resentments at the cadres who began arriving from the North. The fast-talking, condescending northerners imparted an air of superiority, feeling that their culture and patterns of speech represented pure Vietnamese, unadulterated by corrupting foreign influence. Yet they competed with each other to commandeer the most comfortable homes and offices and to land the most lucrative positions—those with a potential for bribes, or what the Vietnamese called "speed money." One Saigonese bitterly remarked, "At least under Diem and Thieu there was honor among thieves. But these Party people are wolfing down everything in sight."

The Party officials cultivated virtues of self-sacrifice and hard work and posted signs bearing such slogans as "Be diligent, parsimonious, honest and upright." But to the

As part of its agricultural plan, the Vietnam government moved hundreds of thousands to New Economic Zones, often located in jungles or other barren locations. Above. At an NEZ being established in 1976 at Lai Khe, north of Ho Chi Minh City, a family gathers its few possessions in a rudimentary shelter. Left. His children in tow, a new farmer at Lai Khe surveys the hardscrabble land.

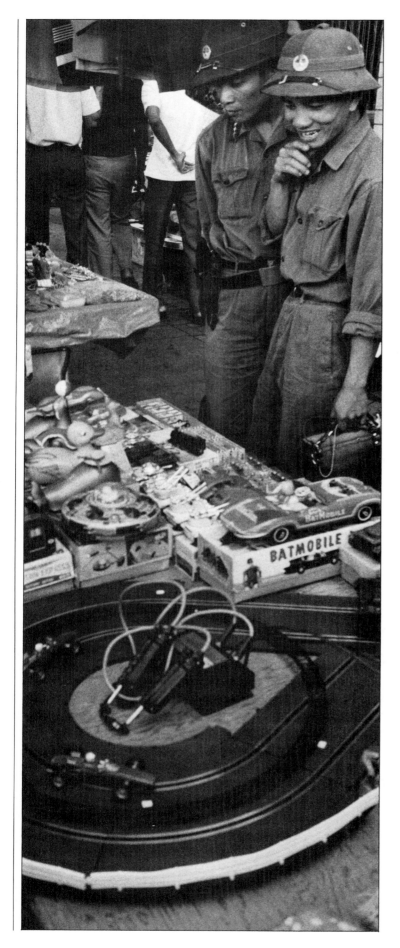

eyes of many southerners the cadres displayed little of those qualities. At one meeting a citizen bravely asked a cadre, "Why are all the best foods, clothes, medicines and supplies reserved for the cadres and Party members?" The presiding cadre answered, "Because they should be spared worries about their material life in order to enable them to devote their time, energy and zeal for the people. What else do the people expect?" The people clearly expected a more equitable distribution of goods, and their disillusionment found expression in cynical black humor. At one time Ho Chi Minh had called on the people of the North to double and triple their efforts to liberate the South. Not long after liberation, people in the South had altered Ho's words to say, "Everybody should double his efforts to buy a radio and bike for the Party officials, and triple his production so that the officials can have a new house and a pretty girl friend." PRG Justice Minister Tang remarked, "It was as if the city [of Saigon] had been invaded by a swarm of locusts."

Vietnam is one country

Early in the summer of 1975, the Lao Dong party Central Committee convened for its Twenty-fourth Plenum in the mountain resort town of Da Lat, home of the ARVN military academy and the locale of many abandoned summer residences including that of former President Nguyen Van Thieu. The Central Committee decided to proceed with formal reunification of the country and to legitimate the process with negotiations and elections. Some Hanoi leaders preferred to hesitate, believing that the possibility of double representation in the United Nations—both North and South Vietnam had applied for membership—was an advantage meriting postponement of formal reunification. On August 11, 1975, however, the question of the two Vietnams arose in the United Nations Security Council, which voted thirteen to one to admit each. But the one negative vote came from U.S. Ambassador Daniel P. Moynihan, and it carried the weight of a veto, the first time the United States used its veto to block admission of a new member. The objections to reunification harbored by some Hanoi leaders were thus swept away.

On November 15 two negotiating teams, one from the North and the other representing the South, met at the former Independence Palace to discuss reunification. Pham Hung, fourth-ranking member of the Politburo, and head of COSVN, led the southern delegation. Some members of the PRG and NLF accompanied Hung as deputies. Truong Chinh, a leading advocate of rapid reunification, headed the delegation from Hanoi. Former first secretary of the Lao Dong party, Chinh was the Party's leading ideologue

Left. *Delighted North Vietnamese soldiers look over the children's toys, many imported from the West, at a Ho Chi Minh City street market.*

and second-ranking member of the Politburo. Hence the "negotiations" over reunification consisted of the Party's second- and fourth-ranking members talking to each other.

North Vietnam, Truong Chinh said, echoing a statement made during the Third Lao Dong party Congress held in 1960, was actively building socialism, whereas the South had not yet completed the stage of national democratic revolution. But, Chinh asked rhetorically, should reunification wait until the South had caught up to the North? "I think that is not necessary," he concluded, making rare use of the first person singular in discussing a major policy decision. After a week-long charade of discussions, the conference announced that elections would be held in April 1976 for a general assembly that would adopt a "Constitution for a united Vietnam." The capital of the country would be Hanoi. According to Truong Chinh, "The composition of the National Assembly must reflect the spirit of broad unity of the whole people within a national front on the basis of the worker-peasant alliance, directed by the working class." Those opposed to socialism or reunification were thereby disenfranchised.

The campaign for the elections bore little resemblance to Western-style electoral campaigns. Although balloting was to be secret, candidates were selected by various Party committees on the basis of their behavior during the war. Campaigning was prohibited, on the grounds, said one official, that "if candidates are not permitted to wage electoral campaigns, they have to be known for their merits or their revolutionary activities." In evaluating the election process, Wilfred Burchett, a pro-Hanoi Australian journalist, frankly explained, "There was no pretense that there was to be any risk of losing the fruits of 30 years of armed struggle on some sort of electoral gambling table." Voting was compulsory; the penalty for not voting was loss of one's ration card.

On April 25, 1976, a few days short of the one-year anniversary of North Vietnam's conquest of the South, elections took place, and voters ratified the choices of 492 out of 605 candidates to the National Assembly. The highest

Consumerism also touches the North. A group of young men and women in the port city of Haiphong admires a shiny Russian Volga sedan.

Indochina Blood Baths

After Ho Chi Minh and his Communist followers took power in North Vietnam, they killed an estimated 50,000 of their countrymen while enforcing the land reform campaign of 1955–56. When the Vietcong held Hue for twenty-five days during the 1968 Tet offensive, they massacred some 2,800 people. Throughout the war, the Vietcong carried out a "violence program," killing those with ties to South Vietnam's government, including village, district, and provincial officials, and such minor functionaries as teachers.

This pattern of killing in the name of political repression prompted a Rand Corporation researcher in 1970 to predict a "bloodbath of very large proportions" in the event of a Communist military victory—100,000 or more executions. In the latter stages of the war, his warning was taken up by U.S. strategists and South Vietnamese officials, thus contributing to the panic of the final days of the Vietnam War in April 1975.

Yet no vast campaign of public summary executions followed the Communist takeover in the South, and the absence of a blood bath became an article of faith among postwar Vietnam observers. One of many to deride the blood bath warning was Senator George McGovern, who in 1976 called it "one of the great false alarms of all time." In 1979 liberal writers Noam Chomsky and Edward S. Herman reaffirmed, "There has been no bloodbath." Conservative Norman Podhoretz agreed, writing in 1982, "The 'bloodbath' that had been feared by supporters of the regime did not occur." *New Yorker* writer Robert Shaplen, considered the dean of

journalists who have covered Vietnam, wrote in 1985, "Though there was no bloodbath, an indeterminate number of former southern political and religious leaders died in prisons or in reeducation camps."

Since then testimony has arisen to suggest that something akin to a blood bath did indeed happen. According to a study conducted among 831 Vietnamese refugees interviewed in the United States and France over three years, a campaign of executions for political reasons did take place in Vietnam.

When Professors Jacqueline Desbarats and Karl D. Jackson of the University of California at Berkeley began their interviews, they did not expect to hear much about political executions (as opposed to deaths from accidents, such as clearing minefields, or from starvation or disease). But they increasingly heard tales of political killings and retributions, two-thirds of which occurred in 1975–76.

Sensitive to charges that refugees tell interviewers whatever they want to hear, Desbarats and Jackson applied strict criteria in talking to the Vietnamese. Whenever possible, for example, they obtained names and dates, which helped to eliminate duplications. Overall, 37 percent of the respondents knew or had heard of one or several persons executed for political reasons. Interviews among 615 refugees in the United States turned up 47 who had actually witnessed executions.

The witnesses described killings such as the disembowelment of an anti-Vietcong village chief; the shooting of a drunken man shouting anti-Communist slogans; inmates killed for attempting escape from reeducation camps, including one who was buried alive; an execution for violation of camp regulations; refugees shot attempting to flee Vietnam by boat.

Desbarats and Jackson wrote in 1985 that the weight of evidence accumulated over three years was "sufficient to exhaust our skepticism about whether or not widespread killing took place in Vietnam after 1975." Using conservative statistical projections, they concluded that a minimum of 65,000 people had been killed for political reasons following the Communist takeover.

In examining the blood bath theory in 1980, sociologist Peter L. Berger, formerly

an antiwar leader, suggested that statistics were not the sole basis on which to evaluate the question. The "merciless system of totalitarian control . . . with the familiar machinery of terror" had inevitably produced victims. In addition to those who died directly from execution and torture, or indirectly from hunger and exhaustion in the camps, Berger noted the "unspeakable horrors" of nearly 1 million boat people. According to relief agencies, the number of boat people who perished at sea ranged from 15 to 33 percent.

"The moral difference between killing people directly or driving them into the sea to die is not clear to me," Berger wrote. Taken together, the executions combined with the deaths of those in camps and at sea constituted for Berger substance enough that, for him, "the 'bloodbath' theory then has been broadly validated."

No such philosophizing is required with respect to Cambodia, where stacks of skulls and bones, and the museum of torture at Tuol Sleng prison, attest to the grim reality of the murders that took place during the three-and-one-half-year regime of Pol Pot and the Communist party of Kampuchea (see chapter 3).

Estimates of the total number of deaths from executions, hunger, and illness vary from a low of 400,000 by one respected Cambodia scholar to a high of 3,314,768—a figure absurd in its specificity and in its size—announced by the Vietnam-sponsored Heng Samrin government. The CIA, with very scant data, postulated 1.2 million deaths.

Because there are few accurate birth and natural death records, figures are impossible to determine precisely. The only nationwide census taken in Cambodia, in 1962, counted 5.7 million people. By 1970, demographers estimate, the country's population was just over 7 million. A decade later, following the five-year civil war (in which an estimated 500,000 people died) and the Pol Pot repression, Cambodia still had a population of nearly 7 million, according to the Heng Samrin government.

Thus it is unlikely that 2 or 3 million people died under Pol Pot, figures used so frequently they have become commonplace. Rather, it appears that the victims of the Cambodian blood bath may have numbered 1 million or less.

vote getter was Madame Nguyen Thi Binh, the PRG foreign minister, who was marked on 97 percent of the ballots. Nguyen Huu Tho was also named to the assembly.

When the National Assembly convened in June, it adopted a constitution—the 1959 Constitution of the Democratic Republic of Vietnam, or North Vietnam—and appointed a government. With the arrival of the new government, the PRG simply ceased to exist. The assembly named North Vietnam Premier Pham Van Dong, third-ranking member of the Politburo after Le Duan and Truong Chinh, premier of all Vietnam. Huynh Tan Phat, former PRG premier, was appointed one of several vice premiers, and Nguyen Huu Tho became a vice president. Madame Binh assumed the post of education minister. PRG Justice Minister Tang was asked to serve as vice minister of nutrition, but he declined. "I had no intention of taking part in a regime that was imposing itself on the South after the betrayal of so many promises," he later wrote.

The meeting of the National Assembly formalized the reunification of the two Vietnams into one. Ho Chi Minh's often-quoted aphorism, a rallying cry during the long war, had come to pass: "Vietnam is one; the Vietnamese people are one people; rivers go dry, mountains wear away, but this truth cannot be changed." To mark the event, and to emphasize the goals of the revolution, the assembly voted to change the name of the reunified country from the *Democratic* Republic to the *Socialist* Republic of Vietnam.

Home from the war. A northern soldier with a present bought in Saigon nears his village.

The Lao Dong, or Vietnam Workers, party scheduled a congress for December 1976, its first in sixteen years. The 1960 Third Party Congress, meeting in Hanoi in September that year, had endorsed a Central Committee decision to create the National Liberation Front as a means of liberating "the South from the atrocious rule of the U.S. imperialists and their henchmen." Party statutes called for a congress every four years but allowed postponements in "special circumstances," and the one and one-half decades of war required to achieve those goals had indeed amounted to special circumstances.

The new congress, held December 14 to 20, 1976, celebrated reunification, and, like the National Assembly, initiated a name change. To honor Ho Chi Minh, the Party "reassumed" the name Vietnam Communist party, as Ho had designated it in 1930. The Party's title, like the country's new name, gave expression to the nation's political and economic goals.

The Party injected new blood into the Central Committee by expanding its membership from 77 full members and alternates to a total of 133, among them several who specialized in economics. The Central Committee's ruling Politburo also added 4 new full members and 3 new alternates, all but 1 of whom were younger than the average sixty-six years of age for the 10 veteran members. Under wartime conditions, the Party itself had swelled to 1.6 million members, out of a unified population of some 50 million. According to Le Duc Tho, the Party over the years had "recruited people with low political awareness, thus in reality lowering the standards of party members and adversely affecting the class and vanguard nature of the party," so the congress resolved to purge cadres deemed to be inadequate or marginal in talent or energy. New members had to be recruited as replacements, especially in the underrepresented South, which had only 130,000 Party members, but a Central Committee report warned, "Particular caution must be exercised against the reactionaries and spies who try to infiltrate the party."

The most important act of the congress was to approve a five-year plan for 1976–80 that called for industry and agriculture to be developed simultaneously but with agriculture given priority. One goal of the agricultural plan was to reclaim 1 million hectares and restore 3 million to agricultural production (amounting to a total cultivated area in Vietnam of 10 million hectares by 1980, up from 6 million in 1976). To achieve this, the Party was counting on its rustication plan for moving some 4 million people from urban areas and overpopulated northern provinces to New Economic Zones.

The Party leaders noted that the population of reunified Vietnam ranked the country third largest among Communist nations and sixteenth largest in the world. The Fourth Party Congress laid out its blueprint for transforming this developing nation into a modern, socialist state. As Politburo member General Van Tien Dung had presciently commented on the day of victory, that transformation was to be "filled with hardship." The Vietnam Communist party leaders were to prove more adept at waging war than at accommodating to peace.

Exodus Vietnam

In the final days and hours of the Republic of South Vietnam, some 130,000 of her citizens fled the country in crowded transport planes, helicopters, and troopships, and on fishing boats, rickety sampans, and barges that drifted out into the South China Sea toward the U.S. fleet and international shipping lanes. The vast exodus of refugees, most of them destined for the United States, filtered through three principal staging areas at Clark Air Base in the Philippines, Wake Island, and Guam. Within twenty-four hours army engineers bulldozed the brush and trees from an abandoned Japanese World War II airstrip on Guam, clearing a 500-acre flatland for a tent city that could hold 40,000 jam-packed refugees. Soon eighty U.S. immigration officers had flown to Guam where, working twelve- to sixteen-hour days, they began the laborious process of admitting the refugees from communism to new lives in the United States.

The Vietnamese evacuated in U.S. Operation Frequent Wind were prominent political and military figures and those whose American or Saigon ties marked them for Communist retribution. More than a third of family heads spoke fluent English. The first wave of refugees also included the professional class of doctors, lawyers, office workers, professors, and journalists, and members of their extended families, in many cases ten to fifteen people. "They were the VIPs, the cream of the crop, all first-class passengers," said an army doctor on Guam. "Some of the women even wore jewels to the physicals." Not all the elite went to Guam. President Nguyen Van Thieu, with three family members and ten tons of baggage, had gone to Taiwan en route to an exile home in London. He turned his back on the United States, which he felt had turned its back to South Vietnam.

The second wave of refugees to arrive at Guam presented a much different spectacle. Down the gangplanks of their rescue ships trudged ordinary soldiers, fishermen, and farmers, who abandoned their homeland with their families and little else. Their leave-taking was not an act of last-minute panic but a decision long pondered. Most were originally northerners, and Roman Catholics, who had moved South in 1954, when the Communists had taken over North Vietnam. Now they were resuming their flight from communism. Said a sympathetic U.S. immigration official, "All they have is wrapped up in a piece of clothing. God help them."

As the refugees moved on to camps in the United States—principally Camp Pendleton, California; Fort Chaffee, Arkansas; and Eglin Air Force Base, Florida—it appeared the majority of the American people did not want to admit them. While slightly more than a third of Americans questioned in a Gallup poll favored resettling the Vietnamese in the United States, 54 percent opposed. Some opponents feared that the Vietnamese would take away jobs from Americans in a stagnating economy where unemployment and inflation were already high. Chicago civil rights leader Rev. Jesse Jackson, for example, wanted the Vietnamese kept out of the country because "there are now nearly nine million jobless in this nation." Some opposition arose out of pure racial prejudice. Republican Representative Burt Talcott said many of his constituents in the Salinas, California, area felt, "Damn it, we have too many Orientals." High-school students near Eglin Air Force Base joked about forming a "gook klux klan." In Barling, Arkansas, near Fort Chaffee, a group of residents felt especially venomous. "They say it's a lot colder here than in Vietnam," said one woman. "With a little luck, maybe all those Vietnamese will take pneumonia and die." But a Georgia State University teacher and Vietnam veteran named David Collins thoughtfully expressed the ambivalence of many Americans when he said, "Vietnam seems a long way away to me now and I don't think we want to be reminded of it."

The resettlement process

The opposition of his fellow Americans, and their representatives in Congress, infuriated President Gerald Ford. When Congress balked at his request for $507 million to resettle the refugees, the normally placid Ford exploded. America's hostility "just burns me up," he told Republican Congressional leaders. "We didn't do that with the Hungarians; we didn't do it with the Cubans. Damn it, we're not going to do it now." With the moral dimension added to the president's political argument, Congress approved a trimmed-down proposal of $405 million for resettlement.

To orchestrate the enormous effort, Ford had appointed a former ambassador to Jordan, L. Dean Brown, to head up the Interagency Task Force, an umbrella organization

Preceding page. *Vietnamese boat people, attacked earlier by Thai pirates, clamber aboard a ship manned by a medical team in the South China Sea, November 1981.*

for twelve agencies including the Departments of State, Justice, and Health, Education, and Welfare. The Justice Department waived the normal time-consuming security checks required by the Immigration and Naturalization Service. Ambassador Brown pointed out that only about 30 percent—roughly 35,000 people—were heads of households and would thus need jobs. AFL–CIO President George Meany said, "If this great country can't absorb another 30,000 people and help them find a way to make a living, it will be denying its heritage." The government set a deadline for the end of 1975 to have the refugees in the United States resettled.

Voluntary agencies and church groups plunged into the task of finding sponsors for the refugees. As if to compensate for the initial hostility shown the newcomers, the press was soon filled with stories of Americans opening their homes to refugees. Every Lutheran church in northern California, for example, offered to sponsor a family, and the churches pooled their efforts to provide interpreters, health care, clothing, and English classes for the new arrivals. Another necessity was guidance for such tasks as obtaining driver's licenses or shopping in supermarkets. E. Michael Gutman, a Vietnam veteran from Winter Park, Florida, organized a community drive that settled forty-five refugees. David Hume Kennerly, President Ford's personal photographer and a bachelor, "adopted" a family of six whom he had befriended when he covered the war.

But there were people who took advantage of the refugees. One dispute arose at a South Royalton, Vermont, chicken-processing plant where twenty-eight veterans of South Vietnam's navy had gone to work for the then-minimum wage of $2.10 per hour, minus $10.00 deducted weekly for housing. The job—pulling the entrails out of birds moving along a production line—left their fingers battered and swollen, so nineteen of the recruits soon quit.

To the recorded refrain of "America the Beautiful," 373 tired South Vietnamese refugees debark May 4, 1975, at Florida's Eglin Air Force Base.

"It was very bad conditions," said Vo Van Quang, a thirty-three-year-old former military policeman. "Because the birds move very fast, we got injured. The boss did not pay for us to see the doctor." But owner Harold Jacobs called their work ethic into question. "They sent us a bunch of young men who never worked," he said, adding that their hands and arms would have adjusted to the work after a month. "The bleeding hearts [told them] they shouldn't have to work like regular refugees." Late in November the task force reported that sponsorships had broken down in only 2 percent of resettlements, but some believed the figure was higher.

The settlement program proceeded on schedule. Camp Pendleton refugee camp closed October 31, having processed 50,426 refugees in six months. The camps at Eglin Air Force Base and Fort Chaffee closed as planned before Christmas, as the total number of Indochina refugees resettled in the United States came to 129,775. Some 6,000 were Cambodian, and 7,000 had come from Laos. The Interagency Task Force disbanded, and in January 1976 the refugees came under the supervision of the Department of Health, Education, and Welfare. Propelled by their fundamental values of family, education, and thrift, the new Americans began to earn their way in society.

Not all the refugees had accepted resettlement. About 1,500 Vietnamese on Guam, many of them military men serving as crew members aboard evacuation ships, requested repatriation to Vietnam, mainly because they had left without their families. Staff members of the Interagency Task Force scrupulously screened them to ascertain that they were acting voluntarily and had no past or current association with the Central Intelligence Agency, a possible link suggesting that they might be seeking repatriation to act as spies or potential fifth columnists. In October they boarded the South Vietnamese cargo ship *Thuong Tin* and steamed for home. There the authorities promptly arrested them and, accusing them of being CIA agents, dispatched them to a reeducation camp in Dong Xuan District, Phu Khanh Province. According to a refugee report, the *Thuong Tin* passengers were still interned in 1981.

A trickle of refugees

As the Indochina refugees from April 1975 dispersed throughout the United States—and other countries, especially Canada and France, where a total of 6,629 had resettled—it seemed as if the flight of refugees from the new Communist state was a one-time phenomenon. Following the great exodus of April, only another 377 refugees turned up in other countries such as Thailand or Malaysia during the remainder of 1975.

But the following year the total number of refugees rose to 5,619. Most of those refugees had escaped Vietnam in fishing boats or other coastal craft and sailed west

30

Life in the U.S.A.

Nguyen Quy Thuan and his pregnant wife Gai arrive with their six children in Gainesville, Florida, where community sponsors offered food, clothing, and shelter for a year. Even under the best of circumstances, homesickness, economic insecurity, and cultural barriers make resettlement difficult. Thuan is eager to support his family, but with a $2 hourly wage, the prospects are dim.

Right. *Vo Thai Gai (center) waits in food stamp office with translator Nhung Fullen. Husband Thuan is the only family member who speaks English. Left. Thuan finds that an affordable rental house, at $70 per month, is little more than a vandalized shell. Above. At work at an auto dealership, cultural barriers keep Thuan from joining in lunchtime camaraderie.*

31

through the South China Sea and the Gulf of Thailand toward the Malay Peninsula. The numbers given for refugees, of course, counted only those who had arrived in the so-called country of first asylum; others may have been lost at sea or been apprehended trying to escape. Refugee officials estimated that one-third of the refugees may have died at sea, victims of weather, unseaworthy craft, or a host of other perils, including dehydration and piracy.

These were the "boat people." Most left in boats that were dangerously overloaded, and few of the refugees had navigational skills or charts. At best the boat had a fisherman for a captain who knew only the coastal waters of his native province. Despite the risks they faced, however, the boat people set out confidently. "We didn't like living under the Communists," explained one old man, who with fifty-five compatriots docked at an island in Malaysia in November 1976 after a voyage from Cam Ranh Bay in a thirty-foot trawler. Fifty more people scheduled to make the trip had been caught at a roadblock on the night of the escape. Those caught escaping usually wound up in jail or a reeducation camp. According to a statement from one security office, Vietnamese lived in "independence, liberty and happiness," hence any refugee by the very act of trying to leave was criticizing, even slandering, the regime and the Party; this made him or her a counter-revolutionary.

In 1977 the total number of refugees from Vietnam jumped sharply to 21,276, precipitating a minor international crisis. Merchant ships that had once responded to distress calls now by-passed the refugee boats. The mariners' customary code of chivalry at sea, with the rescued seafarers deposited at the first port of call, began to disappear when various countries began to refuse the refugees, leaving them as the responsibility of a ship's captain and owners. As one disabled boat drifted helplessly for days off Malaysia, the thirty-three refugees aboard pooled their urine and drank it. A two-year-old baby and then a four-year-old boy died of dehydration. Twelve other children lingered near death. Phan Van Thieu, a former U.S. aid official, reported that at least sixty ships, including some with Japanese and French registration, passed them by. "We waved white cloths and called for help," Thieu said, "but not one of them stopped. They all saw us. Some of them passed within a hundred meters." Finally a Norwegian freighter picked them up and steamed on to Singapore.

U.S. policy had been to admit 300 boat people per month. But in the growing crisis, the State Department sought permission for a one-time admission of 15,000 refugees and prodded other countries to loosen their immigration quotas as well. Yet the number of refugees fleeing Vietnam throughout 1977 remained but a trickle compared to the torrent that was to come.

As their numbers grew, the plight of the boat people got worse. The few refugee camps in Thailand and Malaysia were crowded, so coastal patrol craft from those countries began to turn away refugee boats after allowing them to replenish supplies. Overcrowded Singapore soon followed suit. The boat people sailed precariously on until they could find landfalls or places that would take them in. Several boats made it all the way to Australia, a distance of some 8,000 kilometers, where they were allowed to stay.

The refugees' vulnerability brought back an age-old seafaring menace—piracy. In 1976 stories of pirate attacks were rare; but the helplessness of the refugees soon became widely known. Unable to obtain weapons under the Communists, the refugees were usually unarmed. They had converted their resources into easily carried and concealed gold and jewelry. Those factors made them prey for pirates. Most of the brigands were Thai fishermen, who found cover in the large Thai fishing fleet—40,000 to 50,000 small boats—and abundant hiding places in the hundreds of islands along the southern peninsula. To make matters worse, long-standing racial antipathy between Thais and Vietnamese prompted the pirates to act with great savagery. Rapes, killings, and kidnapings became commonplace. U.S. officials interviewing victims in the camps often entered the initials "RPM" in their case histories. It stood for "rape, pillage, murder." An American official estimated in 1979 that 30 percent of all boats leaving southern Vietnam had been boarded by pirates; perhaps a third of those suffered RPM. In 1981 the United Nations high commissioner for refugees (UNHCR) reported that women on 81 percent of the boats reaching Thailand had been raped, most of them many times over.

Vuong Viet Kieu, twenty, left Vietnam by boat early in 1979. After only one day at sea, the boat was boarded by Thai pirates who robbed all the refugees, then sent the nine women aboard below decks, where they raped them repeatedly before letting them go. One doctor who interviewed rape victims reported: "All they could sense at the time was the stark fear of being faced by naked, sweating, foul-smelling men; the look on the rapists' faces as they laughed and leered; the shock of slappings and beatings; and finally the tearing pain as violation after violation took place in the most forceful and crude manner." Like many victims, Vuong Viet Kieu became pregnant. She planned to have the baby and then join her parents in the United States.

Not all victims were let go. Pirates routinely carried women off their boats, some to be kept as concubines, others to be sold to Thai brothels where they were kept as prisoners. Pirates kidnaped Nguyen Phuong Thuy, fifteen, and another young girl and then sank the refugee boat, drowning sixty-seven other Vietnamese. "I can't forget the look on my little sister Tran's face when she slipped below

An overladen boat carrying 162 refugees sinks just a few meters off the coast of Malaysia in December 1978. Most of the refugees swam ashore or were rescued.

the water," Thuy said later. The pirates kept her in a dark locker below decks, fed her a subsistence diet of rice and water, and came in to gang-rape her as many as thirty times a day. Her companion was treated similarly and then thrown overboard. Thuy was bartered to other boats and after three and one-half months was finally put ashore, where she made her way to a refugee camp. While recovering from her ordeal, she wrote home to her mother: "Don't think about coming by sea. Escape or not, you surely will be dead, but I think it's better to be dead in Vietnam."

The refugees were defenseless against the armed pirates. Men trying to thwart rape or kidnaping might be killed or thrown overboard, with their hands bound, to drown. A refugee who hesitated to give up a wedding band might have his or her finger cut off. Many boats

---

This seriously burned woman on Bidong Island was disfigured by boiling water thrown by a family member when she refused to become a prostitute.

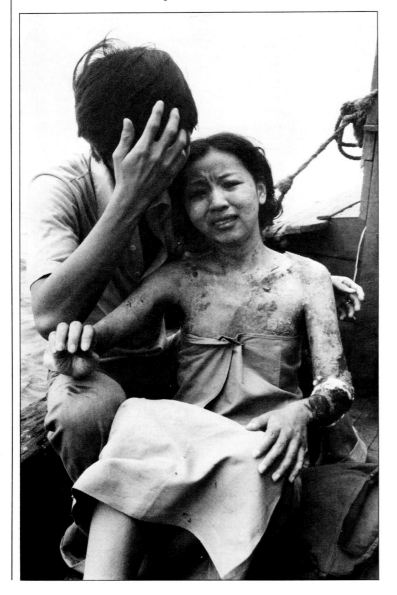

were attacked more than once, and the refugees suffered vengeful brutality when by the second or third boarding they had nothing left of value to surrender.

Refugees also risked danger from their fellow travelers. Under the most difficult circumstances of exhaustion, starvation, and thirst, people thrown together with no common purpose other than the desire to escape grew fearful and suspicious and might fall upon each other. A fifteen-year-old orphan boy named Pham jumped on a boat leaving Haiphong for Hong Kong. The eleven refugees aboard had accumulated twenty kilograms of rice and forty liters of water, but those gave out during the voyage that lasted fifty-two days. Four people "fell" overboard after fighting with the captain. As Pham related to *Time* writer Roger Rosenblatt:

The boatmaster wanted to eat me. . . . [He] told a boy who was a neighbor of mine to take a hammer and hit me on the head, so that they might eat my flesh. . . . They put a shirt over my head, and they hit me with something hard. I felt the men come over to lift off the shirt. But I was still conscious. I heard the boatmaster order another man to cut my throat. At the moment they took the shirt off my head, they saw that I was conscious, and that tears were on my face. I did not know what they were thinking. Then someone said, "Pham, do you want to live?" And I said, "Yes, of course I want to live." So they untied me and took me into the cabin. . . . The next day the boy who used the hammer on me was himself found dead. After the body was discovered, the boatmaster pulled it up out of the hold. Then he cut up the body. Everyone was issued a piece of meat about two fingers wide.

Who were the refugees?

Of the Vietnamese who fled from the South, most were associated in some way with the government or other institutions that had existed prior to the Communist victory. They included politicians, members of the military, civil servants, as well as businessmen, teachers, technicians, and professionals. Many worked on escape plans for years. A university teacher and political dissident named Nguyen Long, holder of a 1973 doctorate from Berkeley, elected against the wishes of his wife to remain in Vietnam. Like tens of thousands of other professionals, he wanted to help build a new country. "A month after the fall of Saigon, I still thought the NLF was a powerful political organization composed of Southern patriots even though many had joined under Northern Communist pressure, . . . " he later wrote. "But the NLF was only a satellite, mobilized and dominated by the Communist Party. . . . By late 1975 . . . I had come to see the true face of Communism." Long lost his position and worked at various jobs, including that of mechanic and private tutor. After two failed attempts a year apart, Long and his family escaped from Vietnam by boat in 1979.

Relatives of "class enemies" also had trouble. The daughter of an ARVN intelligence officer, La Thi Thuy

Quynh, finished her college studies in chemistry but was denied her graduation certificate until she had served as a teacher in a New Economic Zone in the Mekong Delta. Her husband, Pham Bao Quang, was also ordered to a NEZ, but one closer to Ho Chi Minh City. Some Vietnamese who felt disenfranchised in the North likewise looked for ways to escape. One refugee's father had served in the French army and in 1964 had been sent to a labor camp for nine years. Because of that tainted family background, the son was deprived of education and took work as a laborer. "Not that I was afraid of working with my hands," he said. "If I could have made a decent living, I would have, but as a laborer you don't make enough money to smoke even the cheapest cigarettes. One of my brothers is a ditch-digger, the other a pedi-cab driver in Hanoi. . . . Once out of frustration I volunteered to join the army, but even for that I was refused." This man fell into illegal activity and spent time in prison for trafficking in gold and opium before escaping from Vietnam.

Because of the number of people fleeing Vietnam by boat, it soon became difficult for people living inland to win permission to travel to the coast. Several family members might obtain travel permits, but others could be denied in order to lessen the possibility of the entire family leaving. Black market prices of boats and motors rose astronomically high, necessitating the pooling of resources and leading in turn to dangerously overcrowded boats. Those with mechanical or carpentry skills enabling them to rebuild an engine or refurbish a boat proved very valuable. City dwellers who made it to the coast had to act circumspectly as they inquired about boats or sought out groups preparing an escape. One Saigon doctor who spent four weeks on the Ca Mau Peninsula searching for passage related that to avoid arousing suspicions of the police, he cut his hair and changed his style of clothing to appear to be a local resident who worked outdoors.

A woman raped during a 1979 boat crossing from Vietnam to Malaysia is attended by doctors on the French hospital ship Ile de Lumière.

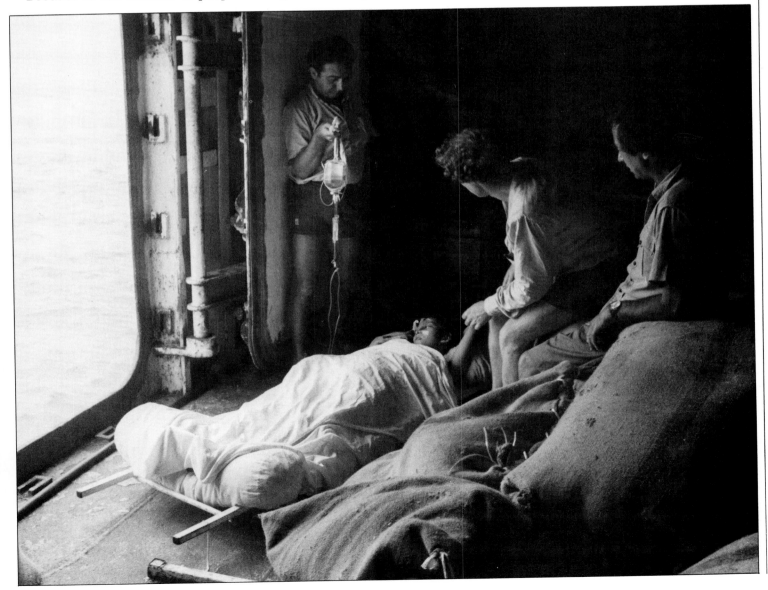

Provoked by economic distress or social ostracism, or dissatisfied with other aspects of life under communism, more and more native Vietnamese sought a means to leave their country. Beginning in 1978 the ethnic Chinese living in Vietnam found themselves confronted with economic pressures and racial antagonisms that made life intolerable.

Rooting out the compradors

In Vietnam, the five-year plan approved by the Fourth Party Congress in December 1976 to "build socialism" was lagging. Among its other goals, the ambitious economic plan called for a 7.8 percent annual growth in agriculture through water conservation, increasing mechanization, and opening new lands to cultivation by consigning millions of people to New Economic Zones. The state encouraged farmers to increase their food production by double-cropping and developing subsidiary crops. Still, farmers in the South were reluctant to sell their grain to state organizations at artificially low prices. They held back their stores, forcing the government to import grain. Moreover, a disastrous cold snap in 1977 was followed by the worst typhoons in thirty years. These circumstances collided head-on with the new government's determination to impose on the South the collectivization of agriculture as already applied in the North.

Collectivization could not proceed until private commerce had been totally abolished. In the first months after liberation, Hanoi had taken over distribution of rice, wholesale meats, fish, vegetables, and gasoline and nationalized such industries as communications and transportation, hotels, rental housing, and pharmaceuticals.

These industries were controlled by so-called *comprador* capitalists. *Comprador* was a Portugese word, meaning a native agent for foreign or colonial traders. Most of them were ethnic Chinese, or *Hoa*, as the Vietnamese called them. Of the 1.7 million ethnic Chinese in Vietnam, 1.4 million lived in the South, where for generations they had prospered in commerce and dominated the banking, wholesale, and retail trades. Some people referred to them in derogatory phrases such as "the Chinese cyst," or "the Jews of Asia." "Compradores belong to the capitalist class. . . . They live off the misfortunes of the people, especially in time of war," said an editorial in the Party-line *Saigon Giai Phong* in 1975. "They are profiteers of treason, the closest collaborators of the puppets." Most ethnic Chinese were citizens of South Vietnam, but they spoke their own language and preserved their schools and their way of life. After the war, the government allowed the Chinese schools to reopen only after teachers had undergone "reeducation" in Communist ideals. The *Hoa* were viewed with suspicion by the government, not only for their capitalist proclivities but because Hanoi believed the *Hoa* reserved their true loyalty for China.

After two years of the gradualist approach to limiting private commerce, the Communists found in 1978 that some 400 private factories and 15,000 small businesses and shops accounted for 65 percent of total industrial production in the South. In cases where the Party had attempted to combine state control with private enterprise, the small entrepreneurs had not cooperated with the doctrinaire Party officials. The continuing private sector production within the larger state-controlled economy induced hoarding and price speculation, and this led to shortages of consumer goods and flourishing black markets. A comparable absence of state control over agriculture led to hoarding and shortages of grain and rice in rural areas. "One need not be a learned scholar or a shrewd politician to see that the deterioration of the living conditions of people in South Vietnam is not wanted by the revolutionary administration," read one commentary in the *Vietnam Courier*. Party planners realized that such economic fluctuation could not be allowed to continue.

In June 1977, at the Second Plenum of the Fourth Party Congress, the Central Committee voted to begin the transition to complete socialism in the South. In July First Secretary Le Duan announced that the government would soon act to seize industry and commerce in South Vietnam and that rural collectivization would follow. The Party established a Committee for the Transformation of Industry and Trade in South Vietnam. This produced very limited results, so on March 23, 1978, the government declared an end to all "trading and business operations." Only small private traders such as handcraft workers were allowed to continue private operations. Earlier government actions against the *comprador* capitalists had been thwarted when merchants dispersed their wares among families and friends, so that the government could not take inventories. This time the Party organized in advance of its proclamation thousands of youth squads, supplemented in many cases by PAVN soldiers, to descend on shops and examine their contents. All seized goods were to be purchased at the state-controlled price, plus a profit of 10 percent if bills of sale could be provided, a price far lower than the open market value of the goods. Many businessmen were ruined overnight. A month later the government further tightened its grip by issuing a single new currency for all Vietnam, which wiped out the savings of the middle class and the wealthy—many of those being Chinese.

These extreme measures did what years of persuasion had not done. Do Muoi, the chairman of the Committee for the Transformation of Trade, announced that private industry in the South had been "basically destroyed." Traders who did not switch their efforts into productive labor were pressured to leave the cities and move with their families to New Economic Zones. Many of them, however, especially ethnic Chinese, chose to take to the sea and leave Vietnam with the connivance of the government. The government decided to make money from the exodus.

Trafficking in refugees

In June 1978 small, out-of-the-way offices operated by the Public Security Bureau—the political police—began to sell departure permissions. Authorities passed word to various Chinese organizations that sea passage could be arranged for a fee. Chinese middlemen were encouraged to organize groups of would-be emigrants and provide them with boats. The price was five taels of gold per adult (half-price for a child), payable to the government, and an equal amount to cover the cost of a boat, supplies, and bribes for local officials—about $3,000 in all. (Vietnamese gold came in thin, beaten strips called taels. Weighing 1.2 ounces, a tael was worth an average of $300 in the gold market of 1978-79. Officially it was illegal to possess gold in Vietnam and police were under orders to confiscate it upon discovery.)

The Chinese flocked to the middlemen and paid for "going abroad officially." The well-to-do were happy to pay in order to leave Vietnam. Impoverished Chinese borrowed from the wealthy with promises to repay the sums once they had resettled overseas. "For us it was a good opportunity to get out of hell," explained Tran Vy Hien, a former merchant from Nha Trang who had been jailed after one failed escape attempt. "For my children, it was a chance to have a better future. . . . All they had to look forward to was the life of a water buffalo, working in the fields for the rest of their days."

Vietnamese also took advantage of the government-sanctioned bribery scheme by passing for Chinese. A brisk business soon developed in false identification cards, election papers, and birth certificates. False papers generally cost one tael. The Vietnamese learned enough of the Cantonese language to fool officials who confronted passengers with questions in Cantonese. The Chinese middlemen had wide discretion and often charged far more than the going rate. "The boat organizer's greed is one thousand times worse than the cruelty of the Communists," said Tran Quoc Tuan. "Three hundred and sixty people were squeezed onto a boat that was originally supposed to carry only 170. Two days out an exhaust fan below broke and two people suffocated. We tried to return to shore, but at nine in the evening we hit a sand dune and capsized. Only 110 people survived."

Because of the clandestine nature of the arrangements, disagreements readily occurred between the middlemen and their passengers and between the middlemen and those officials who checked the passengers and often confiscated more gold and valuables that they carried with them. Also, officials in different jurisdictions competed for their shares. According to Nguyen Long, who posed as Chinese to escape with his family:

Those in one city would permit an officially registered boat to set out, only to have their comrades in a neighboring city stop it as the boat moved into their territorial waters. Both civil and military officials were authorized to detain boats for security reasons in their area of jurisdiction; and the exportation of boat people at times led to skirmishes between cadres and soldiers who disagreed about their share of the gold and money collected.

To avoid such squabbling, Public Security Bureau agents sometimes escorted the boats out to sea, beyond the reach of local authorities.

Vietnam found the "business" so profitable that by late 1978 the fishing trawlers and coastal barges leaving Vietnam were joined by larger tramp freighters. Packed to the gunwales with refugees, they cruised through the South China Sea looking for a port that would take them in. The first was the *Southern Cross*, which appeared off Malaysia in September 1978 with 1,220 Indochinese aboard whom the captain claimed to have rescued from their foundering ship. Malaysia refused to admit them without assurances that some other country would accept them for resettlement. The *Southern Cross* then steamed to the uninhabited Indonesian island of Pengibu, between Malaysia and Borneo, where the crew marooned the refugees. Indonesia reluctantly accepted them.

A month later another freighter, the 1,600-ton *Hai Hong*, appeared off Indonesia carrying 2,500 refugees who, the captain claimed, had clambered aboard the ship as it lay at anchor for engine repairs in the Vietnamese-owned Paracel Islands. Denied permission to stop in Indonesia or Singapore, the *Hai Hong* steamed for Port Klang, Malaysia's main commercial shipping port, where it an-

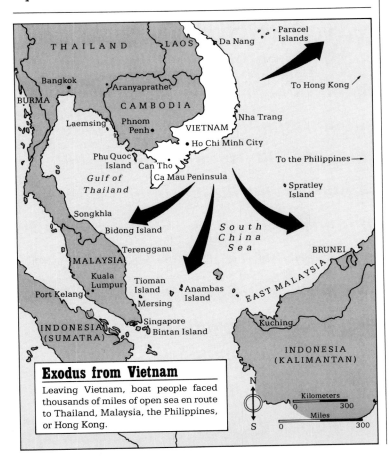

Exodus from Vietnam

Leaving Vietnam, boat people faced thousands of miles of open sea en route to Thailand, Malaysia, the Philippines, or Hong Kong.

chored until Malaysia accepted the refugees. After both the *Southern Cross* and *Hai Hong* disembarked their human cargo, the stories of the refugees' passage began to come to light. Rather than having been picked up at sea, the refugees said they had boarded the ships in Vietnamese ports under the eyes of well-paid Vietnamese authorities.

In December 1978 the *Huey Fong* became the third freighter to focus attention on Hanoi's refugee trafficking when, packed with 3,318 refugees, it anchored off Hong Kong. The *Huey Fong* remained at anchor for almost a month before Hong Kong authorities permitted it to sail into the harbor. Hong Kong accepted the Vietnamese refugees but pressed legal proceedings against the crew for bringing in refugees by "illegal pretense."

The case went to trial in June 1979 and exposed the behind-the-scenes organization of the refugee trafficking. One of the accused, a Chinese middleman named Kwok Wah-leung, described how he had piloted the *Huey Fong* into Vietnamese waters and met two Vietnamese gunboats off Vung Tau. He had traveled with the Vietnamese to Ho Chi Minh City where he met with officials who sat counting and weighing gold tael leaves, rings, and chains that the prospective *Huey Fong* passengers had surrendered as their fares. The *Huey Fong* was supposed to carry 1,500 passengers, but the Vietnamese had loaded more than twice that number aboard. Hong Kong authorities had found 3,500 taels of gold, worth $1.05 million, hidden in the engine room. Found guilty, the *Huey Fong* crew members received prison sentences ranging from fifteen months to seven years.

Hanoi denied that it had a hand in the refugees' departures and argued that the government could not be expected to patrol the country's 2,000-kilometer coastline. The government blamed the refugee traffic on a "clandestine organization" with ties to the United States. According to a long 1979 commentary in the government-published *Vietnam Courier*, "ships are plying clandestinely, taking away those who wish to leave the country—businessmen seeking fortune elsewhere, counter-revolutionary agents who feel insecure." Intellectuals and technicians traveled for free, the article claimed, draining talent from Vietnam. As to the question of any money changing hands, the same commentary explained, "There may be cadres who have availed themselves of the situation to get their palms greased, but this is not government policy. What government can claim that none of its employees has ever been tempted in certain circumstances to fill his pockets?" With an air of one being unjustly accused, Foreign Minister Nguyen Co Thach tried in 1979 to rationalize Vietnam's predicament. "In 1975, we forbade [refugees] to go out,"

Refugees bunk down amid their meager possessions aboard the Hai Hong, *a 1,600-ton freighter, while awaiting the Malaysian government's decision to admit them.*

he said. "We were criticized by the West. We thought it over. We decided to give them the freedom to go. Now [Vietnam's critics] say we are exporting refugees."

Vietnam's protestations fell on disbelieving ears throughout the world. As Barry Wain, a reporter for the *Asian Wall Street Journal*, wrote, "Hanoi's denials defied common sense. Did anyone seriously believe that in a totalitarian state 135,000 people in three months could be organized, ticketed, transported to departure points and allocated boats—a major logistical exercise and one that a nationwide travel agency in any Western country would be proud to equal with the assistance of computerized bookings and international airlines—without the government's knowledge?" In June 1979 Hong Kong Information Secretary David Ford suggested that Vietnam regarded the refugee trade as a leading source of foreign exchange. "Indeed, it is now said to have overtaken their largest export earner, their coal industry," said Ford. If the program continued until every ethnic Chinese had been expelled, the foreign exchange earnings from the refugee traffic might amount to $3 billion. As one Chinese publication summed up, "Humans, it has been said, have become the country's leading export earner."

Calluses on the heart

The flood of boat people washing up on the shores of the Southeast Asian nations put tremendous strains on the resources of Malaysia, Thailand, Indonesia, and Hong Kong, where authorities established refugee camps with the help of the United Nations high commissioner for refugees. Overcrowded Singapore, the city-state on the southern tip of the Malay Peninsula, had taken a singularly tough-minded approach to the refugees; it turned them away unless they could guarantee rapid resettlement in other countries. Said Prime Minister Lee Kuan Yew, "You've got to grow calluses on your heart or you just bleed to death." Singapore resupplied and refueled the boats and cast them off.

Malaysia initially proved to be a relatively hospitable country of first asylum, and the southwesterly course to Malaysia avoided the perils of piracy in the Gulf of Thailand. Almost 40 percent of the boat people landed in Malaysia where, until late 1978, fishermen and villagers often helped the refugees, sometimes for a fee but more often spontaneously offering aid. Eventually the influx of ethnic Chinese refugees created tensions in the multiracial, multireligious fabric of Malaysia, officially a Muslim country with a 35 percent Chinese population. The three states on the northeast coast of Malaysia, which provided landfall for most of the refugee boats, were predominantly Muslim, and by the end of 1978, local residents were discomfited by the stream of Chinese refugees, who, residents complained, drove up the cost of living. Residents of the conservative Malay communities took to stoning refugees as

they came ashore. Soon the Malaysian navy was turning refugee boats away or towing them out to sea. In June 1979 Malaysia's deputy prime minister threatened to enact "shoot on sight" legislation to permit the navy to drive off boats trying to land. In the first six months of that year Malaysia towed out to sea 267 boats carrying more than 40,000 refugees. Many of them tried again, or drifted south to Indonesia. This castaway policy created another class of Indochina refugees, dubbed "beach people," who ran the blockades, scuttled their boats, and swam ashore. Once they made it to land, they were permitted to remain. Many of the refugees, especially ethnic Chinese, were urban residents who, living away from the coast or rivers, had never learned to swim. Drownings were frequent.

To ease tensions between Malays and the refugees, the authorities located the United Nations–run camps away from the population, usually on uninhabited islands. One of the largest camps was on Pulau Bidong, an unpopulated tropical island thirty kilometers off the coast with coral sand beaches and hills covered with jungle. Over the next year, however, 453 boatloads containing 52,516 refugees docked at Bidong, and the island was soon stripped of all trees and vegetation to provide building materials and firewood. Within a year only 10,500 refugees had qualified for resettlement in the United States, Australia, and Europe, with the remainder settling into life in the refugee camp. Australian writer Bruce Grant described it:

One stepped ashore into a violent, tragic, sordid, but also indestructibly resilient world. Bidong was a dangerously congested slum; a tropical island ghetto; a chunk of South Vietnamese society pre-1975, unrepentantly capitalist, anti-communist and predatory, grafted onto a bit of offshore Malaysia; a shantytown with a population of 42,000 confined to a living area of less than one square kilometer.

Pulau Bidong's housing consisted of shanty tenements, some three stories high, constructed of timber from the hillsides, cardboard, and tin sheets. An average room of little more than three by two meters might hold several families. Heaps of refuse despoiled the beach until an incinerator could be built, and the smell of human excrement fouled the air. "We have run out of space to bury rubbish," said Le Ngoc Trieu, a Catholic priest from South Vietnam. "We had to fill in some of the old latrine pits to build more houses over them." Because of the shortage of water (120 wells had been dug, but only 20 remained usable for long), long lines formed for the water that arrived every few days on barges. The United Nations provided each resident 900 grams of food every three days—rice, condensed milk, canned meat, fish, and vegetables. Those with money could supplement their diets or other tastes on a booming black market. Grant noted that "tailors, barbers, mechanics, pawnbrokers, bakers, cakemakers, and hawkers of all kinds sold their skills, brawn and goods. There were woodcutters, watch repairers, acupuncturists and artists." Black marketeers swam offshore at night, pushing homemade boats ahead of them. Out on the water they rendezvoused with Malaysian fishermen who smuggled food and goods to them.

Not every camp was beset by conditions as squalid as those in Pulau Bidong. In Hong Kong, which by September of 1979 had a refugee population of some 67,000—the largest single concentration of boat people in Asia—authorities allowed the UNHCR to administer the camps, and his staff did an excellent job. Refugees had freedom of movement, and to relieve a labor shortage in the territory, Hong Kong authorities curtailed food subsidies, thereby encouraging refugees to find employment outside the camps while awaiting resettlement.

Many of the refugees arriving in Hong Kong were ethnic Chinese from North Vietnam. Like their fellow countrymen in South Vietnam, many of the 300,000 *Hoa* in the North engaged in commerce in a kind of sub rosa economy that Hanoi seemed to find ineradicable. Contrary to the *Hoa* in the South, however, most had not taken citizenship, though many had participated in society to the extent of joining the military and intermarrying with Vietnamese. Their proximity to China permitted many of the northern *Hoa* to maintain close ties with their heritage and families in China; visits to China were approved about once every three years. *Hoa* living in the mountainous border regions regularly smuggled goods back and forth for the North's black markets.

In 1978 relations between Vietnam and China were worsening, and they deteriorated even further when Vietnam abolished private trade in March and set off the flight of the southern boat people. As tensions arose between the two Communist neighbors, the northern *Hoa* began to feel the backlash. Rumor campaigns questioned the loyalty of the *Hoa* in the event of a war. Hanoi seemed to consider the ethnic Chinese a potential fifth column. Some *Hoa* bowed to the pressure, and to the increasingly virulent propaganda campaign between Peking and Hanoi, and fled on foot across the border. Then in February 1979 came China's invasion of Vietnam, setting off a destructive seventeen-day war and more heated propaganda exchanges. This made even more precarious the position of the ethnic Chinese in northern Vietnam. Following the Chinese withdrawal, Vietnam accused some ethnic Chinese of having aided the enemy. Gathering the *Hoa* into groups, government officials informed them that to protect Vietnam against espionage, and to protect the *Hoa* themselves against repercussions, the ethnic Chinese would be removed to other parts of the country, where they would farm or perform other "productive labor," in other words, removal to New Economic Zones. The other option available to them was emigration. This was the option most of

Malaysian authorities under strict orders not to admit Vietnamese boat people stand ready to refuse entry to the refugee boat approaching from the left.

them chose. Virtually the entire Chinese population left northern Vietnam. China alone repatriated and resettled 276,000 of them. The remainder left Vietnam by boat, usually hugging the coastline of China as they sailed northeast until they reached Hong Kong.

The crisis eased

In 1967 the Association of Southeast Asian Nations was formed, allying Thailand, Malaysia, Singapore, Indonesia, and the Philippines—the so-called dominoes of Southeast Asia. When the ASEAN foreign ministers met at Bali, Indonesia, in June 1979, their main preoccupation was Vietnam and the refugees. Hard-pressed Malaysia had ceased calling the boat people refugees and now classed them as "illegal immigrants." More than 350,000 refugees awaited resettlement in Hong Kong and ASEAN transit camps, and the numbers rose daily. Evoking the "domino theory," Singapore's Sinnathamby Rajaratnam charged that refugees, packed into "floating coffins," represented "political warfare" on the part of Hanoi, which sent them as "time bombs to destabilize, disrupt and cause turmoil and dissension in ASEAN states." According to the Philippines Foreign Minister Carlos Romulo, every ASEAN country's resources were "strained to the limit."

The ASEAN countries were particularly annoyed at the half-hearted response of the developed world, especially the United States. President Jimmy Carter, who took office in January 1977, had made human rights the cornerstone of his foreign policy. On a visit to refugee camps in Thailand in early 1978, Carter's vice president, Walter Mondale, said, "There is no more profound test of our government's commitment to human rights than the way we deal with" the Indochina refugees. The fact was that by April 1978 the United States had accepted 160,000 Indochina refugees, but nearly 80 percent of that total had come in the few weeks following the fall of South Vietnam and Cambodia. Only 26,000 more had been admitted in the three subsequent years, about the same as the number of Filipinos and South Koreans admitted each year to the U.S. France had accepted 42,000 Indochina refugees and Australia and Canada about 7,000 each. The United States had established restrictive immigration categories, admitting only refugees with close relatives in the country, former U.S. government employees, and other refugees who could be admitted for "compelling reasons." Although the categories seemed broad enough to cover the boat people, refugees from the first two categories quickly filled the limited quotas. This caused President Carter in April 1978 to increase to 7,000 the number of Indochina refugees admitted to the country each month.

Pulau Bidong refugee camp, a shantytown of multistory tenements run by the U.N. on an island off Malaysia, teems with Vietnamese awaiting resettlement.

The June 1979 declaration by the ASEAN nations that they would no longer accept refugees transformed the plight of the boat people from a regional to an international crisis. U.N. Secretary-General Kurt Waldheim convened a two-day ministerial conference in Geneva of representatives of sixty-five governments to confront what he called "one of the most tragic experiences which the world has faced." To compound the problem, United Nations High Commissioner for Refugees Poul Hartling foresaw a deficit in 1979 of $56 million for the fund that was supposed to succor the mass of refugees.

At the Palais de Nations the Vietnamese delegation, led by Deputy Foreign Minister Phan Hien, repeated its government's insistence that it had no hand in refugee trafficking and bore no blame for the crisis. But Vietnam did promise to abide by an agreement reached in May with the UNHCR to establish a program for the "orderly departure" of persons wishing to leave the country. That was taken to mean that Vietnam would stanch the flow of refugees. The conference also induced pledges totaling $190 million for the UNHCR and a dramatic increase in promised resettlements by Western nations. The United States doubled its monthly quota of refugee admissions to 14,000.

As a part of its campaign to clamp down on refugee traffic, Vietnam in June sent the crew of a Greek ship before a People's Court on charges of attempting to smuggle refugees out of the country. The crew was found guilty and ordered to pay a fine of $5,000 but was allowed to depart two days later without having paid. Early in July Hanoi radio reported that Dang Thanh Dong, director of a fishing enterprise in Tien Gian Province, had been jailed for ten years for arranging escapes. Later, Tran Minh Chau, a former ARVN soldier, was sentenced to death for an attempted boat escape in which a guard had been killed.

As Vietnam undertook serious efforts, the flow of refugees fell off abruptly. In August refugees reaching countries of first asylum fell to 6,770, and in the year's final three months, only 8,680 refugees fled Indochina, and these were bona fide escapees, mainly fishermen and rural residents who obtained small boats and departed surreptitiously in groups of thirty and forty.

During 1980 and 1981 an average of 50,000 Vietnamese refugees arrived in first asylum countries such as Malaysia, Thailand, Indonesia, and Hong Kong. This was still a significant number but far beneath the peaks of 1978 and 1979. Under the orderly departure program, Vietnam released 4,706 emigrants in 1980 and 9,815 in 1981. As the crisis of the Vietnamese boat people eased, however, another refugee problem took on urgency. In 1979–80 some 140,000 Cambodians had crossed into UNHCR camps in Thailand, and another 150,000 were grouped in jungle encampments on Cambodian soil along the Thai border. They were fleeing a series of cataclysms that had engulfed their country from the moment of Communist conquest in April 1975.

Khmer Rouge Takeover

On April 17, 1975, five years of savage civil war in Cambodia came to an end. Except for a few pockets of soldiers hopelessly trading fire with Communist insurgents, the government had collapsed. Phnom Penh stood with its guard down, and the Khmer Rouge, peasant soldiers dressed in black pajamas and dripping with arms and grenades, marched into a city whose people were filled with nervous expectations.

"Everybody, Cambodians and foreigners alike," wrote *New York Times* correspondent Sydney H. Schanberg, "looked with hopeful relief to the collapse of the city, for they felt that when the Communists came and the war finally ended, at least the suffering would largely be over." But, writing after the fact, Schanberg was compelled to add, "All of us were wrong."

Trailed by curious onlookers, victorious Khmer Rouge soldiers enter Phnom Penh.

The hopeful mood of the crowds evaporated as the expressionless Khmer Rouge filed into Phnom Penh, answering cheers with stony silence. Country boys and girls, some hardly taller than their AK47 assault rifles, and older men in their twenties, the Khmer Rouge came in scattered groups, keeping to no military formation. Most of the insurgents wore *chromas*, the red-and-white checked scarves that signified friendship.

The Khmer Rouge exhibited little friendship to the people of Phnom Penh. Before long they began to stop traffic and empty the cars of the occupants. Khmer Rouge soldiers, long used to the privations of the jungle, began looting, pulling Rolex watches and cigarettes and food out of store windows. A truck with cases of Pepsi Cola and a box of ice dispensed drinks to the jungle fighters. "Soldiers drove past in cars heaped high with cigarettes, soft drinks and wine," wrote London *Sunday Times* correspondent Jon Swain. "Few knew how to drive: the crash of gear boxes was the pre-

vailing sound. In other circumstances their efforts to make cars go would have been hilarious. Now they were grotesque: the peasant boys with death at the tip of their fingers were behaving like spoilt brats."

Using bullhorns or simply shouting and brandishing their weapons, the Khmer Rouge began clearing Phnom Penh of civilians. They ordered people out of their houses and herded them down the streets. They offered various stories, that the residents were leaving for three days or ten; that they were leaving because the Americans were going to bomb Phnom Penh or because there was no food. Even the hospital was evacuated, and patients with intravenous bags still attached were wheeled along on gurneys as the streets, wrote Schanberg, "became clogged with a sorrowful exodus."

The Communist party of Kampuchea—the Khmer Rouge—was embarking on a peasant revolution in which city residents, once in the countryside, were to become "new people." Cambodia's calvary had begun.

Above. *On the afternoon of liberation, a Khmer Rouge officer confronts members of the Cambodian government outside the Information Ministry.* "There will be no reprisals," *he assures them. In fact, most, if not all, were to be killed.*

Right. *Walking arsenal: A teen-age soldier of the Khmer Rouge. In the background is an officer, identifiable by his pistol.*

Above. *Long after liberation, the once-throbbing city of Phnom Penh remains deserted.*

Right. *By cart, bicycle, motor scooter, and foot, residents quit Phnom Penh in droves and head for the countryside after the Khmer Rouge order to evacuate.*

Western-style shoes abandoned by Phnom Penh residents symbolize the haste of the 1975 evacuation.

Revolution Against Revolution

To the people of Cambodia, the Khmer Rouge wore a mysterious face. The young, jungle-toughened soldiers who herded 3 million people out of the throbbing city of Phnom Penh on April 17, 1975, wore no insignia or signs of rank. Neither did the older soldiers, presumably officers, who occasionally issued terse orders. The soldiers cited no head of government, no towering Ho Chi Minh-like figure as the avatar of their revolution. Instead they named *Angka*—the Organization—as their authority. *Angka*, they said, would deliver food along the route. *Angka* would provide.

Radio Phnom Penh announced that the Royal Government of National Union of Cambodia had taken over. It was a peculiar name for a Communist regime. The front organization for the Khmer Rouge during the civil war, the RGNUC was ostensibly headed by Prince Sihanouk, the former leader of Cambodia who had been ousted in a right-wing 1970 coup. Although the Khmer

Rouge Communists had opposed Sihanouk—indeed most of its leaders had been chased into exile by him—he joined forces with them as titular head of their organization in his effort to rally Cambodians against the Lon Nol government. But at the conclusion of the civil war, his presence in Peking demonstrated that his role was only that of a figurehead. According to Phnom Penh radio, Sihanouk adviser Penn Nouth held the position of prime minister, while Khieu Samphan, a French-educated intellectual, became deputy prime minister, minister of national defense, and commander in chief of the armed forces. A former minister in Prince Sihanouk's cabinet, Samphan had fled to the forests in 1967 to join the Khmer Rouge movement. In 1975 he became the most quoted official in public announcements over Phnom Penh radio and thus appeared to be the leader of the revolution. The truth was far different, for neither Khieu Samphan nor Prince Sihanouk was running the new government of Cambodia.

The real power was Saloth Sar, secretary since 1963 of the Communist party of Kampuchea (CPK)—the Khmer Rouge. Sar, related to Cambodia's old royal family, was an intense nationalist who, as a student in France, had signed his name "Original Khmer" when contributing to a radical student publication. He became a Communist and

---

Preceding page. *Khmer Rouge leader Pol Pot encourages some of his troops who have been overrun by the Vietnamese in January 1979.*

in 1963 fled to the underground. He had led the Party since then but had always remained in the background, figuratively and literally. When Prince Sihanouk visited the Khmer Rouge in the so-called liberated zones during the civil war, Saloth Sar took a seat behind his colleagues. "I believed very naively . . . that Khieu Samphan was really the master of the movement," Sihanouk later said.

A significant element of the Kampuchean Communist party doctrine was its hatred for the "crime of individualism," which in its view had characterized the Cambodian monarchy, the French colonial period, and the Sihanouk era. The CPK in contrast was shadowy and diffuse, never pushing its leaders to the forefront. The CPK did not publicize its Communist ideology or even its existence. That the new government of Cambodia was Communist went unacknowledged until the CPK's existence was announced in September 1977. Khmer Rouge radio, like the soldiers, like the cadres themselves, referred to the Party as *Angka*.

But as in most Communist parties where power is theoretically shared among the officials in the Politburo and Central Committee, power accrues to the secretary-general. This also happened in Democratic Kampuchea (DK), as the country came to be called. Bolstered by loyal, radical supporters and working against more benevolent, old-style Communists, Saloth Sar labored to consolidate his personal power in the government while instituting a harsh and radical revolution. Ultimately he was to accrue

Democratic Kampuchea

With the "peasant revolution," the Communist party of Kampuchea imposed its harsh ideology. Most people worked in the countryside to increase agricultural production. Religion was banned; intercourse between unmarried persons was punishable by death; communal eating was enforced; forced marriages took place. *Right.* Under guard by Khmer Rouge soldiers, "new people" forced out of the cities till the fields. *Far right.* In a group ceremony, Khmer Rouge soldiers, so-called heroes of the revolution, marry girls they have picked out of regroupment centers.

sufficient power to emerge as the dictatorial head of the country. At that time he was to change his name to Pol Pot.

Saloth Sar's program

Within a week after the "liberation" of Phnom Penh, Saloth Sar and the Central Committee convened an assembly of cabinet ministers and zone and region secretaries and proposed an eight-point program to implement the revolution as quickly as possible. "We made the war and won the victory rapidly," Sar said. "We must thus build the country rapidly too." According to Australian historian Ben Kiernan, who learned of the meeting through interviews conducted in 1980, Sar proposed the following:

1. Evacuate people from all towns.
2. Abolish all markets.
3. Abolish Lon Nol regime currency.
4. Defrock all Buddhist monks and put them to work growing rice.
5. Execute all leaders of the Lon Nol regime.
6. Establish high-level cooperatives throughout the country, with communal eating.
7. Expel the entire Vietnamese minority population.
8. Dispatch troops to the border, particularly the Vietnamese border.

In one sweeping blow, the architects of the peasant revolution aimed to eliminate the bourgeoisie and to institute communism without stopping at any of the required stages of Marxist-Leninist theory, such as first building up an industrial capacity and then proceeding to socialism. "We will be the first nation to create a completely Communist society without wasting time on intermediate steps," said Khieu Samphan. In analyzing the population displacement, which it called "our most important policy" instituted after April 17, a Party memorandum noted, "The city people once scattered in the countryside, would be subjected to control by the basic strata and the [cooperatives]; they would all become peasants."

Saloth Sar's radical program met with disagreement from political opponents in the divided Communist party. Hou Yuon, one of the so-called Three Heroes of the revolution, publicly branded a traitor by Sihanouk in 1967, vigorously dissented. Although a decade earlier he had written that such high-level cooperatives would be advantageous to Cambodia, Yuon, in 1975 the minister of the interior, said now that their sudden and forced establishment was simply not possible. He also quarreled with the policy of abolishing money and wages and the evacuation of the cities.

In the factional power struggles and murderous disputes that characterized Democratic Kampuchea from 1975 through 1978, Hou Yuon became the first important victim. Shortly after liberation, Hou Yuon was sacked from the cabinet, and in August 1975 he disappeared. The exact method of his death has never been discovered, but he was evidently executed by forces loyal to Saloth Sar.

Some of his fellow Party members may have felt that the audacious Hou Yuon merited his fate, and whispers circulated that he had been eliminated for "moral reasons." Nonetheless, officials who may have had dissenting thoughts about the Party Center (a familiar name for the Central Committee) were given a clear message about the fate of those who dared to oppose Saloth Sar.

In foreign policy, Democratic Kampuchea, striving for self-reliance, plunged into a belligerent isolationism. Japan's request for diplomatic relations was rebuffed with the statement that Cambodia would have no interest in formal ties "for the next 200 years." Many of the country's new leaders also harbored deep suspicions toward Vietnam and Vietnamese Moscow-oriented communism. The Khmer Rouge had launched a unique agrarian revolution that for its intellectual basis owed more to Peking and Mao Tse-tung than to Marx and Lenin. Indeed, seeing them as likely subversives, the Khmer Rouge had already killed most of the 1,000 Hanoi-trained Cambodian cadres who had gone into exile in Vietnam after 1954 but who had returned during the civil war. After living in Vietnam, said Khieu Samphan, by way of justifying their elimination, they had "neither the hearts nor minds of Khmers."

In Democratic Kampuchea's national policy lay an urge to settle historical scores with its now vastly more muscular neighbor. Some Khmer Rouge officials even had fantastic illusions of one day reclaiming Kampuchea Krom (lower Cambodia), Vietnam's Mekong Delta, which had long ago been part of Cambodia. According to Prince Sihanouk, Minister of Defense Son Sen considered his army "capable of dealing very easily with Giap's." Within weeks of their taking Phnom Penh, the Khmer Rouge stepped up centuries-old territorial squabbles. Days after the fall of South Vietnam, Cambodia attacked the large Vietnamese island of Phu Quoc and soon launched attacks into the sanctuaries Vietnam had installed along the border. Bilateral talks that summer cooled the atmosphere, but the border between the two countries was to remain hostile territory for as long as Pol Pot held power.

The zero years

Cambodia had already suffered grievously before the Khmer Rouge took Phnom Penh in April 1975. Its economy had deteriorated during the civil war, and its fields and villages had been abandoned in the wake of bombing by the United States and battles between Khmer Rouge and Lon Nol forces. In pursuit of total self-reliance, the Khmer Rouge put the people of Cambodia to work in the fields. As Foreign Minister Ieng Sary explained, "We had to feed that population and at the same time preserve our independence and dignity without asking for help from any country."

In the nomenclature of the peasant revolution, former city dwellers became "new people." People went to work building dikes and bridges, digging reservoirs and irrigation systems, and, in many remote areas, clearing forest land for cultivation. The market system and old economy were dismantled and the Khmer Rouge rationed food, each Cambodian receiving daily one Nestle condensed milk can filled with rice, about 250 grams. Many died either from hard labor or malnutrition. In some areas, "new people" foraged for food, as peasants had always done, to supplement their diet with edible roots or lizards.

There were no machines to help and the war had also taken its toll of draft animals, so in many locales the people themselves worked in harness. Suon Phal, a former student who worked near the western city of Battambang during that first summer, later recalled,

Because of the rains we couldn't hoe and had to work the fields with ploughs. We didn't have any oxen so we formed a team of eight men to pull the plough. Several of my comrades, exhausted by this work, began spitting blood and died.

Women shared equally in this work; one group of women who pulled plows reported that they were frequently beaten by women Khmer Rouge.

Former officials and military officers of the Lon Nol government received especially harsh treatment. The Khmer Rouge asked people to state their identities, falsely assuring them that those who told the truth would not be punished. In one region "new people" were instructed to register on one of three lists, declaring themselves to be either military, civil servant/intellectual class, or ordinary people. Instead of being rewarded for telling the truth, self-proclaimed military officers and civil servants were led away and seldom returned. Some 300 officers who surrendered to the Khmer Rouge in Battambang were loaded aboard six trucks and told they were to be driven to Phnom Penh. As they drove along Highway 5, the trucks turned down a side road toward a hill called Thippadey, and the men were ordered out. The Khmer Rouge killed all of them and left the bodies piled there.

In some areas "new people" were slain for petty grievances or for no apparent reason at all. One evacuee complained to a high-level Khmer Rouge officer that a guard had taken his watch. The officer returned the watch to him, but shortly afterward colleagues of the thief murdered the evacuee. The city people, aware of the intense class hatred fostered by the Khmer Rouge, soon learned to disguise their backgrounds and fabricated histories as menial laborers. Bespectacled people even threw away their eyeglasses lest they be identified as intellectuals. Attitude was a defense: An urban intellectual might not be

The authors use the anglicized name "Cambodia" rather than "Kampuchea," which is a transliteration of the country's name in the Khmer language. The Khmer people are the dominant ethnic group in Cambodia, constituting 90 percent of the population. The country ruled from 1954-1970 by Prince Norodom Sihanouk was called the Kingdom of Cambodia. After the 1970 Lon Nol coup, the country became the Khmer Republic. After 1975 the Khmer Rouge changed the name to Democratic Kampuchea.

During the civil war, the Khmer Rouge leaders lived for years in the jungles. Posing in 1974 are (above from left) Koy Tuon, Nuon Chea, Ieng Sary, and Saloth Sar—later known as Pol Pot. Seated at left (left to right) are Poc Deuskoma, Hou Yuon, Khieu Samphan, Hu Nim, and Tiv Ol. Five of the nine men pictured would fall victim to torture and execution by Pol Pot.

bothered if he adopted the demeanor of a poor peasant, but he faced likely execution if he displayed any of the so-called haughtiness of the urban class.

As the months wore on and collectives became more tightly organized, the Khmer Rouge often punished even a perceived resistance to the new order. Twenty people were sentenced to death for traveling without having obtained the necessary permission and were carried off in a truck for execution. Twelve broke free and escaped; eight died in the shooting. Others were shot for foraging for food when they should have been working. The Khmer Rouge tried to discover who among the new villagers was concealing a past as military officer, government official, engineer, or civil servant. One by one they were summoned to *Angka* and seen no more. Weeks afterward, other villagers or family members might hear soldiers bragging about specific executions, or occasionally stumble upon recognizable bodies in the forest, or notice the clothing of one who had disappeared being worn by the Khmer Rouge. To save ammunition, the Khmer Rouge sometimes used more primitive methods for killing "traitors" and "class enemies." One favored instrument was the pickax.

Some Khmer Rouge picked up nicknames like "A-ksae nylon" for the nylon rope they used to bind up prisoners' hands. The Khmer Rouge seemed not to be concerned about accurate identification. "Better to kill an innocent person than leave an enemy alive," they were heard to say. The value of life sank so low that refugees heard Khmer Rouge say, "Nothing to gain by keeping them alive, nothing to lose by doing away with them."

The severity of the Khmer Rouge revolution did not, however, cast a uniform blackness across the country. Phnom Penh seems to have given local Khmer Rouge discretion to deal with urban evacuees as they wished, so conditions varied widely according to the ideology and governing experience of local leaders, the work goals for new settlements, or the fecundity of a region's rice fields. Cambodians came to distinguish between "good" and "bad" areas. According to Cambodia scholar Michael Vickery, prior to 1977 relatively "good" areas existed in one-half to perhaps two-thirds of the country. In making those distinctions, however, Cambodians established a time factor because conditions changed drastically with the continuing cycle of senseless killing and political purges.

But within the first year, enough refugees had escaped from "bad" areas and told their horrific tales to provoke condemnation throughout the world. On the first anniversary of the Khmer Rouge takeover, *Time* magazine commented, "There is now little doubt that the Cambodian government is one of the most brutal, backward and xenophobic regimes in the world. . . . [Refugees] describe the revolution as a chilling form of mindless terror . . . an estimated 500 to 600 thousand people have died from political reprisals, disease or starvation."

The appearance of Pol Pot

Within a year of Saloth Sar's takeover, in April 1976, Phnom Penh radio announced the dissolution of the government ostensibly headed by Prince Sihanouk and the formation of a new one. At its head stood Khieu Samphan as chairman of the State Presidium, with So Phim as first vice chairman. The Presidium was a figurehead group, however. Real power resided in the cabinet and in the ruling Politburo, and the prime minister was announced as "Pol Pot."

This nom de guerre had never been heard before, and its use confused all but his closest associates about the identity of the nation's prime minister. One foreign ministry official hastily concocted a sketchy, and false, biography of the new leader and forwarded it to the Cambodian mission in Paris. The mysterious Saloth Sar simply disappeared; the names Sar and Pol Pot were never linked. Saloth Sar's brother, Saloth Suong, only learned of Pol Pot's identity in 1978 when pictures of the leader were posted in communal dining halls. As late as March 1978 a delegation of Yugoslav journalists asked the Cambodian leader, "Comrade Pol Pot, who are you?"

Pol Pot's emergence as strongman did not stem political intrigues within the Communist party; jockeying for power continued unabated throughout the summer and into the fall of 1976. In the end, although it is not known exactly what transpired, Pol Pot marshaled sufficient political force to overcome his opponents, whom Foreign Minister Ieng Sary later characterized as "Vietnamese and KGB agents." By mid-October Pol Pot and his supporters were in firm control of the Party Center. Beginning in the fall of 1976, Pol Pot inaugurated a string of brutal political purges to destroy his enemies—real and imagined—and to purify the Communist party of Kampuchea of ideological contamination. Old-line Communists who maintained contact with the Vietnamese, or who favored a less radical form of communism, became his targets.

The first notable victim was Keo Meas, a Communist since the 1940s and, during the civil war, ambassador to Peking. Security forces seized him September 20, 1976, as he worked in the office of the Party Central Committee. Next came Non Suon, head of the Communist party called Pracheachon in the 1950s and current minister of agriculture. Pol Pot forces arrested him as he returned from a trip abroad. Before long they were joined by Sien An, ambassador to Hanoi during the civil war and thus obviously tainted by exposure to Vietnamese communism. Several other diplomats who also had connections outside Cambodia soon followed.

To accommodate the prominent victims of the purges, the government security unit, "S. 21," established a prison and interrogation center named Tuol Sleng in the former Ponhea Yat High School in Phnom Penh. Here inquisitors required their prisoners to write out lengthy autobiographies and "confessions" of their ideological heresies and treacherous misdeeds. When their writings failed to satisfy the interrogators, the traitors were tortured under the watchful eye of a Pol Pot loyalist, Khaing Gek Iev, alias Deuch, a former high-school teacher. Prisoners invariably succumbed and under torture spun out lunatic fantasies professing to have served the CIA, KGB, or the hated Vietnamese. Some of these bizarre documents later became public. On one of them, a confession by Information Minister Hu Nim, arrested in April 1977, the torturer offered a memo that says, "He said that he is an independent CIA officer who buried himself for a long time." Nonetheless the interrogation continued. "I have tortured him to write it again," the interrogator added.

Pol Pot and his allies evidently believed the outlandish conspiracies that torture elicited, especially schemes deriving from the close relationship between veteran Cambodian Communists and the Vietnamese, for the Vietnamese were to Pol Pot the "hereditary enemy." At the very beginning, the interrogations of Non Suon, for example, centered on his activities as a Communist before 1962, not on his duties as a minister in the Democratic Kampuchean government. As the torture victims implicated more and more comrades in their allegedly traitorous schemes, the Pol Pot forces widened the purges.

Pol Pot had long suspected the Northern Zone of dissidence, and in January 1977 he had zone Secretary Koy Tuon arrested, along with his subordinates, and brought to Tuol Sleng. Ke Pok, a Pol Pot ally and commander of the zone military forces, replaced Tuon. But the turbulence in the zone sparked an uprising by embittered peasants in the district of Chikreng, which troops brutally suppressed at a cost of 8,000 to 10,000 lives. The insurrection was blamed on pro-Vietnamese sympathizers.

In one of the first photos out of Democratic Kampuchea, a "class enemy" of the revolution is bludgeoned to death in early 1976 by a Khmer Rouge soldier wielding a pickax.

Hu Nim, who worked closely with Koy Tuon, followed him to Tuol Sleng. One of the "Three Heroes" of the revolution, along with Khieu Samphan and the already liquidated Hou Yuon, Nim served as Democratic Kampuchea's information minister, with responsibility to propagandize on Phnom Penh radio the Party line and the revolution's positive accomplishments. Arrested in April, Hu Nim soon confessed to a host of ideological crimes, including having spoken well of the Northern Zone, formerly led by the treasonous Koy Tuon. In one confession Nim declared:

So I am a traitor to the Party, I am a traitor to the Party's secrecy policy, a traitor to the Organization's instructions which forbid people to contact one another and do not permit people to go in and out from one Ministry to another.

After writing out seven confessions and undergoing repeated ordeals of torture, "Hero of the Revolution" Hu Nim was, in the political vernacular used at Tuol Sleng, "crushed to bits" on July 6, 1977.

Before the terror ended, 242 top-ranking officials and nearly 20,000 lesser figures entered Tuol Sleng, never to emerge. Many were photographed, the pictures neatly filed along with their torture-induced confessions after the prisoners were "crushed to bits." In reality the executioners beat or tortured them to death, hanged them, starved them, or cut their throats. The prison bureaucrats often took photographs of individual corpses, with nameplate and date of death across the chest—eerie mug shots to be sent to high Party officials to show that the "traitors" had been executed.

Pol Pot and the Party Center turned to other elements of their revolutionary program that had been ignored during the Party struggles. The communal eating that was instituted in January 1977 permitted better control of the people and of food distribution, and it constituted an ideological attack on what Pol Pot called "privateness." Pol Pot bolstered his forces at the borders and then in January launched Cambodian attacks into several Vietnamese border provinces. These attacks continued sporadically for two months, escalating into a full-scale border war in March 1977, when Phnom Penh issued orders to attack Vietnam along a wide front. Before long four divisions of Cambodian troops were fighting at the border.

Though little noticed or even known to the outside world, the war continued throughout 1977, with Cambodian forays across the border, long-range artillery shellings, and Vietnamese counterattacks. In one incident, the Cambodian 3d Brigade, comprised of loyal troops from the Central Zone under the personal control of Defense Minister Son Sen, crossed into Vietnam's Tay Ninh Province and massacred some 300 civilians. A Hanoi source described the killings as "worse than the My Lai massacres," and Vietnam hurriedly sent a film crew to the scene.

Vietnam hesitated to retaliate because Pol Pot was then on a state visit to China, Cambodia's major benefactor,

and the Vietnamese were concerned that a counterattack might antagonize the Chinese. But Defense Minister Vo Nguyen Giap traveled to the border area in late September to draw up plans for a counteroffensive. On December 16, 1977, Vietnam put those plans into action; elements of eight divisions with armored columns crossed the border into the Parrot's Beak. At first the Cambodians fell back in disarray, then their resistance stiffened, and they began to make the Vietnamese bleed for every inch of ground. "Hit the enemy where he is weakest," declared Phnom Penh, ordering troops to adopt Maoist guerrilla tactics. The conventional Vietnamese troops bogged down, for all their armored personnel carriers, air cover, and captured U.S. Huey helicopters. One Western military expert observing events from long range in Bangkok commented, "The Viets are making U.S. mistakes. They were much better when their only equipment was an AK47 and a pair of thousand-milers (Ho Chi Minh sandals)." The Vietnamese had grown top-heavy, and its infantry performed poorly.

The Cambodians regrouped and counterattacked, forcing a slow Vietnamese withdrawal. As many as 100,000 Cambodians living in the border regions seized the opportunity to flee Cambodia ahead of the Vietnamese. One who had already deserted his post to take refuge in Vietnam was Heng Samrin, commander of the 4th Eastern Brigade, who had fled a political purge of the military in November 1977. Heng Samrin was to become the nominal leader of the Pol Pot opposition among Cambodian refugees in Vietnam.

Phnom Penh broke off diplomatic relations with Hanoi, and in the wake of the Vietnamese departure both sides waged propaganda war. Radio Phnom Penh hailed the "great historic victory" of its troops in expelling the "aggressor forces" from Cambodia and charged that the Vietnamese had stolen property and raped and killed Cambodian women. Vietnam countered with its first charges of "systematic genocide" on the part of Cambodia's leaders and detailed the "utterly inhuman crimes" of the Khmer Rouge, "raping, tearing fetuses from mothers' wombs, disemboweling, cutting off the heads and tearing out the livers of adults, massacring children and throwing their bodies into flames." Hanoi also warned that General Giap had returned to the border area of Tay Ninh Province, ostensibly to plan a broader attack, and an editorial in the Party newspaper ominously said, "We have acted with extreme patience. But even to patience there is a limit."

Treason in the Eastern Zone

Pol Pot and his colleagues in the Party Center believed that problems underlying their revolution lay in Vietnam and Vietnamese communism and in Cambodians who sided with the Vietnamese, like So Phim, secretary of the Eastern Zone, first vice chairman of the State Presidium,

Tuol Sleng

Tuol Sleng, a Phnom Penh high-school complex of four three-story concrete buildings, became in 1977 a political prison and torture center under the Communist party of Kampuchea. At any one time Tuol Sleng held 1,000 to 1,500 prisoners; no one was exonerated. With their penchant for bureaucracy, the jailers photographed the prisoners before inducing confessions under torture, which, transcribed or typed, they had the victims sign. They then neatly filed the confessions and photographs and executed the victims. One prisoner tortured to death was found shackled to the iron bed (below) in January, 1979; the torturers had continued working as the Vietnamese approached Phnom Penh. After the takeover, Tuol Sleng was turned into a museum, and the bed was roped off for display.

Overleaf. *A few of the 20,000 Tuol Sleng victims.*

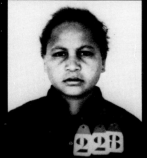 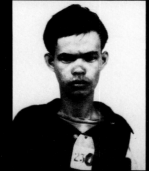    

  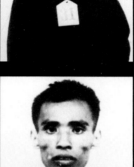  

and fourth-ranking member of the Politburo. A long-time Communist underground leader and military commander, So Phim had worked with the Vietnamese during the First Indochina War, and, from his base in eastern Cambodia, he had maintained close connections with the Vietnamese during the civil war. He saw no reason to be hostile to them or to their brand of communism.

In the nightmarish landscape of Pol Pot's Cambodia, the Eastern Zone run by So Phim seemed a comparative paradise. Food was, if not plentiful or varied, at least sufficiently nourishing so that starvation did not threaten. Many people received two 250-gram cans of rice per day, double that of other areas. With the exception of high-ranking Lon Nol officers who were executed, "new people" from the cities suffered no persecution. Civil servants, engineers, lower-ranking soldiers, and other class enemies were interned in prisons or reeducation camps, where they received political education and gradually toughened their bodies for work in the fields. Very few arbitrary killings took place in the Eastern Zone, according to most witnesses. "The Khmer Rouge were only looking for their enemies and did not kill ordinary people in those years," said one peasant.

Pol Pot viewed such lenient behavior as treason, not just loyal opposition, and he moved cunningly, and systematically, against So Phim and zonal and regional deputies. Pol Pot and the Party Center filled positions of responsibility in the Eastern Zone with their own loyalists including Ke Pok, who was installed in the Eastern Zone with a division of his own troops from the Northern Zone. Security agents arrested military and political officials, tortured them until they concocted conspiracies against the Communist party of Kampuchea, and then widened the circle of arrests. Early in 1978 Tuol Sleng prison filled up with officials from the Eastern Zone. Of over 1,200 prisoners incarcerated at Tuol Sleng on April 20, 1978, for example, more than one-third came from the east.

So Phim soon felt so threatened that he established a second headquarters in secret where his own loyal agents controlled security. According to a woman who observed So Phim, "He did not dare [do anything]. He was being watched very closely by Pol Pot's people. . . . He couldn't get away. . . . Regional, district and military cadres were being taken away one after another, everywhere. . . . He told everyone to watch out, to be careful." So Phim's world was crumbling. As Ben Kiernan has reconstructed, So Phim felt that the revolution, in his eyes a historical inevitability for which he had labored more than twenty years, was being betrayed. He had tried for years to avoid a confrontation with the Party, but now, Party stalwart to the end, he resolved to confront Pol Pot directly.

But before he could act, troops under Pol Pot loyalist Ke Pok struck on May 25, 1978. Two brigades crossed the Mekong River to attack the troops of the Eastern Zone. More soldiers began closing from the southwest. Eastern Zone soldiers, most of their senior officers already liquidated, threw up resistance, using hit-and-run guerrilla tactics. As Tea Sabun, an Eastern Zone political officer, recounted:

If we wanted to survive, we had to make a revolution. I called in the militia from Vihear Luong, Chong Kraung, Anchaeum, Sralap, Lo Ngieng and Kor subdistricts. There were about three to four thousand of us in the forest. . . . We hit [Pok's forces] east of Suong at three in the morning of the 26th. There was fierce, close-in fighting for three days and three nights. We fell back and regrouped, then attacked again and drove them out of Suong.

As the rebellion spread, So Phim tried in vain to contact Pol Pot by radio. Taking his family and bodyguards, he left his base and drove toward Phnom Penh, carefully skirting the northward advance of the southwest troops. When his small caravan reached the Tonle Toch River, So

Phim sent a messenger to Pol Pot, evidently asking for a meeting, and moved on to Prek Po, on the Mekong River above Phnom Penh, where he settled down to await Pol Pot's response.

A week passed before So Phim received his final rebuff. On June 3 two ferries filled with Center troops docked at Prek Po. Pol Pot was not among them. As the soldiers came for him, So Phim told two of his men, "You must rise up and struggle. They are traitors. You keep up the struggle; I can't solve this." So Phim took out a pistol and shot himself in the chest. The shot did not kill him, so he put the muzzle in his mouth and pulled the trigger. His bodyguards slipped away and scattered. The Center troops killed his wife and children.

In his loyalty to the revolution, So Phim had in his life avoided taking a public stand against the Party or Pol Pot, yet his suicide rallied people of the Eastern Zone who dis- liked hearing him denounced as a "traitorous chieftain." According to one follower:

After So Phim's death the people in Region 22 and in Komchay Meas rebelled in anger. . . . The people had long wanted the pri- vate system back again instead of the Party's communitarian system, and they supported the rebellion. They stopped eating communally and were distributing ox-carts and other things among themselves. Cadres still faithful to the Party line were afraid to remain in place for fear that the people would kill them.

For months Party Center forces viciously fought the in- surrection, killing rebels who gave themselves up and massacring villagers they suspected of harboring traitors. They killed everyone—120 families—in So Phim's head- quarters village. The Center forces uprooted remaining villagers, moving them in forced marches toward the northwest. Perhaps a third of the population was moved. Tens of thousands died from starvation, and many of those

Cambodian refu- gees from the East- ern Zone—princi- pally women, children, and old men—pour across the Vietnam border into Tay Ninh Prov- ince in August 1978. The Pol Pot forces brutally suppressed the Eastern Zone in- surrection, sending tens of thousands fleeing for safety.

who survived were killed when they reached their destinations. Villagers fled to the forests, joining the rebels in the maquis. As the resistance dwindled, losing men and ground to the superior Communist party forces, the rebels retreated, low on ammunition and food, toward the mined and patrolled Vietnamese border. They began to make contact with Heng Samrin and other former Khmer Rouge who had fled from Pol Pot.

With the orgy of killing that suppressed the Eastern Zone rebellion, the Party Center had seemingly gained control of the Party and of the country. Toward the end of 1978 Pol Pot and his allies planned to soften political purges because they considered *Angka* to have been 50 to 70 percent purified. Through terror, Pol Pot had consolidated control over his depleted party. One Eastern Zone rebel described the loyalty of some Pol Pot supporters as a kind of slavish indoctrination:

Some of our cadres ... said: "I am not a traitor. I will not betray the people, the nation, the Party. If the Party kills me while I remain loyal, I will die a patriot."

One group of more than twenty youths aged about fifteen was arrested. They did not try to run away. They just said: "I am faithful to the Party. I obey the Party. If I die, I die faithful to the Party and loving it." And all those youngsters were executed. The Party was more than a god to them.

Pol Pot had achieved dictatorship of the Communist party, with himself at the head, and next came what Communists call "a cult of personality." Portraits, busts, and statues of this leader went on display. Cambodia had become Pol Pot's country—for a brief time.

"Blossoming lotus" in Cambodia

In his ascendancy, Pol Pot had created an implacable enemy, one that, unlike his ideological opponents in his own country, was vastly superior in force to him. In February 1978, in the wake of the dismal Vietnamese military performance in the Cambodian incursion, Vietnam's Politburo voted to support the overthrow of Pol Pot by dissident Cambodian troops. The brutal suppression of the So Phim–inspired rebellion, followed by widespread population relocation and massacres, had eliminated the ingredients necessary for a successful insurgency, so in June 1978, as the fighting continued in eastern Cambodia, Hanoi concluded that their own Vietnamese forces must invade Cambodia and overthrow Pol Pot. Although Vietnam later claimed that it acted in order to preserve Cambodians from Pol Pot's "genocide," its decision was in fact prompted by the continuing border war. As Foreign Minister Nguyen Co Thach admitted to U.S. Congressman Stephen Solarz of New York, "Human rights was not a question; that was their problem. . . . We were concerned only with security." The General Staff under General Van Tien Dung began planning the campaign. Hanoi realized that its action could bring Vietnam into conflict with China.

As protection against possible conflict, Vietnam chose to move closer to Moscow, Peking's other antagonist and neighbor, whose 650,000 men on China's northern border might cause China to hesitate before acting against Vietnam. Accordingly, Vietnam moved late in June from observer status to full membership in the Council for Mutual Economic Assistance (COMECON), thus officially joining the Soviet bloc. Negotiations also concluded November 3 with the signing of a twenty-five-year Treaty of Friendship and Cooperation between Hanoi and Moscow. The treaty clearly identified China as the bête noire of the new allies; Moscow and Hanoi pledged to "oppose all schemes and maneuvers of imperialism and reactionary forces"—the latter being the standard Hanoi phrase for China's leaders. Article 6 stated that the signatories would "consult each other" if either was attacked or threatened with attack, but no specific measures were disclosed.

Vietnam also sought during the summer to establish diplomatic relations with the United States, at a time, coincidentally, when China was also courting the United States. The talks proved fruitful after Vietnam dropped its demand for major aid commitments, and the two countries reached an accord in principle in September 1978. "Everything was agreed upon, except for the writing down," said Vietnam Foreign Minister Nguyen Co Thach. But then, according to Assistant Secretary of State Richard C. Holbrooke, the United States, beset by questions about Vietnamese tensions with Cambodia, the refugee exodus, and the strengthening Vietnam–Soviet Union ties, decided to back off. "I think [Washington] would [have liked] to arrange normalization with China and normalization with Vietnam, and the China card prevailed above the normalization of Vietnam," Thach said later.

Hanoi took a decisive step toward war preparations on December 2, 1978, when it sponsored the formation of a Cambodian insurgency group called the Kampuchea National United Front for National Salvation (KNUFNS). The front was created at a meeting in Snuol, Cambodia, attended by some 2,000 people. With former Khmer Rouge brigade commander Heng Samrin as president, the KNUFNS broadcast an eleven-point democratic program over clandestine radio that promised an antidote to the harsh reality of life in Cambodia. Among other proposals, the program aimed to abolish communal eating, to restore family life, and to bring an economy "progressing toward socialism" with wages and an eight-hour work day. But its principal goal was the overthrow of Pol Pot.

From among the 150,000 Cambodians who had fled across the border, Vietnam recruited soldiers and formed them into perhaps six battalions. They would carry the KNUFNS banner against Pol Pot, enabling the Vietnamese to claim that the insurgency was domestic. Indeed, the Vietnamese wanted to hide their role in Cambodia, though under the circumstances this was impossible to do.

On December 21, 1978, Vietnam struck, in what Defense

Minister Vo Nguyen Giap called a "strategic offensive" geared "to exterminate the enemy and seize control." Beneath heavy air cover, Vietnamese troops flowed out of the central highlands into the remote northeast province of Ratanakiri, driving along Route 19 through Andaung Pech to Stung Treng on the Mekong River.

On a second front opened on December 25, troops attacked along Highway 7 toward Kratie, a key port on the east bank of the Mekong. Kratie fell in just four days. Then Vietnamese units crossed the swift-flowing Mekong on pontoon bridges and sped south to capture Kompong Cham, a west-bank town on the Mekong and an important communications link between Phnom Penh and the eastern front. The Cambodian army in the east now found itself outflanked by the enemy's lightning moves; Vietnamese were attacking from the border, and other Vietnamese units already occupied Kompong Cham behind them, loosing barrages of artillery toward Cambodian positions.

Vietnam opened a third front in the south. Beneath air cover provided by Russian-built MiG-21s and captured American A-37s and F-5s from the former South Vietnamese air base at Can Tho, motorized Vietnamese forces closed quickly on Takeo on Route 2, while other units headed for the port city of Kompong Som. Then the southern front troops advanced along three routes—Highways 1, 3, and 4—toward Phnom Penh.

Vietnam's strategists had clearly learned a lesson from their plodding defensive counterattack the previous year. The current campaign bore the unmistakable imprint of army Chief of Staff General Van Tien Dung. Architect of the 1975 conquest of South Vietnam using what he termed "blossoming lotus" tactics, Dung liked to avoid enemy positions at a city's perimeter and strike directly into the city to eliminate the enemy's command post. Then his troops could "blossom" out to the perimeters to destroy the enemy outposts. A military adage dictates that if one can force an enemy to stall his own offensive and attack back toward his own lines, the battle is won. Dung's tactics accomplished just that by outflanking Cambodian positions and racing for the nerve center of Phnom Penh.

On January 7 Vietnamese forces, trailing the Cambodian "rebels" of the KNUFNS, marched into a deserted, defenseless Phnom Penh. Pol Pot had fled two days earlier, but some members of the government, including Deputy Prime Minister Ieng Sary, departed only two hours before the city's fall. The Vietnamese fanned out, taking possession of government buildings and archives, including Tuol Sleng prison where torturers, still at work as the Vietnamese approached, had left mangled corpses chained to iron beds. Democratic Kampuchea had come to an end. The new regime, installed by Vietnamese guns, was called the People's Republic of Kampuchea.

As the Cambodian armies fled west to hastily organized base areas, Ieng Sary slipped out of Cambodia

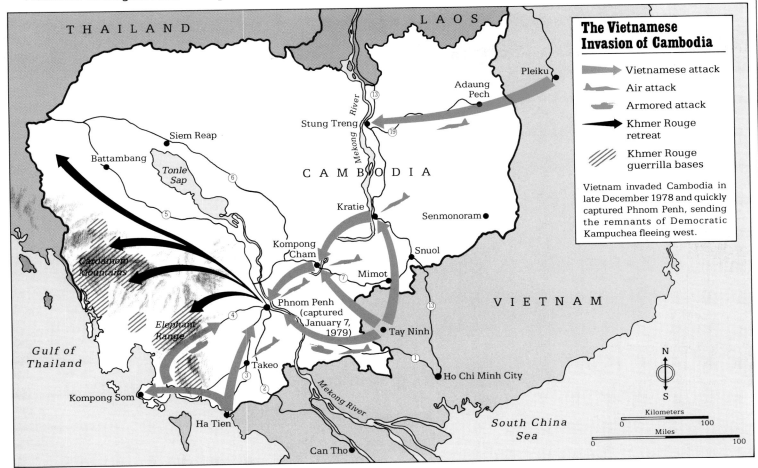

The Vietnamese Invasion of Cambodia

- Vietnamese attack
- Air attack
- Armored attack
- Khmer Rouge retreat
- Khmer Rouge guerrilla bases

Vietnam invaded Cambodia in late December 1978 and quickly captured Phnom Penh, sending the remnants of Democratic Kampuchea fleeing west.

THAILAND

LAOS

Pleiku

Adaung Pech

Stung Treng

Mekong River

Siem Reap

Battambang

Tonle Sap

CAMBODIA

Kratie

Senmonoram

Snuol

Kompong Cham

Mimot

Cardamom Mountains

Phnom Penh (captured January 7, 1979)

VIETNAM

Elephant Range

Tay Ninh

Gulf of Thailand

Takeo

Ho Chi Minh City

Kompong Som

Mekong River

Ha Tien

South China Sea

Can Tho

N / S

Kilometers
0   100

Miles
0   100

bound for Peking, presumably to discuss the continuation of Chinese aid to the deposed government. The Thai government picked up Sary at the border in a military helicopter and flew him to Bangkok, where he boarded a commercial airliner for Hong Kong—flying first class and sipping champagne—and thence to Peking. En route Sary told a reporter that the hatred of the Cambodians for the Vietnamese "is even greater than that for the Americans during the war. . . . We have known the perfidious nature of the Vietnamese for a long time. We hoped after the war, they would let us live in peace, but you see. . . . " The guerrilla resistance, he added, would continue with Pol Pot as head of Democratic Kampuchea.

"Cubans of the Orient"

Shortly after the People's Republic of Kampuchea was proclaimed, China's Vice Premier Deng Xiaoping journeyed to the United States for a nine-day good-will tour to mark the January 1, 1979, resumption of full diplomatic ties after a thirty-year hiatus. Basking in the attention of the clamoring press and television people, Deng seemed partly like a foreign leader on a technology shopping trip and partly a politician seeking reelection. He toured a Ford Motor Company assembly plant, looked at paintings and sculpture at the National Gallery, and donned a ten-gallon hat for a Texas rodeo. Beneath the gaiety, Deng's mind turned often to Southeast Asia, and, perceiving Moscow as Hanoi's sponsor, he frequently baited the Soviets by denouncing "hegemonism," the Chinese term for Soviet expansion. That the United States did not object to his remarks persuaded Deng that Washington supported them.

In private talks, Deng informed President Carter of China's plan to launch a punitive strike into Vietnam. "I tried to discourage him," Carter later wrote, "pointing out that the Vietnamese were increasingly isolated in the world community and were being condemned because they were aggressors." A Chinese attack was certain to embarrass the United States, since the world would assume that Deng had secured Carter's blessing while in Washington. Undaunted, Deng stopped in Tokyo on his way back to China and talked publicly about taking "punitive action" against Vietnam, "those Cubans of the Orient." Tentative war preparations had gone forward in Deng's absence, and upon his return the Military Commission of the Central Committee held three days of conferences from February 9–12, 1979. The Chinese leaders decided to invade Vietnam.

China, with its population of nearly 1 billion, boasted a staggering military force. The People's Liberation Army consisted of some 3.6 million men-at-arms and was

In a picture distributed by the Vietnam News Agency, anti-Pol Pot Cambodian guerrillas, part of a "front" created by Vietnam, liberate Phnom Penh on January 7, 1979.

backed up by an armed militia of over 7 million, plus millions more men and women fulfilling civil defense roles in the militia. The PLA's weaponry, however, compared unfavorably to the modern tools of war possessed by Vietnam. China's numerous but outdated T34 tanks were extremely vulnerable to the Sagger antitank missile. Largely an infantry force, the PLA had last seen extended action during the 1950–53 Korean War; some troops gained limited experience during a month-long incursion into India in 1962. During the Korean War, the Chinese had relied on their great numbers to conduct human wave assaults, and, considering the aged General Staff, it seemed unlikely that Chinese tactics had greatly evolved.

Chinese men and equipment, some of it pulled in horse-drawn vehicles, continued moving to the front until nearly half a million troops occupied the southern provinces. Perhaps 160,000 soldiers in eighteen divisions poised in the mountain passes of the irregular 1,400-kilometer border with Vietnam, while some 340,000 remained in a primarily defensive reserve in case a Vietnamese counterattack should penetrate China. The battle plan called for eight divisions to launch initial attacks, with the others having follow-up roles. The air force deployed some 700 military aircraft, including Chinese-made F-9 ground attack planes, MiG-19s, and MiG-21s, to ten airfields that had long runways capable of handling military traffic. Despite the size of China's air force, the advantage in the air probably rested with the Vietnamese, who, after the defeat of South Vietnam, had procured about 120 sophisticated MiG-23s and a few high-altitude MiG-25s from the Soviet Union. In addition, Vietnam had succeeded in maintaining and operating about one-third of the 75 American-built F-5 fighter-bombers captured in South Vietnam.

Vietnam hurriedly strengthened its defenses. The People's Army of Vietnam (PAVN), 615,000 well-equipped, disciplined, and experienced men in twenty-five infantry divisions and several independent regiments, was spread very thin. The invasion of Cambodia occupied fourteen divisions, while six were stationed in Laos. Only four PAVN divisions protected Hanoi. Yet along the Chinese border Vietnam also had a Border Security Force of 70,000 men, equipped with artillery and a backstop in the form of a 50,000-man militia. Vietnam had heavily mined and booby-trapped many of the frontier mountain passes and had also registered artillery and mortars on them. In spite of its conventional military prowess, Vietnam did not ignore its guerrilla heritage. Border guards and villagers planted fields of bamboo punji stakes; entire bamboo groves in Thanh Hoa and Nghe Tinh Provinces were said to have been razed in the drive to carve the spikes.

Vietnam's plan, orchestrated by Defense Minister Vo Nguyen Giap, was defensive and required a calm hand. Giap planned to do nothing with his regular troops until the thrust of the Chinese attack became clear, at which time he could deploy his divisions from the Hanoi region. The Border Security Forces, falling back as needed, could chew up the Chinese infantry in the mountains with artillery and air power while his Soviet-supplied surface-to-air missiles and air force could contend with any Chinese threat from the air.

The Chinese "lesson"

In the predawn hours of February 17, 1979, Chinese artillery began to fire at Vietnamese border towns, and at 5:00 A.M. Chinese troops poured across the craggy, mountainous border at twenty-six points stretching from the Gulf of Tonkin to the jungles of Laos. Waves of infantrymen, walking behind tanks, flowed through the mountain passes. According to some reports, mounted cavalrymen picked their way along seemingly impassable trails. Passing through some border towns, soldiers rounded up water buffaloes and herded them along the roads to trip mines. Most frequently encountered were Chinese-made plastic mines given to the Vietnamese for use against the Americans. Owing to poor field communications—the Chinese still relied heavily on runners and bicycles to pass messages and controlled attack formations with bugles and whistles—the divisions advanced on a "granular" principle, each moving forward without regard to action on its flanks. Although some planes took to the air—500 sorties were reported in the first week—China did not pit its air force against Vietnam's, and air power played no significant role.

The timing of the attack may have caught Hanoi's leadership off guard. The previous day Premier Pham Van Dong, Chief of Staff Van Tien Dung, and other officials had flown to Phnom Penh to formalize Vietnam's relationship with the nation it had conquered. The premier signed "a treaty of peace, friendship and cooperation" with the government of President Heng Samrin, which Vietnam had installed in power. The pact accorded Vietnam the right to station troops in Cambodia, obviating any further need for Vietnam to maintain that all the fighting had been done by Cambodian rebels opposed to Pol Pot.

While Hanoi's leaders toured Phnom Penh, the Chinese fought their way through the mountain passes against intense opposition from bands of Vietnamese firing from steep hillsides, caves, and a manmade tunnel system. The Chinese called the Vietnamese "cave rats" and took to blowing up the caves and tunnels. The Chinese had pioneered tunnel tactics in the war against the Japanese, and defensive tunnel warfare had been a favorite theme of Mao Tse-tung. The Vietnamese had learned Mao's lessons well and slowed the Chinese advance. The hills, ravines, and jungles of the jagged mountain country presented ideal conditions for ambushes. According to the Vietnam army newspaper, *Quan Doi Nhan Dan*, the ambushes were highly successful. "The corpses of enemy troops and wreckage of military vehicles are littering roads, fields, and hills in Vietnam's northern border areas," it said.

By the end of the second day, Chinese divisions had pushed salients ten to sixteen kilometers inside Vietnam's territory, then paused to wait for more ammunition, supplies, and reinforcements. Ultimately China had some 85,000 troops on Vietnam's soil. There was concern in many capitals that the border war between the two Communist nations would draw in the Soviet Union and instigate a far broader war, but from the opening salvo China expressed its limited objectives. Characterizing the action as a defensive counterattack, Peking declared, "We do not want a single inch of Vietnamese territory." The Foreign Ministry declared that Chinese troops "would be withdrawn after Vietnam had been taught a lesson." China, Deng Xiaoping said, could not tolerate Vietnam's "swashbuckling in Laos, Kampuchea or even on the Chinese border."

Within twenty-four hours of the initial attacks, Moscow warned that it would "honor its obligations" to Vietnam under the recently signed treaty. It said, "Those who decide policy in Peking should stop before it is too late." The Soviet Union dispatched the 15,000-ton cruiser *Admiral Senyavin* and a guided-missile destroyer from Vladivostok to the South China Sea to join the Soviet flotilla of eleven surveillance ships already watching China. Moscow also sent a delegation to Hanoi to "consult," as their treaty dictated, but the U.S.S.R. took no military action along its 7,200-kilometer border with China, where Chinese troops had been placed on maximum alert.

After a pause of three days for resupply and reinforcement, China's People's Liberation Army resumed its advance. The attacks narrowed to six major thrusts. China controlled all the frontier passes, as well as the provincial capitals of Cao Bang and Ha Giang, although gaps between the Chinese salients permitted Vietnamese infantrymen to slip into Chinese territory near Lao Cai and along the coastal route to conduct harassing counterattacks in the Chinese rear. Militiamen fired on the Vietnamese, claimed the Peking press, and they "fled helter-skelter back to Vietnam." Although Chinese troops continued their attacks along the entire front, the battle for the provincial capital of Lang Son, 20 kilometers below the border and 130 kilometers above Hanoi, soon developed into the most important clash of the war. A market town of 46,000 people, the now-deserted Lang Son, situated on a historical invasion route, controlled entry to the Red River Delta. Surrounded by mountains, Lang Son offered the setting for a classic "battle for the pass," in which the defensive forces on high ground would have the advantage.

With troops already posted above the city, China sent two divisions into the coastal plain, with a third division held in reserve, and it appeared the troops might wheel toward Lang Son. In Hanoi General Giap followed his patient plan and saw his Border Security Forces and militia slow the Chinese attack. But as the Chinese closed on Lang Son, Giap had to act. He rushed one division, the 308th, which had fought at Dien Bien Phu, to join the battle. Troop transports and vehicles hauling weapons, ammunition, and fuel soon jammed Highway 1A from Hanoi to Lang Son, as tens of thousands of civilians streamed south to escape the fighting. Some PAVN trucks pulled American 105MM howitzers captured during the war. Giap then moved another regular division north from Da Nang to join the fighting in the coastal area of Mon Kai and to protect the key delta port of Haiphong.

The Chinese attacked Lang Son on February 27 with an artillery bombardment on the high ground of Khau Ma Son, a natural screen north of the city, followed by a tank-infantry assault. A crucial battle developed early for an elevation known as Hill 303. Chinese tanks pounded the hill, then, according to Peking's Xinhua news service, "Chinese infantrymen charged forward and captured enemy positions on [Hill] 303 in just about ten minutes." As the Chinese took the hill, Vietnamese gunners trained their artillery on their old positions; the Chinese tanks dueled the Vietnamese artillery, and the tank-led infantry advanced forward toward other hills. According to Xinhua, "Well-coordinated actions by Chinese infantry and tank forces enabled them to capture all the heights around Khau Ma Son Mountain before they made the final assault on the main peak. The enemy put up a desperate fight

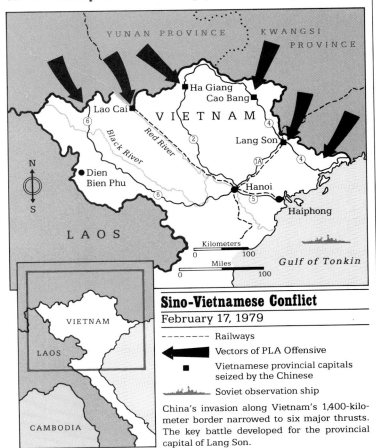

Sino-Vietnamese Conflict
February 17, 1979

-------- Railways

➤ Vectors of PLA Offensive

■ Vietnamese provincial capitals seized by the Chinese

Soviet observation ship

China's invasion along Vietnam's 1,400-kilometer border narrowed to six major thrusts. The key battle developed for the provincial capital of Lang Son.

Chinese Invasion

Historical antagonists China and Vietnam had last battled in 1788. During the Vietnam War, they had been allies, "as close as lips and teeth." But in February 1979, after months of mounting tensions, eight divisions of Chinese infantry poured across the border. The invasion was intended "to teach Vietnam a lesson" for meddling in Cambodia and to show Peking's displeasure at Hanoi's deepening ties with Moscow.

Left. *Near Lao Cai, a Vietnamese soldier carries to the rear a militiaman, wounded in hand and foot by shrapnel from Chinese artillery.*

Above. Chinese artillerymen fire a 100MM antitank gun toward Vietnamese positions near Lang Son, the embattled provincial capital.

Right. After several days of fierce battle, Chinese infantrymen enter Lang Son. Soldiers carry an AK47 (background) and Type 56-1 light machine gun.

Top. Vietnamese guard Chinese prisoners. Many soldiers fought to the death rather than face capture. Above. Before departing Lang Son, Vietnamese-speaking Chinese propagandist leaves a message: "If you don't bother me, I won't bother you."

from the commanding height, firing from all pillboxes and hidden bunkers. The summit was enveloped in smoke that blurred visibility." But the Chinese finally prevailed.

With a key position now in Chinese possession, other PLA forces broke down their massed formations, sending off battalion- and regimental-sized units around the flanks of Lang Son, fighting frequently at night and at close range. As it had for the Americans, darkness eliminated the conventional superiority of the Vietnamese since artillery proved useless. As for range, China's PLA tactics called for an "embrace" of the enemy, and infantry training emphasized use of the bayonet. According to a Western analyst in Bangkok, the Vietnamese 308th Division got "pretty badly chewed up" in the fight for Lang Son.

Chinese troops entered the deserted city on March 2, while fighting continued in the hills south and west of the city. The PLA found rocket launchers, weapons, and ammunition abandoned by the retreating Vietnamese. They also found calendars in the houses of Lang Son still showing February 27, the day of the Chinese attack. A pro-Peking report gleefully noted, "Not a single calendar of the Vietnamese was turned to February 28, which means that the Chinese attack was such an overwhelming surprise that the Vietnamese . . . were hardly given enough chance to breathe, let alone turn their calendars."

With the capture of Hill 413, southwest of the city, on March 5, China's PLA took full control of the Lang Son region, and the Red River Delta containing the key cities of Hanoi and Haiphong lay open to attack. Four hours later, however, Peking unexpectedly announced that the "self-defense counterattack" forces had attained their goals and would begin a withdrawal to Chinese territory. The seventeen-day "lesson" China inflicted on Vietnam had concluded, and the PLA began a cautious retreat calculated to last two additional weeks, almost as long as the advance. "Pulling out is more difficult militarily than advancing," one Peking official said.

To cover their retreat, Chinese troops scorched the earth as they went, blowing up bridges and railroads and taking anything of value, including clothes, household utensils, farm machinery, and cattle. They destroyed Vietnamese military installations that posed any threat to the border, as well as a phosphate mine that provided much-needed fertilizer. The Vietnamese issued empty threats—"If the Chinese troops continue their acts of war, they will be duly punished"—and announced a quite belated nationwide military mobilization, but in general PAVN merely trailed the withdrawal in lethargic pursuit and kept up harassment by means of artillery fire and small raids. The Vietnamese had no desire to slow the withdrawal or provoke a counterattack, and the Chinese wanted to leave Vietnamese soil before the April rains came. The Chinese press spouted stories of heroic counterattacks against the Vietnamese pursuers, but the withdrawal was nevertheless completed in ten days. On

March 15 the last Chinese troops left Vietnam.

Each side published wildly contradictory casualty figures for the campaign, inflating the other side's while understating its own. After the fact, Western analysts estimated a total of 35,000 dead for both sides, with Vietnam losing more than China. Total dead and wounded including civilians, probably exceeded 75,000. The relatively small number of prisoners—238 Chinese prisoners were later exchanged for 1,636 Vietnamese—was attributed to the effectiveness of each side's propaganda, which had stirred the troops to avoid capture. Chinese guards killed some wounded Vietnamese who put up resistance on their way to Chinese field hospitals.

As his divisions pulled back across the border, Chinese Vice Premier Deng Xiaoping boasted that PLA forces "could have gone all the way to Hanoi if they wanted." That claim was highly doubtful, given the reserve strength and air force still available to Vo Nguyen Giap, not to mention the formidable air defenses that Hanoi had erected during the American bombing campaigns. Privately the Peking Politburo recognized China's military deficiencies and expressed disappointment that the PLA had proven incapable of waging a modern war. As Drew Middleton, military correspondent for the *New York Times*, noted, "The Chinese army had numerical superiority over Vietnam in almost every category—men, guns, tanks—but it was unable to score the smashing victory that it sought because of the relatively slow pace of an offensive carried out by what was basically a marching army."

Politically, Deng was perhaps entitled to his swagger, for China had pulled off a bold gamble at a relatively small cost of manpower. Using a favorite image of Chairman Mao's in referring to the Soviet Union, Deng said, "You can't know the reaction of the tiger if you don't touch his arse." China, he added, had shown that the Soviet "tiger" was "not so powerful." According to the Peking press, the war had "dealt a telling blow to the Soviet scheme of aggression and expansion in Southeast Asia."

Ironically, the war may have achieved just the opposite, the strengthening of the Vietnam-Soviet alliance. Early in March Soviet ships patrolling in the South China Sea docked at Da Nang, showing the hammer and sickle in the first call ever made in Vietnam by Soviet warships. And in May 1979 the first Soviet submarine visibly entered Cam Ranh Bay, the deep-water harbor constructed by the United States, from which the Soviet Union could project its naval presence into the Pacific. But Vietnam's granting of naval facilities to the Soviets was probably inevitable after the signing of their pact, and by its invasion China had made not only its annoyance clear but also its propensity to take action. As a Western diplomat in Hong Kong said, "China has demonstrated that it is a regional power willing to back up its diplomacy with military might. There's a message there for Vietnam, for Laos and certainly for Taiwan."

Cambodia Aftermath

After the Vietnamese conquest, the curtain rose slowly over the ruins of Pol Pot's Cambodia, in which the "peasant revolution" had gone insanely awry. The most horrific emblems of the Communist party regime were the piles of skeletons in prisons and in the "killing fields," where as many as 1 million people perished from execution or starvation. As one journalist described Cambodia, "In this parched land abandoned towns are littered with skeletons and the debris of war, and hundreds of thousands of tired and dazed people crisscross the country seeking missing relatives and trying to reach their native villages."

Near Pailin in the west of Cambodia, the remains of executed inmates lie in a temple that was transformed into a prison.

Phnom Penh

Following the evacuation of Phnom Penh in 1975, the capital remained all but empty. Officials of the Communist party operated in ministries there, and Tuol Sleng prison functioned in an outlying district. Some technicians and workers remained, along with a few diplomats who were kept cloistered. A group of touring Scandinavian diplomats called it a "ghost city."

After the Vietnamese invasion, Cambodians drifted back to Phnom Penh, where for months they lived as scavengers amid the debris. Slowly they began the gargantuan task of restoring the city to life. As one visitor to Cambodia, a French journalist, wrote, "In Phnom Penh itself there is no drinking water, no post or telephone, no transport, no registry office, no money, no markets. . . . The city itself is so silent that bird song has a sinister ring to it."

More than a year after the Vietnamese invasion, a back street of Phnom Penh remains littered with debris and garbage. Smoke rises from open cooking fires.

Famine

The Vietnamese invasion of December 1978 disrupted the semiannual rice harvest. Retreating Khmer Rouge troops even mined some rice fields. Moreover, the vast migration that followed "liberation" interfered with rice planting. The inevitable result of these events was a tremendous shortfall of rice and a famine that shook the conscience of the world. Private agencies and the United Nations spent nearly $600 million over a period of eighteen months to bring food, medicines, and farming implements to the shattered nation.

Although the international effort relieved the famine, permanent growth has proved difficult to sustain; in 1983 the World Bank listed Cambodia, once a nation of bounty, as the world's poorest country.

In May 1980, famine–stricken Cambodians cross into the Nong Chan refugee camp in Thailand to collect their biweekly supply of rice. Each cart carries sacks of rice and some farming tools.

Coalition Forces

Guerrilla war continued. As Pol Pot had predicted, Khmer Rouge forces escaped the Vietnamese, and from bases near the Thai border they carried on a war of harassment against the Vietnamese troops stationed in Cambodia. But the estimated 35,000 Khmer Rouge fighters, outfitted by China, were not alone. Non-Communists of the Khmer People's National Liberation Front (KPNLF) fielded some 15,000 guerrillas, supplied covertly by ASEAN nations and the U.S. Another 9,000 guerrillas loyal to Prince Norodom Sihanouk added to the resistance.

The guerrilla war waged by the three-group coalition created a stalemate in Cambodia. The guerrillas could not defeat the Vietnamese, yet neither could the Vietnamese withdraw from Cambodia, allowing the Khmer Rouge, dominant members of the coalition, to resume control of the country.

Five hundred Khmer Rouge rally at their base in northwest Cambodia to celebrate a victory in 1981 against Vietnamese troops.

The Shape of Indochina

Although the Chinese "lesson" had been administered at great cost to Vietnam, it did not alter the course of events in Cambodia. Led by Heng Samrin, the Vietnam-sponsored People's Republic of Kampuchea early in 1979 labored to extend some degree of government across the country. The central leadership of the PRK consisted of a small handful, perhaps twenty-five people, who eagerly sought to enlist anyone with a high-school education who might prove capable of administration. So depleted was the population, and so poor were communications, that an initial draft netted only 106 Cambodians with minimal qualifications. Within two months, the PRK established "people's self-management committees" in sixteen of nineteen provinces, but those committees imposed no more than nominal administration beyond major cities and towns. For months no semblance of government reached into vast parts of the country, especially in the north and west.

Cambodians at first welcomed the Vietnamese as liberators who abolished the Pol Pot terror, freed them from arbitrary killings or political purges by Khmer Rouge soldiers, and allowed them to leave the collective farms and villages into which they had been herded. The Vietnamese occupiers encouraged people to go home, and weakened refugees from a three-and-one-half-year nightmare set out by the hundreds of thousands.

People clogged the highways, carrying their few possessions or pulling them in bullock carts and makeshift wheelbarrows. They crossed a landscape littered with skeletons and the debris of two wars within eight years. Perhaps one-half the population of Cambodia migrated during 1979, hundreds of thousands of undernourished people crisscrossing the country. Their journeys usually took weeks. Often they returned to their native villages to find only ruins and no family or friends; peasants had to wait to see if other relatives might show up. In the meantime they scavenged for food and built or repaired shelters. No rice seed was available for the rainy season rice crop that should be planted in May and harvested in December. When in late February it recognized the scale of the migration, the Heng Samrin government broadcast an appeal over Phnom Penh radio urging the population "to quickly settle down somewhere and stabilize . . . family life in order to engage in production." But as the planting season approached there was no evidence that the people were heeding the government's appeal.

The result was famine. The only aid reaching Cambodia during the first six months of the Heng Samrin regime were inadequate shipments of rice from Vietnam and the Soviet Union. Foreign Minister Hun Sen issued a letter requesting aid and stating that the lives of 2 million Cambodians were at stake.

Such a challenge to the international community could not be ignored, and governments and individuals began to contribute aid. A French campaign called SOS Cambodia raised $2 million; President Carter relaxed the Trading with the Enemy Act that had embargoed aid to Communist Cambodia and pledged $69 million in emergency relief. In a great outpouring of mercy, individuals

---

Preceding page. A Vietnamese soldier bearing an AK47 casts a shadow across a Khmer relief at Angkor Wat.

Images of Khao I Dang, just inside Thailand, the largest camp for Cambodian refugees from 1979 to 1981. A bulletin board (right) displays the notices of refugees searching for lost relatives. A Cambodian child unable to speak (far right) conveys the terror of Pol Pot's regime through a drawing.

around the world sent millions of dollars in contributions to organizations such as the Red Cross and Oxfam. Food was distributed slowly because of the almost complete deterioration of the nation's infrastructure—airport facilities, docks, cranes, trucks—but by early 1980 the famine seemed to have been arrested. Rice seed that constituted part of the aid had made possible new plantings. In February 1981 the new Reagan State Department, observing that famine no longer threatened, reimposed the Trading with the Enemy Act embargo, forbidding delivery to Cambodia of any aid that might lead to the "rehabilitation or development" of the country.

The Vietnamese presence

Although the Vietnamese had freed the Cambodians from the Pol Pot horrors, and blocked the return to power of the Khmer Rouge, many Cambodians inevitably came to resent the occupation of their country by their historical antagonists. Some 160,000 Vietnamese troops, numerous political and administrative officials, and tens of thousands of Vietnamese civilians—some of them former Cambodia

residents evicted in 1970 by the anti-Vietnamese government of Lon Nol, others new migrants—also moved into Cambodia. Those from the cities had constituted a merchant class, and they resumed their jobs in commerce as traders, owners of restaurants and cafés, and technicians. As they or their forebears had for generations, some Vietnamese turned to fishing on the Tonle Sap (Great Lake), often pushing the Cambodians off to the tributaries while they fished the lake, thus restoring the Vietnamese dominance that had existed for centuries.

Although Hanoi maintained that the Vietnamese settlers were merely returning to their pre-1970 lives, Cambodians insisted that the Vietnamese were mostly newcomers and that Hanoi was carrying out a plan to colonize Cambodia so that whatever the ultimate political settlement in Cambodia, Vietnamese would always exert a powerful influence in Cambodian affairs. The impact of the Vietnamese in Cambodia did indeed become pervasive. As one U.S. writer observed, "Teaching of skilled occupations is done only in Vietnamese or Russian. Cambodians who wish to advance in civil service are encouraged to marry Vietnamese. Rice farmers are expected to

feed and quarter Vietnamese soldiers in the countryside." The Vietnamese-sponsored government of Heng Samrin fostered the impression that the Vietnamese remained in Cambodia at the behest of the people. But one civil servant reflected the feelings of most Cambodians when he said, "That's not true. The Vietnamese are not welcome here."

Yet the Cambodians' dislike for the Vietnamese seemed to exist in inverse proportion to the threat they saw from the Khmer Rouge. The Heng Samrin army consisted of but 30,000 conscripts trained by the Vietnamese. One U.S. writer in 1985 described a Cambodian army contingent as "a rag tag collection of elderly men and young boys clad in assorted scraps of khaki. Most lack shoes. All lack guns." They proved to be useless in contesting the guerrilla activities of their countrymen and former masters. The political leaders of the Khmer Rouge, along with thousands of soldiers, had escaped the Vietnamese "blossoming lotus" in early 1979. Bringing their families with them, and also bringing—or driving—hundreds of thousands of peasants who feared the Vietnamese, they had fled to the southwest Cardamom mountains and to remote refugee encampments along the Thailand border. As many as 1 million Cambodians may have joined this exodus. Scarce foodstuffs went to the soldiers first, so tens of thousands died during the march or in the mountain camps. Buffeted by war, disease, and now starvation, many Cambodians began to quit the Khmer Rouge and cross into Thailand or to join other groups of non-Communist Cambodians. By late 1979 Thai authorities estimated that 600,000 Cambodians had arrived at the border, fleeing starvation, and that they were slipping into Thailand at the rate of 8,000 per day. The overwhelmed Thais herded many of them back across the border.

Within a year, the number of civilians and soldiers in the camps had shrunk to some 250,000. The Communist Khmer Rouge, with an estimated 30,000 soldiers, occupied the more southern mountainous camps. Because the Khmer Rouge leaders were deemed to constitute the legal government of Cambodia, overthrown by an invading force, Democratic Kampuchea retained its seat at the United Nations despite horrific stories that surfaced about the slaughter during the reign of terror. To legitimate its claim to the seat, however, the Khmer Rouge had to maintain its camps on Cambodian soil and avoid being driven totally out of the country. A group of non-Communists at the border, with perhaps 20,000 fighters, occupied refugee settlements more to the north. These non-Communists organized as the Khmer People's National Liberation Front (KPNLF), under the leadership of a former Cambodian prime minister named Son Sann. Another small group of non-Communists, perhaps 10,000 strong, professed its loyalty to deposed Cambodian leader Prince Norodom Sihanouk, who was living in exile in Peking. In a June 1982 meeting in Kuala Lumpur, Malaysia, these three groups—

Khmer Rouge, KPNLF, and Sihanoukists—joined in a tripartite coalition they called the Coalition Government of Democratic Kampuchea (CGDK) with the stated goal of ousting the Vietnamese from their country.

Vietnam's Vietnam

Armed by China and the ASEAN countries, via an overland route through cooperative Thailand, the guerrillas of the three anti-Vietnam groups slipped out of their hideaways and penetrated into the Cambodian interior, ambushing Vietnamese patrols and planting mines. Although some large-scale clashes took place, principally during the annual dry season offensives mounted by the Vietnamese beginning each November, most of the fighting consisted of skirmishes and ambushes.

Members of the KPNLF patrol for signs of their Vietnamese adversaries near the Nong Chan camp early in the Vietnamese 1984 dry-season offensive.

In counteracting the guerrillas, the Vietnamese soldiers puzzled over tactics, much like the conventional American troops in Vietnam a decade or more earlier. "If we send out a five or six-man team," said one Vietnamese officer in western Cambodia, "it runs the risk of ambush. If we send a battalion, they'll make so much noise that they'll never find the enemy. So most of the time we try to use a company." Despite the elusiveness of the enemy, the Vietnamese had to keep up frequent patrols, often going out after dark. "If we don't [the guerrillas will] soon be back planting mines," said one soldier. Duty in Cambodia proved hazardous enough—due as much to malaria as to enemy ambushes—and long enough to sap the morale of the Vietnamese soldiers, many of whom put in three or more years in Cambodia without home leave.

It was not until 1984 that a break came in the stale-

mated cycle of annual dry season offensives, during which the Vietnamese launched diverse attacks beginning in November or December only to fall back with the onset of the rainy season in May. Under Le Duc Anh, a senior Vietnamese general and Politburo member in command of military operations in Cambodia, Vietnamese forces struck hard, moving in late November of that year against the more lightly armed KPNLF. The Vietnamese attacked Nong Chan, a KPNLF stronghold of 20,000 rebels and captured it quickly as the KPNLF withdrew. Other Vietnamese troops overran two other KPNLF camps, and then on Christmas morning Vietnamese troops, backed up by

T54 tanks, armored personnel carriers, howitzers, and mortar fire, attacked and soon captured Nong Samet, the KPNLF's largest guerrilla camp. Early in 1985 the Vietnamese besieged and took the KPNLF headquarters and military training school at Ampil, leaving the KPNLF without any visible symbol of their political legitimacy on Cambodian soil.

The KPNLF policy of falling back before the superior Vietnamese firepower had in fact minimized the non-Communists' casualties, and from their new positions inside Thailand and along the border Son Sann and his military strategists considered initiating mobile guerrilla warfare rather than harboring a civilian population and trying to defend fixed positions. The KPNLF had suffered setbacks but was clearly not beaten.

Observers who wondered why the Vietnamese had chosen to attack the non-Communists and ignore the more heavily armed Khmer Rouge had their answer in mid-February 1985, when the thrust of the Vietnamese attacks shifted south. Le Duc Anh threw elements of four divisions into the attack against the Phnom Malai complex, a series of guerrilla and civilian encampments spread out over 300 square kilometers of rugged terrain on the Thai border. Employing tactics like those of the KPNLF, the Khmer Rouge evacuated their civilian population and most of their soldiers into Thailand or south to the Cardamom mountains, leaving a rear guard to contest the Vietnamese.

Premier Pham Van Dong at the prime minister's residence in Hanoi. His 1978 good-will tour to ASEAN capitals backfired.

Le Duc Anh hoped to control the border areas and to prevent guerrillas from infiltrating into the Cambodian interior. But sealing any land border, as the Americans learned during the Vietnam War, was an enormously difficult task. In February a Khmer Rouge communiqué spoke with satisfaction of the "favorable developments," noting that the concentration of Vietnamese troops at the border "leaves inside Kampuchea rather empty, which offers a golden opportunity for our resistance forces to strike deeper."

As the 1984-85 dry season drew to a close, it became clear that the three factions of the Coalition Government of Democratic Kampuchea had suffered losses, and dislocation, but that they remained viable politically and militarily. "While [the Vietnamese] have made some prog-

ress," noted one Western diplomat in Bangkok, "I don't think what they have achieved this year along the border could be described as a major breakthrough."

Although in conquering Cambodia, Vietnam had achieved the aim of securing its own border, its continuing occupation of the country pulled Hanoi deeper into a quagmire. The occupation had a disastrous impact on Vietnam's foreign policy since world condemnation provoked by the invasion did not ease and, as a precondition for establishing diplomatic relations or negotiating trade agreements, many countries insisted that Vietnam withdraw from Cambodia. Yet to do so was impossible, Hanoi knew, because the coalition government could then walk unimpeded into Phnom Penh, and the Khmer Rouge could easily overcome their less potent colleagues to regain control of the country.

Following the ferocious 1984-85 dry season offensive, Hanoi had seemingly moved no closer to solving its dilemma, although it did restate a compromise offer, this time imposing a deadline. Hanoi would allow most of the coalition government—with the exception of Ieng Sary and Pol Pot, the latter out of public sight for several years and rumored to be sick—to take part in the Communist government of Vietnam. That is, they could stand for election but only as members of the People's Republic of Kampuchea government of Heng Samrin, not as members of independent political parties. Hanoi imposed a deadline of 1987 on its compromise offer, after which it implied there would remain no role for them to play.

In September 1985, Khmer Rouge Radio announced that Pol Pot had given up his duties and retired. But China, enjoying the discomfiture of Vietnam in its Cambodian dilemma, continued to support Pol Pot and the Khmer Rouge, having already informed Son Sann and Prince Sihanouk that Peking would not accept a coalition that excluded the Khmer Rouge leaders.

In 1985 Sihanouk, the nominal head of the coalition and for many the true symbol of Cambodia, remained in exile in Peking, growing old and infirm. He supported the guerrillas because the only solution he could envision was to "weaken the Vietnamese on the battlefield" and to persuade them to accept an international conference. "Otherwise," he said, "one day there will be five million

Vietnamese in Cambodia. Cambodia will be lost to the Cambodians, and Cambodia will be a colony of Vietnam."

The upright dominoes

As Vietnam labored to find a solution to its dilemma, its neighbors in Southeast Asia strove to keep Vietnam diplomatically isolated. The members of ASEAN—the 1967 economic alliance that united Thailand, Malaysia, Indonesia, Singapore, the Philippines and, in 1980, the tiny sultanate of Brunei—had been angered by Vietnam's invasion of Cambodia, and not only for the breach of Cambodia's sovereignty. The invasion took place after what the ASEAN leaders came to conclude was a duplicitous fence-mending mission by Vietnam Premier Pham Van Dong in September and October of 1978.

The Vietnamese premier had carried a message of peace on his tour of ASEAN capitals already jittery about Hanoi's policies in the ongoing boat people crisis. In Bangkok, Dong pledged that Hanoi would never aid Thai Communist insurgents, and in Kuala Lumpur he went so far as to lay a wreath at Malaysia's national monument to those killed fighting Malay Communist insurgents. In Jakarta, Indonesia, he sought peaceful economic development; in Manila, he proposed a regional zone of peace; in Singapore, Premier Dong promised that Vietnam's desire for friendship would be matched by peaceful deeds.

Instead of carrying through on those pledges, however, the next month Hanoi signed its twenty-five-year friendship and defense pact with the Soviet Union and promptly invaded Cambodia. Vietnam apparently believed that Pol Pot's reputation was so bad that the world might overlook, and perhaps even approve, its actions. Singapore's United Nations representative T. T. B. (Tommy) Koh reported that Vietnam ambassador Ha Van Lau had told him, "In two weeks, the world will have forgotten the Cambodian problem."

But condemnation was worldwide and the deceived ASEAN nations took the lead in denouncing Vietnam's actions. When the U.N. Security Council convened in January 1979, Tommy Koh threw Pham Van Dong's words about Vietnam's peaceful deeds back in his face: "We regret to say that after Vietnam's armed intervention in the internal affairs of Cambodia, my country will have serious doubts about the credibility of Vietnam's words and about its intentions." Every year after the invasion, the ASEAN nations, joined by China and the United States, led the fight in the United Nations to prevent the recognition of the Vietnam-sponsored Heng Samrin regime.

Ironically, it was these ASEAN nations, growing increasingly strong throughout the 1970s and 1980s, which

A convoy of PAVN troops returning from duty in Cambodia crosses the Vietnamese border.

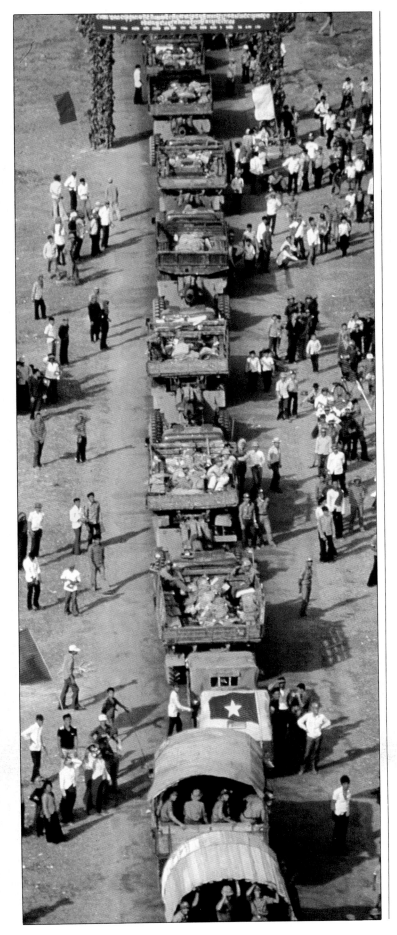

were the countries that prophets in the fifties and sixties said would fall to communism in the wake of a Communist triumph in Indochina. During a press conference in 1954, when the Vietminh was besieging Dien Bien Phu and the U.S. government was considering a bombing mission in support of the French, President Dwight Eisenhower gave definition to the vivid rationale invoked by his successors. "You have a row of dominoes set up," he said. "You knock over the first one, and what will happen to the last one is the certainty that it will go over very quickly."

Eisenhower's imagery, enshrined as "the domino theory," came to dominate America's strategic thinking in the Pacific and to conjure up the danger of communism sweeping across the ocean, engulfing Hawaii and ultimately reaching even California. Twenty-one years later, after the domino theory became doctrine, South Vietnam, Cambodia, and Laos had fallen to communism, but none of the other Pacific dominoes had followed.

That the Southeast Asia nations did not fulfill their domino destiny was due in part to the Vietnam War itself: Those nations benefited from an infusion of billions of dollars into the region and also from what their leaders referred to as "breathing room" provided by the ten-year war for their own postcolonial governments to take root and learn how to govern.

An equally important factor in the strength of the ASEAN countries was the rift between China and Vietnam. The domino theory had assumed a concerted effort on the part of Communist nations, including a reasonable degree of cooperation between Moscow and Peking. "The domino theory rested on the premise that communists cooperate with each other to bring other states into their orbit," said Singapore's long-time leader Lee Kuan Yew. But as a result of the China-Vietnam confrontation, and the rift between China and the U.S.S.R., Peking cut off material shipments and propaganda support to local insurgents. With Vietnam also promising ASEAN nations not to aid local insurgents, domestic Communist opposition wilted.

The country to benefit most from such withering of support was Thailand, whose buffer zone between it and Vietnam—Cambodia—had been abruptly removed by the Vietnamese conquest. With Vietnam now on its doorstep, indeed pursuing Khmer Rouge into Thai territory, and with a domestic Communist insurgency, Thailand was imperiled. But in its plight, Thailand discovered an ally in China.

Peking sought a supply route to the Khmer Rouge, and the only possible route lay through Thailand. The two countries had established diplomatic relations in 1975. This had led to some trade and tourism, but Peking had ignored Bangkok's primary concern—the insurgency by the Communist party of Thailand (CPT) supported by China. Now the Thais had something substantial to bargain, and China soon cut off the pipeline to the Thai insur-

gents. On July 10, 1979, the CPT clandestine radio station, which had broadcast into Thailand from Peking via a relay station in Yunnan Province since 1962, suddenly reached the end of a seventeen-year road. An announcer said, "Dear listeners, we will be temporarily suspending our broadcasts beginning July 11." With its radio quiet and its aid as abruptly cut off, the estimated 11,500 Thai insurgents became demoralized. Soon there was no resupply of weapons, ammunition, medicines, and clothing, and no more safe havens in China for regrouping. A stepped-up counterinsurgency campaign, bolstered by an amnesty program with cash incentives, soon reduced the ranks of the CPT. By late 1982, even senior veterans of more than ten years in the jungle had defected, and the insurgency had dwindled to no more than a few hundred hard-core guerrillas who no longer presented a military threat.

U.S. influence resurgent

In the immediate aftermath of the Vietnam War, ASEAN leaders wondered whether Washington intended to turn its back on Southeast Asia. The level of U.S. aid dropped, with Thailand, for example, receiving just $7.5 million in fiscal 1978 before the Carter administration tripled assistance to $21.6 million the following year. But the rapprochement between China and the United States, culminating in the January 1, 1979, resumption of diplomatic relations after a thirty-year hiatus, meant that the ASEAN nations, concerned about the expansion of Vietnam, could court both the Oriental and Western superpowers as a counterweight to Hanoi.

At the same time the Carter administration realized that the Soviet Union, by virtue of its twenty-five-year treaty with Vietnam, had gained a strategic foothold in the Pacific. With access to the warm-water port of Cam Ranh Bay, built with American millions, the Vladivostok-based Soviet fleet gained the capability for reconnaissance and antisubmarine/anticarrier warfare against the United States Pacific fleet. Moscow soon pressed its new advantage by building up its fleet. In all, the number of Soviet surface vessels in the Pacific grew from sixty to eighty-seven in the decade after the fall of Indochina; the Soviets also expanded their submarine pens at Petropavlovsk on the Kamchatka Peninsula.

In addition to their strategic locations in the Pacific, the ASEAN nations grew into large suppliers of critical raw materials to the United States. In 1980 the United States imported 84 percent of its tin from Malaysia, Thailand, and the Philippines; 91 percent of its chrome originated in the Philippines. Furthermore, Indonesia entered the 1980s providing the U.S. with 6 percent of its oil imports. The possibility that any of those states might fall under Communist control, with the corresponding loss of metals crucial to American industry, prompted the United States during the late 1970s and early 1980s to bolster those nations through a combination of grants and foreign aid.

In 1979 total U.S. financial and military aid in the region amounted to some $1.1 billion and $340 million, respectively. The Carter administration's policy was continued once Ronald Reagan assumed office. Military aid, for example, totaled $335 million in 1981, $352 million in 1982, and $367 million in 1983.

Direct military and economic aid to the region, however, was dwarfed by the trading carried on by Pacific nations and the United States. By 1980, East Asia—the six ASEAN states, along with Japan, South Korea, Taiwan, and Hong Kong—had surpassed Western Europe as America's largest trading region. By 1983, trans-Pacific trade exceeded trans-Atlantic trade by some $30 billion. The ASEAN nations alone accounted for $25.6 billion in two-way trade with the United States in 1984. "It would be hard to pick an area of greater opportunity in the world," said U.S. Trade Representative (and later Reagan labor secretary) William Brock.

The ASEAN nations' capitalist economies flourished, growing at an inflation-adjusted average of 7 percent annually, about twice the global rate. Per capita income increased, to $760 in the Philippines for 1982, $800 in Thailand, and the comparatively astronomical figure of $5,745 for Singapore. By contrast, per capita income for Vietnam in 1982 lagged at a meager $189. Meanwhile, the ASEAN countries' agricultural programs matured, as did a generation of university-trained young people to join the government and society. Regional leaders talked hopefully about an economic surge that would propel them into an "Asian century."

With the exception of the Philippines, where insurgents and dissatisfaction with the regime of authoritarian dictator Ferdinand Marcos rendered the country unstable in the mid-1980s, the ASEAN members and other U.S. allies in East Asia presented Washington with a strong security chain throughout the Pacific. (As a contingency against the possible loss of Clark Air Base and the Subic Bay complex in the Philippines, the United States leased 18,000 acres on Saipan and Tinian in the Mariana Islands for future development.) The United States found itself in a far stronger position in East Asia in 1985 than even the most optimistic strategist might have predicted following the fall of South Vietnam. "Even compared to the end of World War II, it is far better because the countries of Asia are far more self-reliant," said Paul D. Wolfowitz, assistant secretary of state for East Asian and Pacific affairs. "[They] don't look to us as much as they did before; but when they do, we are there."

While the ASEAN and other East Asian nations experienced an economic boom in trade relations with the West, Vietnam, its socialist economy in a shambles, lagged far behind. The invasion of Cambodia was the main reason for the almost complete cutoff of more than $200 million per year from Western European nations and Japan and was a major factor in China's decision to end a five-year-old aid program worth nearly $1 billion. By 1985, diplomats estimated, Vietnam's foreign reserves amounted to a paltry $16 million, and Hanoi was incapable of paying even the interest on its loans from the International Monetary Fund. Since 1975, Hanoi had looked to the Soviet Union for aid, and Moscow complied by sending, according to diplomatic estimates, between $1 billion and $2 billion annually in military and economic aid. In addition, some 7,000 Russians, mostly technicians, and 1,500 East Europeans were stationed in Vietnam. Hanoi sought more aid, but during the 1984 COMECON summit, Moscow made clear its reluctance to increase its commitment. (U.S. aid to South Vietnam in the last years of the war, by comparison, averaged $1.6 billion, accounting for some 70 percent of Saigon's budget.) Despite its heavy obligations to Moscow, the presence of Russian advisers in Vietnam, and the increasing use of Cam Ranh Bay by the Soviet fleet, Vietnam's leaders steadfastly denied that Vietnam was becoming a Soviet satellite. "No other nation in history has ever paid so much in blood for its independence," said Foreign Minister Nguyen Co Thach, adding that an independence so dearly won was not about to be squandered.

In fact, Vietnam desired a reduction in its dependence on the Soviet Union, and Hanoi may have been spurred into action when Moscow and Peking resumed efforts in late 1984 to reconcile their disputes. Rapprochement between Moscow and Peking could leave Hanoi even more isolated diplomatically. After months of high-level debate, the Politburo decided on, and the Central Committee endorsed in December 1984, a more "flexible" foreign policy, aimed especially at improving relations with the United States and attracting Western trade, investment, and aid. Hanoi's new approach also opened the door to a role for Washington in the settlement of the Cambodian problem.

Early in 1985 Vietnam made several approaches to the United States. Meeting in January, the Indochinese foreign ministers, those of Vietnam, Cambodia, and Laos—all of course speaking in a Vietnamese voice—called for normalization of relations with the United States and for the U.S. to play a "responsible role" in Southeast Asia. At the same time, Hoan Bich Son, Vietnam's permanent representative to the United Nations, said in an interview, "If the United States sincerely wishes to establish peace and stability [in Southeast Asia], it will find the Vietnamese forthcoming. . . . We can cooperate with the United States in many fields." Le Duc Tho, second-ranking member of the Politburo, told *New Yorker* writer Robert Shaplen, "We do wish that normalization of relations may come sooner rather than later." In 1984, Pham Van Dong told an interviewer, "Our door is always open. . . . We are a patient people. We can wait. Eventually the U.S. will come through that door." But Washington responded to these

Creating an Economy

Primarily an agricultural country, Vietnam has concentrated in the postwar era on constructing a socialist economy while facing, according to Le Duc Tho, "the destruction in the American war of most of what industry we had." With the support principally of the Soviet Union, Vietnam has sought to revitalize traditional sectors of the economy while expanding its industrial base. The country's major problem, said Le Duc Tho, was a lack of economic managers.

Above. *Vietnamese women process pineapple at a factory in the Mekong Delta town of Kien Giang. Left. Workers receive instructions at a steamroller plant in Gia Sang. Right. A girl weaves a traditional rug at a carpet mill, part of the Minh Khai Cooperative, in 1976.*

openings with little more alacrity than it had in the past; early in 1984 Assistant Secretary of Defense for International Security Richard Armitage had told the Vietnamese that normalization of relations would have to wait until the Vietnamese had withdrawn from Cambodia.

Another key to establishing relations with the United States, especially as U.S.-Peking economic and military ties improved, was for Hanoi to effect a reconciliation with Peking. Yet there remained the Cambodian tangle. China stepped up its aid to the Khmer Rouge during Hanoi's 1984-85 dry-season offensive and even threatened another invasion of northern Vietnam "to teach the Vietnamese a second lesson." In 1984, speaking to a group in New York, Hanoi's Foreign Minister Thach took an ironic approach to the problem of China. "We have waited 4,000 years for normalization of relations with China," he said. "We can wait a few more years, or centuries." Hanoi's leaders knew though, that they could not remain aloof. Thach later adopted a more serious attitude, confidently predicting to Robert Shaplen, "It will happen not in twenty years but within five years."

Vietnam's economic woes

Hanoi's postwar five-year economic plan proved a disaster. Flushed with the speed and totality of their victory, the Marxist-Leninist ideologues in Hanoi had embarked on a program to bring the South "rapidly, vigorously and firmly" to socialism. But the measures Hanoi took were overly ambitious and were conceived with disregard for the attitudes in the South. As one Ho Chi Minh party document defensively noted:

We must strive resolutely to correctly implement correct Politburo resolutions while informing the Politburo of the actual situation so that it may lead us more accurately.

New policies were enacted by decree rather than persuasion, and the recalcitrant southerners failed to comply, resorting to a kind of passive resistance. The economic measures resulted in a litany of failures.

New Economic Zones were intended to reclaim abandoned farmland and clear virgin lands for agricultural production. The forcing of people from the cities to NEZs was also supposed to relieve overcrowding. But of the 400,000 people sent from Saigon alone in 1975-76, almost 60 percent returned to the city within a few months. The abolition of private trade by merchants not only helped to provoke the exodus of boat people but also helped to institutionalize the black market system. China's withdrawal of its advisers, cancellation of aid projects, and seventeen-day invasion had a serious impact on Vietnam. The invasion destroyed half a dozen towns, a railway line, a power station, and the phosphate mine that provided much of the country's fertilizer. Six years later, production had been brought back only to a third. Collectivization of agriculture, intended to ease food shortages, failed dis-

Workers spend their earnings at a Hanoi restaurant. Many restaurants had closed by 1985 due to high taxes.

mally. As the first stage of collectivization, some 13,240 production teams were established in 1979 to work thirty to fifty hectares each. Within a year, 10,000 of them had collapsed, the victims, Party publications noted, of poor planning and the peasants' passive resistance.

After the economic crisis deepened in the wake of the invasion of Cambodia, and China subsequently invaded Vietnam, the Sixth Plenum of the Fourth Party Congress convened in September 1979. In that meeting the Central Committee initiated far-reaching changes in the economy, including practical measures antithetical to socialist planning, such as lifting restrictions on open markets and providing material incentives for peasants and workers.

Perhaps the most significant innovation was the so-called contract system, allowing peasants, and later workers, to sell, after certain quotas had been reached, surplus food or goods on the open market or at preferential prices to the government. Due to continuing debate among high-level Party leaders, however, the contract system did not receive full government approval for more than a year. But even before approval, some officials practiced the contract system at the provincial level.

Within two years the country had, by the narrowest of definitions, begun to feed itself. "By 1983 we had achieved self-sufficiency in food, but only by using the lowest allowable per capita standard—eighteen hundred calories a day," said Professor Tran Phuong, deputy prime minister for planning and one of the few trained economists in the Party hierarchy. Phuong predicted that Vietnam would rise above bare self-sufficiency by 1990, in spite of a birth rate of almost 2.5 percent that added some 1.5 million people per year to the almost 60 million population of the mid-1980s. Still, Phuong marked progress in small stages. Immediately after the war, the North had had to send rice, including imported rice, to the South. But by 1984 that trend had been reversed, and the South sent 700,000 tons of rice to the North. By using the contract system to increase production, Phuong foresaw a time when the South might export rice, as it had done before the war.

The contract system extended to industry, where the government also allowed hybrid cooperatives that combined private and state ownership. In one successful manufacturing cooperative in Ho Chi Minh City, engineers sought out customers for water pumps, for example, designed the machine, and bought and tooled raw materials from the city. This cooperative paid a third of its income for taxes, a third for repairs and expansion, and a third for wages. "It is really free enterprise, and I personally think this contract system will last a long time, especially since the Party has now approved it," said Vo Sau, a coop director who had been a Vietcong political worker. Although the Party had approved such quasi-capitalist ventures, Le Quang Chanh, vice chairman of the Ho Chi Minh City People's Committee, maintained that the Party's economic goal remained "the steady socialist transformation of the economy by gradual increase of the socialist sector and reform of the capitalist one." Chanh added that the Party could easily restrict such enterprises by taxation, registration, or limiting bank accounts. Indeed restaurants, not considered necessary, were taxed as much as 70 percent, forcing many out of business. Farmers, by contrast, paid an annual tax of 8 percent of their production.

Many in Vietnam survived on what was called "the second economy"—moonlighting. The average worker's monthly salary in 1985 was 300 or 400 dong, which converted to 30 or 40 dollars. The official rate was 11 dong per dollar, but on the black market, moneychangers, reflecting an artificially controlled currency, offered up to 200 dong per dollar. Consumer goods were beyond the reach of workers who did not supplement their incomes. A girl's embroidered blouse in 1984 cost an average month's pay. Men's trousers cost from 250 to 400 dong. Bicycles, a primary mode of transportation, cost from 15,000 to 23,000 dong. Even with rationed food and regulated housing costs, the average worker required an additional 1,000 dong per month to live at all well.

In addressing many of these domestic problems in 1984 with the *New Yorker*'s Robert Shaplen, the first American to whom he had spoken since the 1973 Paris peace accords, Le Duc Tho suggested that it would take time for Hanoi to overcome its problems.

Kissinger used to tell me that we know how to wage war but not peace. But it's not that we don't know how to deal with peace. Our problem has been lack of time and experience—how in the short space of a decade to sort out the objective and subjective conditions, and, particularly, how to handle our shortcomings in economic management. ... We have had to devise new methods of dividing the responsibilities for action, by levels, and we are doing this progressively, step by step, in advancing to socialism.

Prospects for the South

Le Duc Tho also remarked on a different "cast of mind" among southerners and implied, with the firm conviction of the ideologue, that it was not a question of whether Hanoi could impose its will on the South but only when. "Like everything else in a period of transition, it will take time," he said.

In the decade after the fall of South Vietnam, the South had scarcely been absorbed by the North. In fact the reverse may almost have been true: North Vietnamese said, half-jokingly, that although they had conquered Saigon militarily, Saigon might ultimately conquer them with graft, soft living, and bourgeois customs. In Ho Chi Minh City, which virtually everyone but leading Party officers continued to call Saigon, the capitalist spirit proved irrepressible, and the black markets were filled not only with goods available in Vietnam, or left over from the American period, but also with the latest radios, television sets, and phonographs smuggled into the country from Singapore, Bangkok, Tokyo, and Hong Kong. Every plane bringing northerners home from Saigon was filled with consumer goods unknown in the more austere North.

Le Duc Tho and his fellow Communist planners faced the nearly insurmountable task of inspiring the Communist Vietnamese to work as hard to rebuild their country as they did to oust the Americans and their client governments and to persuade the defeated southern Vietnamese to join in building socialism on a Vietnamese model. What had characterized the northern Communists during their long revolutionary struggle was a sense of unity and discipline. Although ranking members of the Party had often disagreed, and engaged in spirited debate in Party publications, once the Politburo had reached a decision, it was carried out zealously down to the lowest cells. But much of the Communists' ability to inspire had been used

Posters in Hanoi remind the younger generation of the struggles that led to victory.

up in the war. "Everything since the war here has been anticlimactic," said one Western diplomat stationed in Hanoi. "What kept people going so long, against the French and then against the Americans, was the siege mentality, and it provided a remarkable drive and force. But now that the big wars are over there is no substitute for its élan, and this accounts for the malaise—for the lack of ambition, ingenuity, and imagination."

The character of Vietnamese in the South had always been more self-interested and prideful, traits that confounded the Americans and that the northerners had not grown comfortable with in a decade. Some thought the solution lay in something other than Hanoi's efforts to impose its will. "Socialism simply doesn't work for the Vietnamese," said an international aid official who had spent much of his four postwar years in Vietnam in the South. "They are far too individualistic. The state can run the railways and the utilities, but it's got to get out of retail trade, including marketing and distribution. Despite the heavy influence of the Soviet Union, not one Vietnamese I know has any interest in a system as a system. They all search for ways to get around any system—to cock a snook at authority. This is true from the government level down to the moonlighting worker."

Although economic reforms such as the contract system had been enacted, the prospect for workable economic and social programs on a national level resided with the top Party leaders in Hanoi, some of whom steadfastly refused to accept differences between North and South.

Some of the aging ideologues in the Politburo may have been gradually giving way, at least intellectually, to younger, more reform-minded colleagues. Senior Party leaders Le Duan and Le Duc Tho, in 1984 aged seventy-five and seventy-three respectively, endorsed the reform measures of Politburo member Vo Van Kiet, head of State Planning, and his deputy, Professor Tran Phuong. If the trend toward reformism continued, Kiet was seen as a possible successor to Prime Minister Pham Van Dong.

But in the mid-1980s, the conservative faction, with some concessions to economic necessity, seemed to be holding sway. To Huu, an ideologue in his early sixties, was seen as a more likely successor to Pham Van Dong. Huu was joined by Truong Chinh, an aging hard-line theorist who had once been number-two man in the Party to Ho Chi Minh, and by General Van Tien Dung, defense minister and successor to Vo Nguyen Giap, who stepped down from the Politburo, or was demoted, in 1982. Dung disciple General Le Duc Anh, Vietnamese commander in Cambodia, favored an uncompromising line there. Pham Hung, another Politburo hard-liner, served as minister of the interior, and his conservatism was rooted more in his concerns about national security than in political ideology.

Pham Van Dong, acutely aware of the imminent passing of his generation of revolutionary leaders, acknowledged that his main concern was "how to make all the generations go forward with the flame that has been handed down from Ho Chi Minh." Dong confidently predicted that Vietnam would suffer no "generation gap" and that its youth would rise to the challenge. He said:

We know that young people have their aspirations—that they want better clothes, some up-to-date fashions, a richer culture. These things should be welcome. That's progress, and we're not fighting it. But their minds and spirits are important. We must keep their minds and spirits Vietnamese, and the achievement of our young people will then be great. In ten years' time, we shall see.

Another of Hanoi's concerns remained reeducation camps, to which those who had served the American and South Vietnamese governments and military had been consigned. Ten years after the war, opinions varied widely about the numbers still detained. Vietnam claimed to be holding 7,000 "irreconcilables" in 1984, but the U.S. State Department annual report on human rights suggested that as many as 60,000 remained incarcerated. In a 1984 interview, Pham Van Dong criticized America's concern for the political prisoners, whatever their numbers, and threw down the gauntlet for Washington. "We are quite prepared to allow all of those left in the camps to leave tomorrow for the United States," he said. "But the U.S. government has rejected that suggestion. They prefer to leave these criminals free in Vietnam but not in the United States."

Some people were free to leave Vietnam. Under the Orderly Departure Program, instituted in 1979, some 84,000 people had left Vietnam by 1985, 30,000 of them for the United States. But a backlog existed of more than 40,000 Vietnamese who had been granted exit visas yet failed to win resettlement in a foreign country.

Others who could not leave Vietnam legally still took to the open sea. Although in later years the numbers of Vietnamese boat people did not approach the proportions of the 1979 crisis, Vietnamese still escape clandestinely by sea: Some 2,000 Vietnamese boat people arrived monthly in countries of first asylum in 1984. Le Thanh Dau, a medical doctor who in 1980 escaped in a small boat with his wife and 80 other people, added a mournful postscript to the story of those fleeing. Their boat stole away after midnight from the Ca Mau Peninsula, heading west to Thailand, and by 6:00 A.M. the refugees could still make out the coast. But others could also see them. A fishing boat filled with undercover policemen chased them. With a burst from an AK47, a policeman wounded a nineteen-year-old engineering student in the head. The police seized the refugees' maps and compass and then allowed the boat to continue on its way. An hour later, the student died of his wounds, and his fellow refugees conducted a burial at sea. "We put his body out over the side," Dau related "and it floated beside the boat for three to four hours. Some believed it was because his soul wanted to come with us away from Vietnam."

Vietnam Ten Years After

The North

Ten years after North Vietnam pushed toward Saigon in its final offensive, hundreds of American and foreign correspondents, many of whom had once covered the war, flocked to the country to observe the anniversary and to inquire into the first decade of Communist rule in Vietnam. One visitor was Tim Page, a British photographer who spent years in the hottest areas of the war zone and who collected several wounds, including a near-fatal head wound, for his efforts. Hanoi granted Page, whose photographs comprise this essay, an unusual degree of freedom to travel about the country.

What Page, and others, found in the North was a region that, while no longer at war or subject to bombing raids, had by no means entered an era of prosperity. In fact Vietnam's economic problems and the quagmire of its Cambodian occupation were two of the major topics of the decennial anniversary. Visitors found Hanoi relatively unscathed by bombing. Its French architecture, said one journalist, gave Hanoi "the look of a sleepy French provincial town. It is ... nothing like a capital."

Farther north there was abundant evidence of destruction. Although the offensive phase of the 1979 Chinese invasion lasted but seventeen days, the Chinese practiced scorched-earth tactics during their retreat. Even six years later, residents claimed, Chinese troops routinely shelled across the border.

Left. A bomb casing once used as an air raid warning gong in Lang Sen, a village northwest of Vinh, remains as a relic of the war.

Preceding page. A boy races the southbound "reunification train" as it steams toward Thanh Hoa. The train normally takes three days to traverse its route between Hanoi and Ho Chi Minh City.

Above. *With the border of China as near as the background hills, this house in Dong Dang, north of Lang Son, stood in the path of the 1979 Chinese invasion.*

Left. *A former soldier in North Vietnam's army stands before his home in the town of Vinh in the southern panhandle, which was heavily bombed during the war.*

Vestiges of War

During fifteen years of warfare, few locales in South Vietnam escaped untouched. Ten years after the fall of Saigon the rusted wreckage of war still lay on many battlefields. Some of the most heavily pounded U.S. bases, such as Khe Sanh and Con Thien, remained off limits because unexploded munitions still scattered the ground. At other bases visitors were cautioned not to stray from marked paths.

Hidden unexploded munitions posed great hazards for farmers, who risked setting them off while tilling the fields. Hanoi reports that several thousand peasants have been killed since the war by striking unexploded bombs.

Left. Riverine boats probably used by the U.S. 9th Division lie at anchor south of Ben Tre. Above. A South Vietnam army veteran in Dong Ha has been reduced to begging. Right. A girl collects 105MM howitzer shell casings for recycling at the former U.S. Marine base at Chu Lai.

Ho Chi Minh City

In Ho Chi Minh City, which most Vietnamese by habit still called Saigon, the
mad bustle of the wartime era had fled.
New Yorker writer Robert Shaplen wrote
that the city seemed "a dormant mollusk,
its shell closed, waiting for the weather to
change or the tide to come back in. There
was something terribly tentative about the
city, something untold and untellable, not
because of any dark secret but because
the plot was obscure, the future still unclear."

*Above. One of the ubiquitous portraits of
Ho Chi Minh, this one overlooking the post
office in his namesake city. Right. A vendor
offers fruit on Dong Khoi (Uprising) Street,
formerly Tu Do Street, once the locale of GI
bars.*

Vietnam and the American Spirit

Nineteen seventy-six was a year of proud remembrance for the United States. Americans celebrated their nation's 200th anniversary with parades, gala parties and balls, sporting events, concerts, and hometown barbecues. In Washington, D.C., on July 3d, 500,000 people turned out to view the capital's grand parade of more than fifty bands, sixty floats, and ninety marching military units. A flotilla of warships from twenty-two countries sailed into New York Harbor for an Independence Day salute, followed by a procession of 200 high-masted sailing ships. On July 4 almost every major city in the country staged some kind of holiday extravaganza. Americans joined in the festivities enthusiastically. A woman watching the parade in Washington, D.C., expressed the national mood best when she shouted to a friend marching by, "Everything's OK! Lookin' good, lookin' good!"

Despite the recent national traumas, Americans closed ranks during their bicentennial celebration

for a reaffirmation of their national achievements. An editorial in the *New York Times* observed, "Two years after Watergate and four years after Vietnam, friends who were then ashamed of the United States seem to be saying now that they see America's better values surviving. The oldest written Constitution still in effect—and one of the most democratic in its effective guarantees for human rights—assures this nation a solid place in hearts that cherish the world's receding zone of freedom."

Underlying the nation's pride in its past, however, was an uncertainty, an uneasiness about America's present direction and role in the world. Watergate and the Vietnam experience had shaken the country's confidence in the extent and legitimacy of its power and taken some of the luster from its vision of being the preeminent world leader. Moreover, although President Ford in 1975 had urged America to put the war behind it and "focus on the future," the consequences of Vietnam could not be so easily glossed over. The toll of more than 58,000 U.S. troops killed and 250,000 wounded in a futile military endeavor still embittered the nation. Ford himself called the cost of the war in national treasure, more than $180 billion, "staggering." And the price was destined to go higher: in the plight of hundreds of thousands of mentally and physically scarred veterans; the prolonged anxiety of the families of MIAs; a demoralized military establishment; tens of thousands of political exiles, draft evaders, and deserters cut off from home; a stagnant, inflation-ridden economy; and the influx of nearly a million Indochinese refugees. As former Secretary of State Dean Rusk warned on April 30, 1975, "We haven't seen the final bill yet."

The end of an era

A major preoccupation in Washington in the wake of Vietnam was to adjust to the realities of postwar international affairs and chart a new course for American foreign policy. By the time U.S. troops had pulled out of Vietnam, many American policymakers were seriously questioning the efficacy and wisdom of "global containment," the guiding principle of U.S. foreign policy for a quarter century. The Vietnam War had undermined containment's credibility by demonstrating that the American people might not have the will or capacity to combat the spread of communism on all fronts, that they no longer believed every successful Communist move would directly threaten the security of the United States. "Vietnam made clear," said historian George Herring, "the inherent unworkability of a policy of global containment."

The United States's frustrating involvement in Vietnam not only eroded containment, it left in disarray the domestic consensus that for so long had been its mainstay. Leslie Gelb, who had been a Pentagon analyst and then a journalist, wrote, "It is undeniable that American immersion in the Vietnam war was the product of an American consensus to do so. . . . The Vietnam war brought an end to the consensus on containment."

In 1975, therefore, as the U.S. pondered its place and role in the post-Vietnam era, the urgent need for a new consensus impressed itself upon U.S. foreign policymakers. Secretary of State Henry Kissinger asserted, "The present ordeal of the whole nation is too obvious to require commentary." He cited the "exhaustion" of "the consensus that sustained our international participation" and concluded "it must be restored."

The political legacy of Vietnam offered both opportunities and obstacles to building a new consensus. One of the principal effects of the war was a more active participation by Congress in formulating American foreign policy. Congressional reassertion of its foreign policy responsibilities culminated in the War Powers Act. The act, passed over Nixon's veto on November 3, 1973, required the president to report to Congress within forty-eight hours of committing U.S. troops abroad. Congress reserved the right to recall the troops at any time by concurrent resolution, unless the president obtained authorization to extend their deployment.

An evolving partnership of Congress and the president in setting foreign policy seemed the best chance for forming a postwar consensus. But the hostility and distrust generated by Vietnam, and Watergate, made close cooperation between Congress and the White House difficult. In addition, a "Vietnam hangover" beset the rest of America's foreign policy apparatus—the State Department, the CIA, the military. In the post-Vietnam era, tensions in the State Department and Pentagon sparked a debilitating round of what former Secretary of Defense Harold Brown later described as "backbiting." Self-doubt and guilt exacerbated the internal dissension. Zbigniew Brzezinski, national security adviser to President Carter, observed that "the Vietnam War contributed to a loss of self-confidence and moral self-righteousness with which any elite has to be imbued."

The CIA, the so-called eyes and ears of American foreign policy, was parlous. Public revelations in 1974 of the CIA's part in bringing down Salvador Allende's Chilean government badly tarnished the agency's reputation. In 1975, Seymour Hersh revealed in the *New York Times* that the CIA had exceeded its statutory authority by using illegal break-ins, wiretaps, and surveillance against American citizens, many of them Vietnam dissidents. Former CIA agent Frank Snepp's book describing CIA bungling in the final months of the Saigon regime further embarrassed the agency.

After Congressional hearings in the mid-1970s publicized questionable CIA anti-Castro activities in the 1960s

---

Preceding page. *The American hostages, after being seized at the U.S. Embassy in Teheran on November 4, 1979, are paraded through the streets by Iranian militants.*

and similar covert operations against Iran and Guatemala going back to the 1950s, a wave of recriminations overtook the U.S. intelligence community. A CIA shakeup, resulting in the replacement of director William Colby by George Bush, threw the agency into turmoil, and Congressional legislation to impose substantial restrictions on its future operations significantly impaired the CIA's prestige and reliability as an instrument of American foreign policy. "Defenders of any continuing CIA role in the range of American policy options," noted former Assistant Secretary of State William Bundy, "were for a time either silenced or outgunned."

No branch of the U.S. government sank lower in public esteem after Vietnam than the military. The military's deterioration in the later years of the war was a principal source of public disfavor. In 1974 air force Colonel Donaldson Frizzell of the Army War College cited "the backlash against the military in the United States stemming from our national frustration over Vietnam." Admiral Thomas Moorer, chairman of the Joint Chiefs of Staff, deplored "the public's unwillingness to uncouple from the disenchantment of Vietnam." In 1975 Secretary of Defense James Schlesinger also fretted about a climate of disdain for the military forces. "The vitality of the nation's military establishment," he asserted, "for its perceptions of itself, its precision of mission, flow from a sense of purpose deriving from a larger national unity and spirit. ... Vision and confidence have diminished; a vacuum of the spirit has appeared."

Bill Mauldin's Bicentennial cartoon depicts Uncle Sam as bruised by Vietnam and Watergate.

Not surprisingly, the military entered the postwar period dispirited and sulking. The largely self-inflicted wounds of Vietnam, the drug abuse, demoralization, racial discord, and corruption that tore at the fabric of the armed forces, were still fresh in memory. Despite drug rehabilitation and prevention measures, for example, a 1979 Pentagon study concluded that "the Army and the other services still have a drug problem and have failed to resolve it satisfactorily." Racial dissension persisted. At Camp Pendleton near San Diego in December 1976, "organized racial harassment by whites" in the Marine Corps drew a full-scale reprisal by blacks wielding clubs, knives, and screwdrivers. There were exposures of rampant corruption. At five of its eight basic-training bases in November 1975 the army cracked a ring of NCOs who solicited bribes from recruits. In exchange for a weekend pass, a passing exam grade, or an overlooked infraction, NCOs accepted cash or favors. In November 1976 West Point cadets were ejected for cheating.

The combined effect of public scorn and internal breakdown on America's new "volunteer army" was deleterious. Unable to attract qualified recruits, the military began signing up the dregs of the manpower pool to fill its enlistment quotas. After the draft was abolished in 1973, a Marine Corps report disclosed to the Senate Armed Services Committee in October 1978, recruiters were "routinely taking criminals, illiterates, and the physically unfit." Of the 74,888 people who joined the marines between 1976 and 1978, over 10 percent, according to the Pentagon, had to be discharged for medical disabilities and drug habits. By 1979 the percentage of army recruits with some college experience plunged from 13.5 percent in 1964 to 3.2 percent. This coincided with a drop in the number of "Category I" recruits who scored highest on aptitude tests. The general decline of military institutions and traditions alarmed administration and Congressional officials in Washington. Warning about the armed forces' poor combat readiness and its "unhealthy" ramifications for U.S. foreign policy, Democratic Senator Sam Nunn of Georgia, a member of the Senate Armed Services Committee, raised another concern when he stated, "We are losing the confidence of our allies. Talk to some West Germans off the record and ask them what they think of the U.S. ability to fight a war. It's very, very low."

Shorn of a political consensus, its foreign policy establishment in ferment, the United States government entered the post-Vietnam era tentatively, to put it mildly. In 1975 President Ford spoke of avoiding "commitments too far from home." Yet beyond the national conviction that global containment had been unrealistic, as demonstrated in Vietnam, no agreement existed about why and how it did not succeed. What is more, the prospect for a broad review of the "lessons of Vietnam" was dim. There was little enthusiasm in or outside government for a comprehensive probe of the origins, nature, and objectives of U.S. intervention in Vietnam. "Today, it is almost as though the war had never happened," *Christian Science Monitor* columnist Joseph Harsch wrote in late 1975. "Americans have somehow blocked it out of their consciousness. They don't talk about it. They don't talk about its consequences." William Henderson, editor of *Asian Affairs*, lamented Amer-

The Mayaguez Affair

Monday, May 12, 1975, 2:20 P.M. in the Gulf of Thailand. The instant Cambodian gunboat fire rocketed across his bow, Captain Charles Miller, the skipper of the U.S. merchantman *Mayaguez*, knew he and his thirty-eight men had trouble on their hands. Bound for Sattahip, Thailand, laden with commercial cargo and supplies for American servicemen and embassy personnel, the small, unarmed ship had been accosted by two Cambodian gunboats just off the tiny and barren Wai Islands, 100 kilometers from the Cambodian mainland. Unknown to Miller, within the past ten days Cambodia had fired upon or detained some twenty-five ships in the same area, although Thailand and Vietnam also claimed the islands. Radio operator Wilbert Bock got off a desperate "mayday" message just before soldiers boarded the ship and found its radio shack.

Miller's mayday arrived in Washington at the State Department Operations Center at 5:30 A.M. EDT. At 7:40 that morning, National Security Adviser Brent Scowcroft strode into the Oval Office with the news of the nation's first major test of will in the post-Vietnam era.

At an emergency meeting of the National Security Council that noon, President Gerald R. Ford looked on as Secretary of State Henry Kissinger argued that a chance was at hand. "At some point," said Kissinger, "the United States must draw the line. This is not our idea of the best such situation. It is not our choice. But we must act upon it now, and act firmly."

With American destroyers and the aircraft carrier *Coral Sea* too far away to effect an immediate rescue, Ford moved on two fronts, military and diplomatic. The State Department was told to induce the Chinese to pass on to Cambodia an American demand for the ship's release. Militarily, the Pentagon ordered the *Coral Sea* and other naval vessels to steam immediately for the Gulf of Thailand.

The next day the Chinese bluntly indicated that they would not be go-betweens by returning the note the U.S. had given them. Ford also learned Tuesday morning, after hours of contradictory intelligence, that a reconnaissance plane had found the *Mayaguez* anchored off Koh Tang Island, fifty-five kilometers from the Cambodian mainland. Hearing nothing from the Cambodians, and fearing that the merchantman could become another *Pueblo* (the U.S. spy ship captured in 1968 and held with its crew for a year by North Korea), Ford began military planning in earnest. Eleven hundred marines from Okinawa, plus two marine platoons from the Philippines, flew to the Thai air base at U Tapao over vehement Thai objection. That evening, an air force helicopter bound for U Tapao crashed; all twenty-three aboard were lost.

The NSC that evening decided to make one last diplomatic initiative, asking United Nations Secretary-General Kurt Waldheim to mediate. Ford, however, had little faith in that approach, and the military operations continued. The destroyer escort *Harold E. Holt*, the guided missile destroyer *Henry B. Wilson*, and the *Coral Sea* converged on the area.

The decisive meeting of the NSC began Wednesday afternoon. Debate among its members was in full swing when, suddenly, the president, the vice president, the secretaries of state and defense, the director of the CIA, and the chairman of the Joint Chiefs of Staff got advice from a quite unexpected quarter: twenty-nine-year-old David Hume Kennerly, who had been moving silently about the room taking pictures. Ford's personal photographer, who had been in

Battle-ready marines storm aboard the Mayaguez, found at anchor near Poulo Wai Island. The crewmen had been transported to the mainland, however, and the empty ship was taken under tow.

Cambodia just prior to the fall of Phnom Penh, suddenly spoke up, suggesting that the seizure may have been the act of a lone Cambodian commander, acting without orders from the Khmer Rouge.

"Everyone here has been talking about Cambodia as if it were a traditional government," Kennerly said. "It's not that kind of government at all. We don't even know who the leadership is. Has anyone considered that?" In his memoirs, Ford noted that the NSC members were flabbergasted at Kennerly's cheek in offering his unsolicited opinion. For his part, however, the president wrote that he was glad to hear that point of view. Nevertheless, he ignored it. (At a press conference in Bangkok some months after the fact, Cambodian Foreign Minister Ieng Sary confirmed Kennerly's analysis.)

Ford made up his mind, and the orders went out. The *Holt*, now steaming into the Gulf of Thailand, moved to seize the *Mayaguez*, and marines prepared to storm Koh Tang (where intelligence indicated the ship's crew had been taken) and, in Ford's term, "destroy" any Cambodian units that tried to stop them. The *Coral Sea* was then to launch punitive air strikes against the shipping facilities at Kompong Som, on the Cambodian mainland. "We waited as long as we could,"

Ford told leading congressmen in a briefing.

At dawn in the gulf, the mission began and instantly ran into trouble. Because of faulty intelligence, the marines expected only token resistance on Koh Tang, but a company of dug-in Khmer Rouge troops awaited them. Three of the eight helicopters sent to the island were shot down, with 13 marines killed. Enemy fire disabled two other choppers. Of the 175 marines who began the attack, only 110 landed on Koh Tang. But, after a desperate struggle to establish a beachhead, the servicemen found no *Mayaguez* crewmen. The *Holt* had found the *Mayaguez*, and marines wearing gas masks stormed aboard, but the ship was deserted. The *Holt* took it under tow.

At the moment, the *Mayaguez* crewmen were aboard a Thai fishing boat, motoring toward the anchored ship. Capt. Miller had convinced the Cambodians that his ship had no ties to the CIA, and orders had come from Phnom Penh to release the Americans. A reconnaissance plane spotted them frantically waving shirts and other objects.

Meanwhile, Ford, in the middle of a state dinner at the White House, stepped out periodically to receive status reports. At about 8:15 P.M., Scowcroft telephoned the president with word that the Cam-

bodians had just broadcast their willingness to release the captives. Ford held up the first air strike for twenty minutes. Then, because Phnom Penh failed to provide confirmation of the crew's release, he authorized the scheduled air raids. The airport at Ream, railroad marshaling yards, and an oil refinery at Sihanoukville were thus destroyed.

Two anxious hours passed before Secretary Schlesinger called Ford, by now in the Oval Office, with the news that all thirty-nine crew members had been found. A buoyant president appeared in the White House press briefing room at 12:27 A.M. on Thursday to tell the nation that the crisis was over.

The reaction was rapid—and euphoric. "There are limits," said Secretary Kissinger, "beyond which the United States cannot be pushed." At home Ford won almost universal plaudits for his calm and decisiveness under pressure: His standing in the polls shot up eleven points, and he was deemed overnight to have resuscitated his faltering bid for a White House term of his own. A grateful crew later presented him with the *Mayaguez's* steering wheel. Amid these nationwide celebrations, however, one sobering fact remained. To free the thirty-nine men, fifty marines had sustained wounds and another forty-one had died.

The president and his men react to news of the crewmen's release. From left are Robert McFarlane, Brent Scowcroft (back to camera), Donald Rumsfeld, Henry Kissinger, and President Ford.

ica's unwillingness to consider the Vietnam War's foreign policy implications. "What is perhaps more remarkable," he stated, "is the determined effort in almost every quarter to avoid serious analysis of the episode. The American people are still weary of Vietnam."

Americans did, however, make clear that they had learned one important lesson from Vietnam: They would view any future application of U.S. military power abroad warily. A December 1974 Harris poll reported that only 34 percent of those surveyed "favored U.S. military intervention if the Russians took over West Berlin" and "only 27 percent if Israel were being defeated by the Arabs." It also showed that Americans were redefining their defense interests closer to home. Fewer than a third "would sanction military action if Castro's Cuba invaded the Dominican Republic." A majority endorsed military intervention to the north "only if Canada were attacked" by a foreign power. The American public, opinion analyst Burns Roper indicated in 1975, is "almost oblivious to foreign problems and foreign issues."

The reluctance of Americans to embroil the U.S. in another "Vietnam-type" conflict went deeply. A 1978 Gallup poll, for example, found that Americans "showed no inclination to repeat the [Vietnam] experience." "Seared by Vietnam," a 1978 public opinion survey reported, "the country has no desire to act as the world's leading gendarme." Congress also recorded its opposition to a repeat of Vietnam. The Senate, for example, passed by a large majority the "National Commitments Resolution." It conveyed "the sense of the Senate that a national commitment by the United States results only from affirmative action taken by the executive and legislative branches of the United States government by means of a treaty, statute, or concurrent resolution of both Houses of Congress specifically providing for such a commitment."

Vietnam not only affected the attitude of Americans toward military intervention abroad, it also altered their perception of U.S. leadership and influence in world affairs. Losing in Vietnam, and the aloofness and criticism by its allies engendered by the war, shook the United States's once-unbounded faith in its international primacy and toppled America from its moral pedestal, as well. After World War II the U.S. had embarked on its global contest with Soviet-led communism convinced of its moral superiority. In American eyes, containment was a crusade of "good against evil." But the moral ambiguities of Vietnam—civil war versus external aggression, nationalism versus communism—and the international uproar over U.S. tactics—the bombing of North Vietnam, free fire zones, and mass civilian relocations—gradually eroded the moral underpinnings of U.S. involvement. Tragic episodes like

Civil war in Angola. UNITA soldiers gather Communist weapons—many of Soviet make—that were captured during an assault on the town of Luso in January 1976.

the My Lai massacre impelled many Americans to condemn the entire enterprise as immoral. A 1978 Gallup poll divulged that 72 percent of the public deemed the Vietnam War "fundamentally wrong and immoral."

Some American policymakers interpreted these developments as a psychologically harmful consequence of the U.S. defeat in Vietnam. Richard Nixon labeled it the "Vietnam Syndrome." According to Nixon, defeat in Vietnam had sapped U.S. confidence in its ability to defend its international interests and to apply its military power abroad. Americans, according to Harvard government professor Stanley Hoffmann, reacted as if "our failure to do the impossible in Vietnam affected our ability to do the possible and the necessary elsewhere." Richard Holbrooke, a former State Department official, saw the Vietnam Syndrome as symbolic of America's changing perception of itself from "No. 1" to "No. 2." "I grew up in school believing that the United States had never lost a war," he told the *Wall Street Journal*. "My children don't think that. I grew up thinking that the United States was the strongest country on earth. My kids think that maybe Russia is. Suddenly, we became fallible."

Despite such gloomy assessments, America's post-Vietnam spirit, while dampened, was not extinguished. The United States was not, as Richard Nixon's definition of the Vietnam Syndrome suggested, unable or unwilling to maintain its international security interests. After Vietnam, Congress and the American people simply became more selective about national commitments, more vigilant about engaging U.S. military resources, particularly in Third World, former colonial countries such as Vietnam. In this context, the Vietnam-induced "fallibility" bemoaned by Richard Holbrooke signaled not a retreat from responsibility by Americans but the potential for a foreign policy more attuned to both the inherent strengths and the limitations of U.S. power.

It was natural, and perhaps inevitable, then, that Vietnam, in the mind of America, would serve as a litmus test for postwar situations where U.S. intervention might be deemed necessary. This first became evident during the Angolan civil war in 1975. Backed by $100 million worth of Soviet weapons, and 5,000 Cuban combat advisers, the pro-Communist Popular Movement for the Liberation of Angola seemed on the verge of gaining control of that African country. In response, the Ford administration proposed supplying an additional $25 million in arms to the non-Communist forces being assisted by the U.S.

Congress questioned the proposal, suggesting parallels between Angola and Vietnam. While acknowledging the extent of Soviet aid and the activities of Cuban advisers in Angola, Congress had reservations about entangling the U.S. in what was essentially a civil war between rival fac-

Brandishing machetes, Angolan militiamen of the pro-Communist MPLA faction gather for a midnight rally in Luanda on November 10, 1975.

tions. It was also troubled by the involvement of South Africa with the non-Communist group. Senator Dick Clark, then chairman of the Subcommittee on African Affairs, maintained that "the important lesson of Angola is that we should not ignore the African black liberation movements until their victories against the minority regimes are imminent and then back particular factions simply because their opponents are backed by the Soviet Union."

The administration's campaign for Angolan aid recalled the Vietnam policy battles of the 1960s. Proponents used such terms as American credibility, domino theory, regional balance of power, and covert operations. President Ford's rationale for supplying assistance to anti-Communist Angolan forces even echoed that offered by Lyndon Johnson for Vietnam: "The failure of the U.S. to take a stand would inevitably lead our friends and supporters to conclusions about our steadfastness and resolve."

Comparisons between Vietnam and Angola spilled over into the public debate as well. An angry letter to the *New York Times* charged, "Already another Vietnam is being prepared for us in Angola." Journalists and editorialists reinforced the Vietnam–Angola analogy. In *The Nation* Charles Lipson wrote, "Under the whole Angolan episode is a series of flawed policy judgments remarkably similar to those once used to rationalize U.S. intervention in Indochina." Anthony Lewis of the *New York Times* stated, "The point is much larger than the specifics of Angola. Our attitude toward that affair will really indicate whether we have learned from Vietnam and Watergate." On December 17, 1975, Walter Cronkite told a reporter, "America became so heavily involved in Vietnam because the government did not share enough of its decisions with the people. . . . To try to play our small part in preventing that mistake this time CBS News is scheduling a special series on the Angolan conflict."

On December 19, 1975, by a vote of fifty-four to twenty-two, the U.S. Senate prohibited Ford from sending any further assistance to Angola. The president decried the decision: "This abdication of responsibility by a majority of the Senate will have the greatest consequences for the long-term position of the United States and for international order in general. Responsibilities abandoned today will return as a more acute crisis tomorrow."

Foreign Service officer Thomas Enders, who served in Cambodia in the early 1970s, gave this assessment of the impact of U.S. policy toward Angola. "There were major political elements in opposition to the Angola Communists," he wrote, "and they had every reason to anticipate that they would at least hold their own in a civil war. The United States failed to give adequate support to the two main non-Communist groups and, in the end, they proved no match to a Communist-led guerilla force supported by Cuban mercenaries and lavish Soviet material aid. . . . But U.S. aid was vetoed by Congress, and the strongest argument used against the administration was that it was getting us into another Vietnam."

In the 1970s, oil became a powerful instrument of international relations. Above. OPEC officials meet in Algiers in March 1975. Right. Motorists in Boston endure a forty-five-minute wait for gasoline during the first oil shock, January 1974.

Although the Ford administration blamed the Vietnam Syndrome for the Congressional defeat of its Angolan policy, Angolan aid foundered simply because the president did not make a compelling case for it. Neither Congress nor the public were convinced that U.S. assistance to non-Communist Angolan forces would succeed. Moreover, they feared that once the U.S. intervened, failure would lead to an even more extensive involvement. If anything, analogies drawn between Vietnam and Angola had the positive effect of deepening the inquiry into Angolan affairs and avoiding the kind of Congressional "rubber-stamping" of presidential foreign policy that had occurred in the 1960s.

Rather than inhibiting foreign policy deliberations, therefore, reflection upon America's Vietnam involvement could be said to have enhanced and sharpened them. In 1975, for example, American strategists and policymakers began debating whether U.S. military intervention might be necessary to maintain the crucial flow of oil from the Middle East. The 1973 oil embargo and fourfold hike in oil prices by the Organization of Petroleum Exporting Countries (OPEC) seriously endangered the international financial order built upon America's political, military, and economic supremacy after World War II. The United States interpreted OPEC's actions not only as an economic but as a political threat to the security of the American-led alliance system in the West. In 1974 President Ford stated, "Unreasonable action on the part of the major oil produc-ers involves the risk of world aggression, the consequent breakdown of world order and safety, and the rise to power of governments that might have fewer scruples about their international behavior."

Robert Tucker, a professor of international relations at Johns Hopkins University, suggested that it was America's defeat in Vietnam that, in part, emboldened OPEC to exact steep price increases and to risk an oil embargo. "Vietnam," he declared, "was seen by [OPEC] as a successful challenge to the foundation on which the American-inspired postwar order rested." In a provocative *Commentary* article, Tucker explored scenarios for U.S. military intervention in the event of a second oil embargo. He argued "that the Persian Gulf states lack trees and brush foliage—elements that have been cited as impediments to American military operations in Vietnam—thus negating one of the arguments against attempting to conduct limited military operations in the Middle East." This brought angry rebuttals, like that of a former Defense Department official, Adam Yarmolinsky: "If the United States contemplates a cheap and easy way to protect its Middle East oil supplies—doubtfully a vital national interest—we risk another Vietnam, without foliage."

Memories of Vietnam caused the government to think carefully about U.S. options in the Middle East. In January 1975 Secretary of State Henry Kissinger announced that force would not be used in the Middle East oil crisis "in the case of a dispute over prices" and would be entertained

The Newest Americans

During the decade after the Vietnam War, some 1.4 million Indochinese refugees fled Communist regimes in Vietnam, Cambodia, and Laos, and about half of them eventually arrived in the United States. "Our nation's resettlement of over 725,000 Vietnamese, Lao, and Cambodians ranks as one of the largest, most dramatic humanitarian efforts in history," Roger Winter, director of the United States Committee for Refugees, said in 1985.

Though indisputably an enormous effort, the process of absorption was by no means easy, as the new Americans tried against often remarkable odds to fashion new lives and careers from the debris of their old ones. They often encountered culture shock, intraethnic strife, and popular resentment dogging their efforts to fit in. Many of them managed to meet the challenges—and then some. In April 1975, at the age of eleven, Quyen Thi-Hoang Nguyen had fled Vietnam with her father, a colonel in South Vietnam's army. Less than a decade later, in February 1985, "Jean" Nguyen stood proudly at the U.S. Capitol as President Ronald Reagan praised her achievements during his State of the Union address; three months later, she graduated from West Point.

Many of the first 130,000 Vietnamese to arrive in the United States were government and military officials, professionals such as physicians and attorneys, college students, and individuals affiliated with the U.S. government and private American corporations. In 1975 President Gerald R. Ford and Congress anticipated a relatively quick, one-time relief effort to absorb them.

When the flow of Vietnamese receded to fewer than 2,000 by 1977, Ford's expectations seemed justified. Then the yearly totals began rising, reaching a new peak in 1980 when close to 100,000 Vietnamese—the so-called boat people, many with no American ties—were admitted to the United States. Though the numbers again leveled off—24,900 came in 1984—the total of Vietnamese settled in the United States had reached nearly half a million, with Laotian and Cambodian refugees accounting for the remaining 225,000.

Those arriving in America after 1975 differed markedly from their more urbanized predecessors and were much less prepared for Western life. One non-English-speaking family's anticipation turned to frustration upon discovering that the can of Crisco vegetable shortening purchased for dinner did not contain the fried chicken pictured on its label. "It's as if you landed on the moon," said a Vietnamese who headed the Center for Southeast Asian Refugee Resettlement in San Francisco. The Indochinese formed nationwide support mechanisms such as the Cambodian Community Organization of Orange County, California, and the Indochinese Community Center of Washington, D.C. These groups sought to guide those new to the U.S. through the intricacies of finding employment and language training.

The nation's newest immigrants had also to contend with resistance and outright hostility from Americans of longer residency angered by the federal government's seeming favoritism toward "foreigners." Of the 5,000 Hmong from Laos who settled in Philadelphia during the late 1970s, only 650 remained in the early 1980s; most of the rest had been driven out by harassment by unemployed neighborhood youths. Provoked by desperate economic competition, violent conflict erupted in the Gulf of Mexico between Vietnamese and American shrimp fishermen. One Boston refugee told of being chased by a mob calling him "Viet Cong." "It is ridiculous," snapped another. "If we were Viet Cong, why wouldn't we stay in our country and enjoy the victory?"

The refugees also faced threats within their own communities. Vietnamese street gangs in southern California practiced extortion and intramural violence. Data collected on local refugees in 1984 by the Boston-based Vietnamese American Civic Association showed that 76 percent had housing problems and that 82 percent were worried about their personal safety on the street. Equally high percentages of the refugee population felt doubtful about their prospects for education and job security.

And yet many refugees did establish new stakes in America—some spectacularly. Within five years of his arrival with his family in a San Francisco slum, Nguyen Thanh's technical acumen had landed him a personal interview with the heads of Hewlett-Packard—leading in turn to a subcontract for computer cable. By the mid-1980s, Thanh's Vinatekco, Inc. was grossing $4 million a year. Of the eighty-three students on the honor roll of Boston's Brighton High School in 1983, fifty-six were Vietnamese—prompting grumbles from other students that the Vietnamese were winning all the college scholarships. A Houston banker, emerging from a theater late one evening, spotted Le Van Vu and his wife cleaning a bakery. The banker was so impressed he loaned the former Saigon lawyer $10,000 to buy the bakery. Vu parlayed that investment into two French bakeries, a barbecue-sandwich shop, and a liquor store.

Many of the new Americans attributed their success in their adopted home to a native culture that emphasized, insistently, family, education, and savings. Moreover, many of the fields they entered once in America—accounting, engineering, and high technology among them—required relatively little facility in English. And the willingness, even eagerness, of many refugees to take entry-level jobs, plowing the money they saved into investments, also played a role.

Success for a significant number of refugees notwithstanding, many still confronted a difficult road. By the early 1980s, for example, more than 70 percent of all Indochinese refugees in the United States were dependent on some form of public funds. This spurred demands by beleaguered local authorities that Washington put the brakes to the continuing influx of "economic" (as opposed to "political") refugees. But federal officials, pointing to the emergence of an English-speaking younger generation, voiced the expectation in 1985 that the burden on society would steadily decrease. The newest Americans themselves shared that sense of anticipation. They had endured a great deal to get here; they had survived. Most of them now hoped to prosper.

only "where there's some actual strangulation of the industrialized world." President Ford defined Kissinger's "Strangulation Thesis." "If a country is being strangled," he stated, "and I use strangled in the sense of a hypothetical question, that in effect means that a country has the right to protect itself against death."

Newspaper editorials denounced as blatant disregard for the lessons of Vietnam talk of possible military intervention in the event of another OPEC embargo. Economist Charles Schultz described it as a "fantasy no one needs." Others spoke of the Middle East becoming a "super Vietnam." A survey of 2,000 American businessmen, clergy, public officials, educators, and military officers by Professor Ole Holsti of Duke University showed that a majority opposed intervention in the Middle East in the event of another oil embargo.

Although the president left open the option of a move against OPEC, he initiated "Project Independence," a program to conserve fuel and build up a national reserve, as the means of lowering U.S. dependence on Middle East oil. In addition, he pressured U.S. allies to follow suit and preserve Western solidarity. Once again, the Vietnam experience had generated a healthy skepticism about whether U.S. forces would fare any better fighting Arabs in the deserts of the Middle East than Vietcong in the jungles of Vietnam. It also prompted more careful consideration of alternatives to military force.

A national malaise?

During the 1976 presidential campaign, Jimmy Carter promised to release America from what he called its "Vietnam malaise." He pledged to dispel "the disillusionment of the American people following the national defeat suffered in Vietnam [and] the Watergate scandal." "As a citizen and governor," he recalled, "I had shared the people's anger and frustration, but as a candidate I was surprised at the intensity of the pain I found among them, which had quickly become obvious from their bitter comments and probing questions." Carter also vowed to address "the profound moral crisis" produced by Vietnam "that was sapping worldwide faith in our country."

Much of what was determining the serious political and economic difficulties in America during the 1970s and the national attitude toward them could be attributed to Vietnam: The resettlement of refugees, the struggle of veterans, and the psychological jolt of defeat all contributed. But the malaise the president detected in the country was caused by more than repercussions of the Vietnam War. The political disillusion over Watergate, the vulnerability dramatized by the oil crisis, high inflation and unemployment, as well as rising crime rates, were rubbing away at America's morale.

After his election, however, Carter persisted in associating the nation's ills with the Vietnam experience. Furthermore, he adjudged the nation's Vietnam ordeal a redeeming experience and adduced from it a straightforward moral. In his May 1977 commencement address at the University of Notre Dame, he emphasized that "through failure [in Vietnam] we have found our way back to our own principles and values and we have regained our lost confidence." The lesson to be learned, the president continued, was basic. The Vietnam War had violated the fundamentally "humane" and "democratic" values of the American people. And its "intellectual and moral poverty" had eventually turned them against it. No longer, the president said, would the U.S. yield to "that inordinate fear of Communism which once led us to embrace any dictator who joined us in our fear."

Having renounced the values that took the U.S. into Vietnam, Carter laid the groundwork for an outward-looking foreign policy, one in harmony with the "good sense" of the American people: "It is a new world that calls for a new American foreign policy—a policy based on constant decency in its values and an optimism in its historical vision." A Carter adviser explained the administration's "human rights" foreign policy. "We finally decided," he said, "that we didn't have to support every son of a bitch around the world just because he was our son of a bitch." Carter's national security adviser, Zbigniew Brzezinski, hailed the human rights policy for putting the U.S. "back on the moral offensive" around the world.

Through persuasion and financial leverage, the White House chalked up some impressive human rights successes. In December 1977 Guinea's President Sekou Toure agreed to free 300 government officials accused of trying to depose him. U.S. influence also got President Suharto of Indonesia in January 1978 to accelerate the release of 20,000 political prisoners, while in South Korea quiet U.S. diplomacy secured the freedom, on New Year's Day 1978, of five prominent religious and political dissidents. Even in the Soviet Union, dissidents credited Carter's human rights policy with keeping their movement alive. In February 1978 Minnesota Congressman Donald Fraser, head of an ad hoc human rights caucus, said he would "like to see the administration do even more."

For all its initial success and popularity, by 1979 Carter's human rights foreign policy was drifting. The president's inconsistent application of human rights standards was partly to blame. Some critics scolded Washington for paying more attention to repression in right-wing or pro-American regimes like Chile, South Korea, South Africa, and El Salvador than in Cambodia, Vietnam, North Korea, or Poland. In late 1978 Henry Kissinger complained, "The human rights campaign, as now conducted, is a weapon aimed primarily at allies and it tends to undermine their domestic structures." In the fall of 1979 former State Department official William Bundy wrote, "The Carter Administration plainly saw major gains from its decision to make human rights a worldwide element in

U.S. President Jimmy Carter (right) applauds Israeli Prime Minister Menachem Begin and Egyptian President Anwar Sadat after their signing of the "Framework for Peace," the Camp David agreements, on September 17, 1978.

American policy—in giving the American people a renewed sense of idealistic purpose and in enhancing the American image abroad. But in doing so it risked confusions that would have unforeseen consequences and give ammunition to its opponents."

George Kennan, known as the "father of Containment," voiced the growing international discontent with Carter's human rights policy: "Fine, let us make sure that this country stands as a model for all humanity on human rights. But I do not think that any very useful purpose is served by pressing other governments in other parts of the world on this subject. I don't regard us as very good advisers to them. Very often we achieve just the opposite of what we wanted to achieve when we push them along this line."

The main flaw of the human rights policy was its lack of a coherent strategy encompassing military and political, as well as moral and economic, objectives. Having changed America's role from the global policeman of Vietnam to global preacher, Carter was unable to design a strategic alternative to containment for exerting U.S.

power in foreign affairs. A former Carter aide admitted, "Carter is good at detail; he has an engineering mind. But in terms of the tapestry of global diplomacy, there is nothing in his background that prepared him for thinking in strategic terms."

Lacking a workable strategy, American foreign policy zigzagged and flip-flopped, angering U.S. allies. In 1975 U.S. allies had worried about the U.S. turning inward after its failure in Vietnam. That spring a West German newspaper ran the editorial headline: "America, A Helpless Giant." A London *Daily Telegraph* editorial read: "For too long you [the U.S.] have been beating your breast in self-flagellation in the trauma over Watergate and Vietnam. . . . The United States should know that its European cousins and allies are appalled and disgusted. The self-criticism and self-destructive tendencies are running mad."

"To friend and foe alike, America seems to be slipping," contended Thierry de Montbrial, director of the French Institute of International Relations. "For the first time, the U.S. appears to have lost faith in the future."

In Israel, America's closest friend in the Middle East, uncertainty about Washington's defense commitments caused much apprehension. In 1975 the *New York Times* reported "nervousness among Israelis today that the turn of events in Indochina could weaken the credibility of America's support for Israel." In Egypt, Anwar Sadat was also troubled. His quest for peace with Israel relied on a U.S. pledge of support that Egyptian officials now doubted.

Contrary to its allies' fears, the United States did not succumb to a bout of neoisolationism. Instead, both the Ford and Carter administrations endeavored to strengthen ties with their allies, especially in NATO. During the Vietnam War, U.S. preoccupation with Southeast Asia had caused it to neglect NATO, leaving the alliance, as former State Department official Paul Katzenberg has written, in "a sort of limbo." America's European allies thus welcomed the revitalization of their relationship with Washington, while at the same time seeking to take a more active part in Western economic and political affairs.

But the erratic policies of President Carter tended to alienate rather than reconcile America's allies both in Europe and Asia. After pressuring America's NATO allies to deploy the neutron bomb, for instance, Carter turned around and announced the bomb would not be built after all. After proposing to pull more than 30,000 U.S. troops out of Korea, he decided otherwise. "The President keeps reversing himself," said Michael Ledeen of Georgetown University, a specialist in European affairs. "He says one thing today and another thing tomorrow. That's what our allies can't live with."

Europeans were scathing in their criticism. "You can't run a government on the basis of 'let a hundred flowers bloom,'" said David Witt, director of Britain's Royal Institute for International Affairs. An aide to French President Valery Giscard d'Estaing remarked, "Let us say simply that Giscard is disappointed with Carter's performance."

President Carter's wavering foreign policy was seen by some of his foreign and American critics as emblematic of the United States's decline as a world power. The president himself was troubled. After claiming to have banished the "Vietnam malaise" in 1976, in July 1979 he once again cited "a national crisis of confidence." The president's own gloomy rhetoric, however, obscured some major foreign policy successes. In addition to making the United States a respected spokesman, in the view of many Third World countries, for human rights, the Carter administration not only had supplanted Soviet influence in the Middle East but had brought about the Camp David accords between Israel and Egypt, a major step toward peace in that unstable region. Vietnam had not left the United States the "pitiful, helpless giant" once prophesied by Richard Nixon. But as the U.S. approached Thanksgiving in 1979, the president's repeated pronouncements about a "Vietnam malaise" and "a crisis of confidence," coupled with 12 percent inflation and interest rates in the teens, were dampening the usually festive holiday spirit of the American people. For perhaps the first time in decades, many Americans were beginning to shrink from the future, wondering what could go wrong next.

A crucible of faith

Until November 1979 Iran was as remote to most Americans as Vietnam had once been. Then, on November 4, Iran thrust itself into America's consciousness like nothing since the war in Southeast Asia. Student revolutionaries of the Ayatollah Khomeini, who had recently overturned the government of long-time U.S. ally Mohammed Reza Shah Pahlevi, seized sixty Americans at the U.S. Embassy in Teheran. The hostage taking and reports of the rough treatment accorded the kidnaped Americans stunned the nation. In a "shocking image of innocence and impotence, of tyranny and terror, of madness and mob rule," said *Time*, "employees of the U.S. embassy were paraded . . . before vengeful crowds while their youthful captors gloated and cheered."

The Carter administration chose a strategy of economic and political pressure, not military force, as the best way to secure the hostages' release. Accordingly, the U.S. employed international diplomacy, a boycott of Iranian goods, a freeze on Iran's assets in American banks, and a cutoff of Iranian oil imports. None succeeded. As the United States approached a new decade, the 1980s, the sixty Americans remained in Iranian hands. There was little hope in Washington of a swift resolution. After two months of negotiations, the hostage situation stood at stalemate between Iran and the United States. President Carter later said, "The first week of November, 1979, marked the beginning of the most difficult period of my life."

While Americans reeled from the commotion in Iran, the Soviet Union invaded Afghanistan in late December 1979. The hostage dilemma in Iran and the Afghanistan invasion had nothing to do with Vietnam. The Islamic revolution and the anti-Americanism it aroused, not American weakness arising from the Vietnam Syndrome, as some have alleged, produced the hostage crisis. And the Soviet Union chose to intervene in Afghanistan to control a country it considered within its sphere of influence and important to its security, not to exploit America's Vietnam Syndrome or the Iranian deadlock.

Nevertheless, journalists and policymakers critical of post-Vietnam U.S. policy judged Iran and Afghanistan as blatant evidence of the downward slide of U.S. power since the war in Southeast Asia. *Washington Post* columnist Joseph Kraft termed the memory of Vietnam "the American disease." "The seizure of the embassy is clear," he wrote. It "was a blatant act of aggression that took place against a background of organized hostility to this country. . . . There are occasions when the United States has to deal with persons and groups that can only be described as enemies; and unless that is understood—and soon—the American disease could be fatal." Former Secretary of Defense James Schlesinger judged the Iranian impasse "a cataclysm for American foreign policy. . . . It is plain," he added, "that respect for the U.S. would be higher if we didn't just fumble around continuously and weren't half-apologetic about whatever we do. . . . Wild as the Ayatollah seems to be, he would not dare touch the Soviet embassy."

George Will, in the January 21, 1980, issue of *Newsweek*, chided Washington for having drawn some wrong lessons from Vietnam: "In 1977, U.S. paralysis was elevated to the status of policy, even philosophy, when Carter unfolded a new American foreign policy in his commencement address at Notre Dame. . . . His theme was clear: We would rely on optimism and the power of exemplary living. . . . Carter's policies have expressed his and Secretary of State Vance's shared values and lessons of Vietnam: The futility and illegitimacy of power politics, the virtues of moralism and accommodation." One-time State Department adviser Helmut Sonnenfeldt's "lesson of Iran" was the rejection of the Vietnam Syndrome. "We must disabuse ourselves of the notion," he stated, "that whenever we assert our interests, we inevitably get involved in another Vietnam."

President Carter seemed to give credence to this call for reasserting American power by his own comments and actions. During the second week of December 1979, President Carter recommended a 5.5 percent boost in defense spending. Four years before, as a candidate, he had pressed for a $3 to $7 billion cut in the annual military budget. The announcement of NATO's decision to deploy Pershing and cruise missiles in Europe underscored the president's intent to bolster America's strategic posture vis-à-vis the Soviet Union. Said Carter, "We must understand that not every instance of the firm application of power is a potential Vietnam."

Carter also sought to improve America's readiness by trying to reinstate mandatory draft registration of all American males at their eighteenth birthday. The president, said one of his aides, saw his proposal as "a dramatic signal to send to the Soviet Union." Registration entailed no physical exam, classification of service, or the issuance of a draft card. Failure to register could bring a penalty of five years in prison and a $10,000 fine. Congress passed draft registration in June 1980. Despite several antidraft protests reminiscent of Vietnam days (at Stanford University 700 students burned a mock draft

card), 93 percent of the 4 million men affected registered for the draft. This compared to 77 percent during the Vietnam War. Kevin Foust of Greenville, Pennsylvania, for example, said, "I'm for it 100 percent. I think it's more or less my duty to sign up." For others registration was less an affirmation of performing military service than a rejection of protest. As Long Island University student Floyd Thomas in New York concluded, "You can't fight the government."

Meanwhile, American emotions—shame, indignation, and resentment—coalesced into a firm determination to secure the safe return of the hostages. Public demonstrations in support of the hostages did not represent so much a surge of patriotism as an outburst of virulent anti-Iranian feeling. New York Congressman Leo Zeferetti called "for the immediate deportation" of the Iranian students who had dangled a 140-foot banner from the Statue of Liberty demanding: "The Shah must be tried and punished." A week after the embassy takeover in Iran, a group of 1,500 people, waving American flags and carrying a large portrait of John Wayne, marched on the Iranian consulate in Houston. In Beverly Hills, California, a crowd of Americans harassed a band of Iranian protesters, shouting, "Deport! Deport! Deport!"

As the days, weeks, then months ticked by with the Iranians still holding the hostages, pressure mounted on the president, from in and outside of government, for a decisive move to obtain their release. On April 16, 1980, he reluctantly approved a "surgical" operation to rescue the hostages. The plan called for eight helicopters to lift off from American aircraft carriers in the Gulf of Oman, fly 600 miles to an isolated part of Iran code-named Desert One, and then proceed to a landing zone in the mountains north of Teheran. After waiting a night, the ninety-man Delta strike force led by Vietnam Special Forces veteran Colonel Charles Beckwith was to board trucks, procured by friendly Iranians, enter Teheran, overpower the revolutionary guards at the U.S. Embassy compound, free the hostages, and airlift them out.

The mission was scheduled for April 24. But the strike force never even reached the jump-off outside Teheran. Mechanical failures crippled three of the eight helicopters. The plan called for a minimum of six. At Desert One, air force Colonel James Kyle, the overall mission commander, asked Beckwith, "Would you consider taking five and going ahead? Think about it before you answer me. You're the guy that's got to shoulder this." After a brief pause, Beckwith sadly replied, "There's just no way." The mission was aborted.

Failure became tragedy when during withdrawal two helicopters collided, killing eight servicemen. News of the fiasco incensed the nation. "I am still haunted by memo-

In January 1980 Soviet artillery and tanks encircle Afghanistan's capital of Kabul. Some guns face the city, others face guerrilla positions in the surrounding mountains.

America Held Hostage

The ordeal of the U.S. hostages in Iran from November 1979 to January 1981 frustrated Americans more than any event since the Vietnam War. The harsh treatment of the hostages and the Ayatollah Khomeini's refusal to release them not only angered Americans but drew them together. Although they disagreed about the best means of freeing the hostages, Americans joined in expressing sympathy and support for the hostages and their families. In cities across America flags flew at half mast. Millions of people kept vigil in prayer services. The hostages' hometowns tied yellow ribbons to park trees in expectation of their return. And when the hostages finally arrived home after fourteen months, their countrymen accorded them a hero's welcome.

A flag symbolizing the 350th day of captivity of the Americans held hostage in Iran is raised at the Hillcrest Floral Park Cemetery in Hermitage, Pennsylvania, on October 18, 1980. Hermitage residents planted a flag each day the hostages were held.

The Ayatollah Khomeini, spiritual and political leader of Iran, waves to his followers after returning home from exile, February 1979.

Shortly after the takeover of the U.S. Embassy in Teheran, Iranian demonstrators burn a U.S. flag for the benefit of American cameras.

ries of that day," Carter has written, "our high hopes for success, the incredible series of mishaps, the bravery of our rescue team, the embarrassment of failure, and above all, the tragic deaths in the lonely desert."

The hostages stayed captive until January 20, 1981, when Iran, at war with Iraq and financially strapped by U.S. economic sanctions, relinquished them. Even as the planes bearing the Americans lifted off the runway in Iran, the United States was inaugurating a new president, Ronald Reagan, who had ridden into office on the theme of restoring America's power and prestige. Carter later attributed his election defeat to the country's disapproval of his handling of Iran. Others ascribed it to the botched military rescue.

Some political observers attached a broader significance to the Iranian episode. The U.S.-Islamic stand-off in the Middle East, said Senator Richard Lugar of Indiana in December 1979, marked "a very important turning point in American post-Vietnam policy. I think there is a realization that if we are to have any respect in the world, at the very least we must convey the sense of our ability to retaliate." A Congressional expert on military appropriations commented, "We are seeing the theme of readiness taking shape again. The emerging view is that there are real bad guys out there." A Carter administration official noted, "In terms of domestic politics, Iran put an end to the Vietnam Syndrome."

The Iranian hostage confrontation and the failed rescue attempt did raise Americans' concern about the state of U.S. influence in world affairs. The Russian invasion of Afghanistan also focused attention on U.S. military defense capabilities and Soviet activity on several international fronts in Asia, Africa, and Central America. An NBC-Associated Press poll in 1980, for instance, showed a majority of Americans favoring a stronger defense policy, and opinion surveys by Gallup and *Newsweek* revealed that most Americans supported Carter's imposition of a U.S. boycott of the 1980 summer Olympic games in Moscow.

For all their angry reaction to the Iranian hostage crisis and the invasion of Afghanistan, the willingness of Americans to take a firmer stance toward the Soviet Union and Iran did not mean that incoming President Ronald Reagan had a mandate to revert U.S. foreign policy to the cold war posture of global containment. Nor were Americans ready to cast aside the inhibitions of the so-called Vietnam Syndrome in favor of a new interventionism. As Americans viewed foreign affairs in 1980, five years after the fall of Saigon, for all the Reagan administration's talk of a new patriotism and the eagle flying high, caution was still the national watchword.

The wreckage of the hostage rescue effort sits at Desert One (see map, inset) on April 28, 1980. At center are the melded remains of one helicopter and a C-130 plane; they are surrounded by three abandoned RH-53D helicopters.

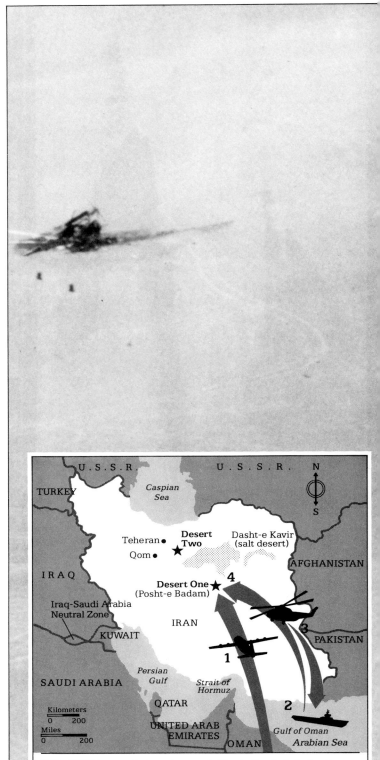

1. Six C-130 transport planes leave Egypt for rendezvous with helicopter force from U.S.S. *Nimitz*.
2. Eight RH-53D helicopters take off from the *Nimitz*.
3. Two helicopters develop mechanical trouble. One is left in the desert; one returns to the *Nimitz*. Six arrive at Posht-e Badam.
4. One helicopter's hydraulic system fails, leaving only five in operation. President Carter cancels mission. During takeoff, one helicopter crashes into a C-130; both burst into flames. The remaining helicopters are abandoned, and the survivors take off in the C-130s.

"When Johnny Comes Marching Home"

January 25, 1981, was like an unproclaimed national holiday. After fourteen months of imprisonment in Teheran, the fifty-two American hostages were home at last (eight were released earlier), and the nation awarded them a hero's welcome. Los Angeles relit the flame at its Olympic stadium. Chicago released 10,000 yellow balloons over its downtown plaza. Washington finally lighted the national Christmas tree, which it had kept dark during the hostages' imprisonment through two holiday seasons. Around the country bells pealed and banners festooned public buildings. New York City prepared a ticker-tape parade to honor the hostages. President Ronald Reagan paid them high tribute. "Those who say we are in a time when there are no heroes," he said, "just don't know where to look."

For Vietnam veterans, the hostages' warm, ceremonious reception was a painful, and galling, reminder of the homecoming they never re-

ceived. Millions of rankled veterans began asking the same question: "Where the hell is my parade?" Complained Ron Kovic, a paralyzed veteran, "All we got was a one-way ticket home to a very difficult situation. You can't welcome 52 hostages home like heroes and forget about 9 million Vietnam-era veterans. . . . We're just feeling left out." "They [the hostages] even got season tickets to baseball games," said a bristling John Callahan, a disabled veteran of the 1st Infantry Division. "Gimme a break! I'd have loved to go to a ballgame once in a while."

A number of veterans banded together to air their grievances. In Indianapolis, Indiana, 300 veterans and their families staged a two-mile march "to protest the hostages' welcome." Another group in Evansville, Indiana, held a news conference to convey the same message. Veteran Gary Cooper of Hammond, Indiana, was so distraught by the accolades bestowed on the hostages that he holed up in his house with a rifle and was killed in a shootout with the police. The newspaper headline said "Viet Vet Goes Berserk Over Hostage Welcome."

In *Newsweek*, Suzanne Wilke, whose husband served in Vietnam, made a plea for America to grant veterans the recognition they deserved: "With the return of the American hostages our country has come alive with a renewed self-respect and sense of unity. . . . During the last few weeks we have also witnessed an outpouring of distress from many veterans of the Vietnam War who have compared the recent festivities with their homecoming and subsequent treatment. . . . They are asking this country to finally acknowledge their sacrifice and service. . . . Must we make them wait any longer?"

Aggrieved Vietnam veterans had a point. Most returned from Vietnam singly or in small groups, unlike their counterparts from World War II who came back with their units on military transport. And there were no formal ceremonies to mark their arrival. For it was only their tour in Vietnam that was over, not the war itself. One veteran remembered the searing solitude of getting back to the

On February 2, 1981, Vietnam veterans march in Indianapolis seeking greater recognition.

U.S.A.: "They let us off on the Oakland side of the Bay Bridge. I had to hitchhike to the San Francisco airport because of a transit strike." Worse than the loneliness for veterans was the reproachful silence that enveloped them, especially after America gave up on the war in 1968. America's growing disgust for the Vietnam War made the soldiers who fought it pariahs. "They came home quietly," said Al Keller, national commander of the American Legion, "sometimes hurt and broken, while the nation looked away in shame."

To their surprise and consternation, returning Vietnam veterans often had to endure insults and nasty confrontations. Veteran Edward Avila recalled, "When I returned home, a young woman, upon learning I was a Vietnam veteran, spit at me in disgust. Two weeks before, deep in the jungles of Vietnam, I had lived like an animal trained to kill at the first provocation. Yet all I could do was stare at this woman in shock." "You know," former marine William Taylor told journalist Joe Klein, "when I got back to California, the hippies in Anaheim spat at me. I was walking along a street. I just couldn't believe it. It made me so goddamn angry."

Stories like these quickly made their way back to Vietnam, and soon homeward-bound veterans expected the worst. "It's really odd," remarked former long-range reconnaissance man Sid Smith. "When I came home in 1967, I had a pistol in my pocket. I was as scared as I've ever been in 'Nam.'" Another vet snapped, "Other people got invited to parties. I got invited to fights."

Even many erstwhile hawks, fuming at America's defeat, turned against the veterans they held responsible. In Seattle in 1969, for example, a man dressed in an American Legion uniform, spotting several Vietnam veterans, hurled obscenities at them. "Losers," he screamed, "candy-ass losers!" While those who backed the war tagged Vietnam veterans "losers," some members of the protest movement labeled them stupid for not being smart enough to evade service. "If you fought in Nam," said former Marine Corps officer Robert Muller, a paraplegic from combat wounds, "you were either a crybaby or a

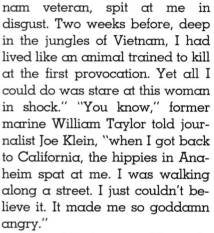

dummy who couldn't find the road to Canada." "The men who came home from World War II were heroes," asserted Dr. Jack Ewalt of the VA, "but the Vietnam vets were different. The public either felt that they were suckers to have gone, or that they were the kids who lost the war."

America's derisive opinion of Vietnam veterans was displayed on television and cinema screens across the country. Prime-time television series and movies in the 1970s regularly depicted veterans as mentally deranged, psychotic killers, hardened criminals, or venal "druggies." On the TV series "Cannon," for example, a Vietnam veteran conspired to blackmail his former commanding officer, who had faked himself into a hero's status. A "Mannix" plot featured a Vietnam veteran characterized as a "drug dealer, sadist, murderer, and deserter." In a 1975 television movie, *Beg, Borrow, and Steal*, three desperate crippled veterans pulled off a perfect art heist. A Hollywood producer explained, "The veteran was not a hero when he came home, did have some re-entry problems, and so it's easy to make him a bad guy. And on cop shows . . . the veteran is a bad guy at the moment."

The facts about Vietnam veterans as a whole, however, belied their image as losers. Despite the handicaps the war forced on them, most Vietnam veterans achieved successful reentry into civilian life. Almost two-thirds of Vietnam-era veterans, compared to just over half of World War II veterans, took advantage of GI Bill education benefits. And against a backdrop of high unemployment and economic turbulence in the early 1970s, hundreds of thousands of Vietnam veterans reentered the job market, resuming old careers or beginning new ones. After peaking at 11 percent in 1971, veteran unemployment by 1978 (5.1 percent) was slightly below that of nonveterans of the same age (6.2 percent). VA director Max Cleland reported that Vietnam-era veterans earned more per capita ($12,680) in 1977 than nonvets of the same age ($9,820).

There was no shortage of Vietnam veteran "success stories." Chuck Hagel built up a good business in the telecommunications field, employing 100 people. Former helicopter pilot Tony Pirrone became a Mobil Oil executive. James Lawrence of Alabama "took a gamble on real estate," rising to the position of branch manager of the largest real estate company in his state. John Kerry served as lieutenant governor of Massachusetts and in 1984 won a term as one of that state's senators in Congress. He is one of fourteen Vietnam veterans serving in the 99th Congress, including Democratic Senator Albert Gore of Tennessee, Republican Senator Jeremiah Denton of Alabama, and Republican Congressman Jim Kolbe of Arizona. Two governors, Robert Kerrey of Nebraska and Charles Robb of Virginia, are also Vietnam veterans. Tom Clay, helicopter gunner turned actor, got roles in major Hollywood films, including *Prime Risk* and *State of Mind*. Rocky Bleier overcame a crippling Vietnam leg injury to play running back for the Superbowl champion Pittsburgh Steelers.

Vietnam veterans chose occupations as diverse as automobile mechanics, computers, sales, law enforcement, engineering, forestry, and teaching. "We're just ordinary guys," said veteran Jerry Dickinson. "We live ordinary lives; we have wives and kids and ordinary jobs. We're ok. But you never hear about us. You only hear about the guys who are messed up." John Dwyer of Dayton, Ohio, demanded "more attention to Vietnam veteran success stories, to those men and women who are today giving their time, energy, and ideas to their communities and states. We are today a valuable resource for our country. We survived the war. We can handle anything."

The "taint" of having fought in Vietnam, however, stuck to veterans whether successful or not. "Making it wasn't easy," confessed Tony Pirrone. "During a job interview with an executive at Procter and Gamble," he said, "the damn guy wanted to see the needle tracks in my arm! It was about the time the drug issue was really starting to come out. . . . I almost decked him." Geoffrey Boehm, executive director of Boston's Pollution Control Commission, used to include his veteran status on job applications and got "flak" from interviewers about whether his participation in the war was "morally right." "I didn't feel that had anything to do with applying for the job," Boehm said.

Some veterans, like Joe DePrimo of New York, began hiding the fact that they were Vietnam veterans. On interviews, he said, "when I said I was a vet they laughed [sarcastically]. . . . Now when I go out for jobs, I don't put down that I was a vet. People think you're a time bomb or an addict."

The insidious legacy

Nearly 100,000 American soldiers left Vietnam with acute physical disabilities. Tens of thousands more—but a minority of the over 3 million men who served in Vietnam—returned with wounds that never showed up on the casualty charts: drug addiction, alcoholism, and an array of psychological disorders such as severe stress, depression, and suppressed rage. They bore no physical scars and received no Purple Hearts for them, but their injured minds and spirits were war wounds nonetheless. And they kept part of these veterans trapped in the trauma of a war that at the time they wanted to forget; this impeded their transition to civilian life.

Between 1968 and 1972 drug use by U.S. forces in Vietnam had reached epidemic proportions. Defense Department statistics revealed that approximately 60 percent of U.S. soldiers during that period smoked marijuana and 30 percent used hard drugs like heroin. One-fifth of all enlisted men in Vietnam in 1970 were addicted to narcotics

Combat veteran Earl Robinson, who lost both legs in Vietnam, watches the Armed Forces Day parade in Chattanooga, Tennessee, May 15, 1976.

"These Skills for Hire"

"Dullsville, U.S.A." That's what Robert Brown, a Special Forces A Team leader, felt when he returned home in 1969 after his tour in Vietnam. In the early 1970s, men like Brown, who had experienced the war's turbulence, sought relief from the tedium of everyday life in a variety of paramilitary, action-oriented groups.

Brown's solution was to found *Soldier of Fortune, A Journal of Professional Adventurers* in 1975. The magazine became the journal of men interested in survivalism, guerrilla warfare, and the mercenary way of life. *SOF* also offered a heavy dose of Vietnam action stories and assessments. Begun on $10,000, within ten years the monthly had attained a circulation of 167,000 at $3.00 per copy.

One of *SOF*'s attractions is its classified section. There, among ads for mail-order medals, camouflage ties, knives, and explosives, would-be soldiers of fortune seek buyers for their skills:

FOR HIRE: 6-year USAF-S.E. Asia Vet. Sharp, knowledgeable professional with diverse background. Personal agent, investigation, missing persons, courier, bodyguard, bounty surveillance, etc. Individual or two-man teams. All projects considered with utmost discretion and confidentiality.

Although the vast majority of *Soldier of Fortune* devotees restricted their activities to sport and survivalism, *SOF*'s mercenary mystique extended beyond mere recreation. The following ad appeared in an early issue of *Soldier of Fortune:*

Wanted: Employment as mercenary on full-time or contract basis. Preferably in South or Central America, but anywhere in the world if you pay transportation. Contact Gearhart. . . .

Six months later, Daniel Gearhart, a thirty-four-year-old veteran, was executed in Angola for participation as a mercenary in that country's civil war.

Vietnam veterans showed up in other conflicts. Several former Green Berets, whose names were not revealed, were involved in the unsuccessful attempt to overthrow the Seychelles government in 1981. And a dozen Americans served in Lebanon with the Christian forces of Major Saad Haddad in the early 1980s.

After he visited Angola in 1976, Roy Innis, national director of the Congress of Racial Equality, tried to recruit a force of black Americans to serve as an unofficial peace-keeping force, a buffer between warring pro- and anti-Communist factions until elections could be held. With great pride, said Innis, 6,000 black Americans, many of them unemployed Vietnam veterans, volunteered. How many actually ventured to Angola? Innis refused to say. However, at least one member of CORE, former Vietnam Green Beret Larry Mitchell, fought as a mercenary in Angola, according to *Time.* "This time," said Mitchell, "I was the Viet Cong."

American soldiers of fortune—many of them veterans—also became involved in the conflict in Central America. In 1983 *SOF* magazine sent several military instructors to El Salvador. The next year, four Vietnam veterans in Decatur, Alabama, also formed an organization called Civilian Military Assistance (CMA) to send supplies to anti-Communist factions in several Central American countries. CMA sent a six-man team, including four Vietnam vets, to Honduras to join the Democratic Force in Nicaragua, an anti-Communist *contra* group. Two men, Dana Parker and James Powell, died in September 1984 when their helicopter was shot down in Nicaragua.

For American citizens serving in other nations' armed forces, U.S. law stipulates two consequences: criminal prosecution and loss of citizenship. The penalties are contingent upon the kind of group being aided as well as the citizen's intent.

What impels these men to risk life, limb, and citizenship in foreign military conflicts? Boredom, joblessness, and sympathy with rightist political views are the most common reasons. Vietnam veterans who became mercenaries had a common view: For them, no stateside experience duplicated the high of combat action. A paratroop captain who lost his commission in the postwar cutback said, "A hundred years ago you could go out and get adventure. But where can you go today? A lot of us are bored." Today's mercenaries, says *SOF* publisher Brown, are "men who are born to fight."

Anti-Communist ideology, reflected by *Soldier of Fortune,* is shared by its readers. Individuals involved with mercenaries dismiss the notion that they are simply adventure-crazed guns-for-hire. "Wanton killers? Horse shit," scoffed Robert Brown in a 1976 *Esquire* article. "Ninety-nine percent of the people who have contacted me about mercenary work are motivated by ideology. They feel we took it in the ear in Vietnam, and consequently they're looking for a chance to get back at the Communists someplace else in the world."

Some who sell their skills describe themselves as "war facilitators" rather than warriors. One of the heads of CMA stressed:

We are not mercenaries. We are not for hire. We're together to fight communism before it comes to the United States. We've drawn our line and that line happens to be in Central America. We're offering our knowledge and expertise and what little material support we can to those who are themselves fighting for the survival of something we believe very strongly in: freedom.

In 1975 Bell Helicopter International dispatched 1,500 Vietnam-era veterans to train pilots of Iran's new helicopter fleet. "We're not mercenaries because we're not pulling triggers," said one former army officer recruited to train the Saudi Arabian palace guard. "We train people to pull triggers."

One former chopper pilot, Barry Meeker, used flying skills developed in Vietnam to help a handful of dissidents escape Czechoslovakia. In September 1975 he took off from Munich airport in a rented helicopter, passed through Austria, and landed in a sparsely populated area inside Czechoslovakia. He avoided radar surveillance by flying as low as three feet above the ground. His helicopter was fired upon by Czech border guards, but Meeker picked up the three dissidents and made it safely back to West Germany.

Dale Dye, executive editor of *SOF,* estimated that more than half of his readers are veterans, most from the Vietnam era. The growth of the activities reported on by the magazine represents a resurgence of veterans' pride, said Dye, if not in the Vietnam War itself at least in their own personal achievements as soldiers.

at some time in their tour. By 1971 drug abuse there accounted for 20,529 of the hospitalized soldiers, four times the number treated for combat wounds.

Military detoxification programs in Vietnam enabled many GIs to kick the habit, but an alarming number departed Vietnam still hooked on dope. According to a 1971 Harris survey, 26 percent of Vietnam veterans took drugs after the war, and at least 7 percent were addicted to heroin or cocaine. In 1982 Tom Pauken, director of the government's ACTION Program and Vietnam Veterans Leadership Project, reported that 1.3 percent of all Vietnam veterans remained drug-addicted after their tours.

Many soldiers in Vietnam had turned to drugs to escape the unpleasant conditions of their service: fear, fatigue, boredom, and homesickness. Drs. Herbert Hendin and Ann Haas in a psychiatric study of Vietnam veteran drug users cited some typical cases (the veterans' names were changed in the published report). Don Gray, "who felt his need to protect himself and his squad demanded that he stay awake, and Tony Marco, who feared getting his throat cut if he slept while on listening post duty, used amphetamines to stay awake and hypervigilant. Tony found it necessary to use marijuana when he did wish to sleep." Drugs also helped the time pass more quickly until the soldiers' departure. Tom Bradley, also mentioned by Hendin and Haas, "stayed up all night and would smoke [marijuana] and sleep all day. That's how I spent the last two months in Vietnam—just waiting to get in that bird and come on home."

For soldiers unwilling or afraid to take drugs, alcohol had been a common alternative. Although the military compiled no statistics on alcohol abuse in Vietnam, in 1971 the Pentagon conservatively estimated between 5 and 10 percent of the soldiers "needed help with a drinking problem." Back in the U.S., alcoholism, like drugs, continued to plague Vietnam veterans. A 1978 Presidential Review Memorandum on Vietnam Era Veterans informed the House Committee on Veterans' Affairs that "Vietnam veterans identified as alcoholics or problem drinkers accounted for 13% of the VA hospital population in 1970 and 31% in 1977."

A 1981 VA report found that combat veterans, even those with no prior drinking problem, were particularly prone to alcoholism. "The frequency of drinking," it concluded, "increases with exposure to combat." Hendin and Haas interviewed more than 100 Vietnam veterans, two-thirds of whom misused alcohol. Ted Ford, "whose sense of himself as a frightened, powerless victim of circumstances beyond his control was reflected in his identification with the baby he accidentally killed when he shot the child's mother, used alcohol heavily during the latter part of his tour in order to cope with his fear." Bill Clark began using alcohol excessively because "of the guilt he felt about having become a 'mass murderer' and his sense that he was out of control."

For thousands of veterans neither drugs nor alcohol could assuage the anger and guilt Vietnam had instilled in them. The moral and political dilemmas of the war—the daily quandaries of distinguishing the enemy from civilians, the creation of refugees, and America's gradual disenchantment with the fighting—all contributed to the erosion of values and morale among U.S. forces. A veteran in San Francisco described the effect of the war's troublesome contradictions: "I must tell you that I still feel tremendous anger. I've been thinking about it and it had to do with my background. I had taken in certain moral values. One was that killing was wrong. A second was respect for women. We even believed some of the moral declarations that racism was bad. But then we were out in the jungle, and told to shoot at anything that moved. We couldn't tell if the people we were killing were men or women, let alone Communists or peasants. . . . Something got broken in me, and I'm still angry about that."

After the war, a small number of soldiers, bereft of self-respect and morally disillusioned, harbored the potential for antisocial behavior and unprovoked violence. In 1974, for instance, Vietnam veteran John Gabron of Los Angeles "went on patrol" in Griffith Park and was arrested for seizing two city park rangers at gun point. He told his captives that "he had lived by the gun and wanted to die by the gun." A VA psychiatrist commented: "There are thousands of John Gabrons in this country, struggling to get their combat experience behind them, but unable to. Their potential for violence is of great concern to them and should be of even greater concern to the whole nation."

Sometimes veterans unleashed their fury on family and friends. California veteran Max Ingelt once woke up after a nightmare to find himself choking his wife. One day he went berserk, got shot trying to rob a store, and was left paralyzed from the waist down. In other cases a veteran's inner rage would simply explode in a "mad minute" of violence. In 1979 John Coughlin of Massachusetts opened fire in a Quincy cemetery, shooting wildly until the police subdued him. No one was injured. In 1974 a VA social worker had ominously predicted, "The Viet vet is angry. He wants society to bleed as much as he has."

Veteran animosities sometimes triggered not only senseless violence but a range of crimes including burglary, dope peddling, and car theft. Crime statistics often referred to "Vietnam-era veterans" but made no distinction between those who actually served in Vietnam and those stationed elsewhere during the war. In 1978 the Carter administration estimated that 29,000 Vietnam-era veterans were incarcerated in federal or state prisons, 37,500 were on parole, 250,000 were on probation supervision, and 87,010 were awaiting trial. In 1976 Vietnam veterans comprised 11 percent of Massachusetts's prison inmates. A 1978 Vermont survey found that 27 percent of its prison population was Vietnam-era veterans, although not all of them had served in Vietnam.

Dr. Charles Figley, a combat veteran of Vietnam and the director of the Family Research Institute at Purdue University, detected a strong connection "between the violence of Vietnam and the crimes committed in its aftermath." The *Legacies of Vietnam*, a 1981 VA study of 1,440 Vietnam-era servicemen, indicated that while most arrested veterans had committed nonviolent offenses, "the arrest rate among heavy combat veterans" was "nearly three times the rate among Vietnam veterans who experienced light combat or no combat at all."

Dr. Figley uncovered what many veteran specialists believe is the critical link between the intensity of combat and violent crimes by Vietnam veterans. It was, he discerned, the absence of a decompression period between when a soldier completed his combat tour and was discharged in the U.S. "What we found particularly significant," he stated, "was the short amount of time between the foxhole and the fireplace, from the time he put the gun down to the time he was back in his living room. Combat troops never got the chance to be consoled by their co-survivors, to compare experiences, to talk about who was responsible for the death of a buddy. . . . These guys hit the streets without any debriefing. They still had the combat mentality with them."

A Vietnam veteran inmate at Walpole state prison in Massachusetts reached a similar conclusion—the hard way. "We came back from a very unpopular war," he said, "and we got caught up in a whole lot of other contradictions. . . . Why are so many veterans in prisons for violence related crimes? . . . The overwhelming majority are men who have been in the infantry, the grunts who have been in combat situations. We came back to this country and there was no mechanism to grab us and detrain us." Another jailed veteran added, "I leave Vietnam on a Monday and that Wednesday I'm walking down Blue Hill Avenue in Boston. . . . I been in the jungles ten months, got shot at and here I am walking down the street in Roxbury."

Troubled Vietnam veterans frequently directed their pent-up violence against themselves. The result: a rash of suicides. In 1974, *Time* reported that nearly one-quarter of the 800,000 veterans in VA hospitals had tried to kill themselves. Although there are no conclusive suicide statistics for Vietnam veterans, a 1978 estimate said "that institutionalized Vietnam-era veterans had a suicide rate 23 percent higher than institutionalized non-veterans of the same age group." Subsequent research by Dr. J. E. Baker, associate chief of the VA's Treatment Services Division, showed that Vietnam-era veterans, though less than 15 percent of those hospitalized by the VA, committed 30 percent of inpatient suicides. Dr. Herbert Hendin, in *Wounds of War*, contended, "The suicide rate would be much higher if the figures were restricted to Vietnam combat veterans." Sadly, the Vietnam War was still taking American lives long after the last U.S. soldier had withdrawn.

"Payback"

Drug addiction, alcoholism, crime, suicide—they all baffled and overwhelmed a VA bureaucracy responsible for meeting Vietnam veterans' needs. Until 1970 the VA had no alcohol treatment units and until 1971 none for drug patients. For much of the 1970s, psychological counseling for the specific disturbances of Vietnam veterans was almost nonexistent. Moreover, only one in five Vietnam veteran prison inmates was able to obtain VA benefits to which he was entitled. "The VA," said VA counselor Don Crawford, "was as confused as anybody about what Vietnam was about."

In 1971, then Administrator for Veterans Affairs Donald Johnson announced a series of VA surveys that "indicated that these [Vietnam] veterans were different in many respects and that if we were to meet their needs, basic changes in VA methods and operations were essential." The VA responded by opening five drug rehabilitation centers at hospitals in New York, Houston, Battle Creek, Washington, and Sepulveda, California. "The VA," said a VA doctor, Joel Kantor, "was plunged into the drug treatment business." The VA also spent $2 billion annually on medical care, including expansion of alcohol and mental health clinics at its 30 psychiatric and 115 general hospitals across the country. After the General Accounting Of-

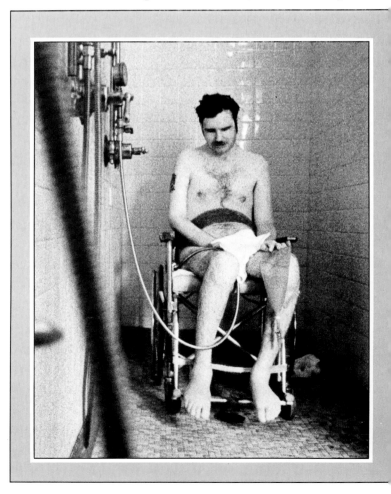

fice informed Congress in 1974 "that the VA could do much better in prisons," the agency passed a regulation requiring counseling visits to every state and federal prison. In 1977 counselors visited 319 prisons and assisted 20,000 veterans. By 1979 the VA disclosed that it was aiding incarcerated veterans in everything from "subsidies for completing high school requirements to payments for work toward advanced degrees."

Overall, the VA's performance in coping with Vietnam veterans' special requirements was mixed. Although the type and number of VA facilities increased, the quality and efficiency of services lagged behind. Drug treatment programs illustrate the problem. "Early growth was chaotic," wrote Paul Starr, author of *The Discarded Army*, a study of the VA and Vietnam veterans, "because there was no time to plan the structure of the program and little relevant experience to draw upon. Typically, a local hospital or clinic was simply authorized to set up a drug center within ninety days, no guidelines or assistance offered. Some ended up with drug-free rehabilitation programs, others with methadone maintenance. The VA had no policy on anything." In Washington, D.C., for example, the VA hospital provided methadone maintenance but no drug-free program. "There's not a whole lot we can do," said hospital director Dr. Norman Tamarkin.

Vietnam veterans in prison encountered similar in-adequacies. A 1979 issue of *Corrections* magazine showed, "Veterans Administration activity is uneven. In one region alone—New England—corrections administrators' assessments ranged from 'outstanding cooperation' to an adamant 'we never see them.' " "When I first came to prison," a Walpole inmate said, "I was told my VA disability stops once I get to prison. I took his word for it and let it go and thought that I had lost my disability." VA officials acknowledged their spotty record. "We're caught in a crossfire," declared VA national director James Cox, "a crossfire between those who say we're not doing enough and the others who are saying 'why are you giving this money to criminals?' "

A communications gap also snarled relations between the VA and Vietnam veterans. The antagonism Vietnam veterans often felt toward the military carried over into their dealings with the VA. Viewing the VA as an extension of the military, they approached it warily and with low expectations. "I thought twice about coming here because of government identification," said one VA patient. Others feared their military discharges or benefit status might be affected by an admission of drug or alcohol dependency. Dr. William Winick, director of the Brockton, Massachusetts, VA conceded, "Vietnam veterans identify us as a quasi-military organization."

A generation gap hampered VA operations as well.

VA Under Fire

During and after the Vietnam War, veterans complained to the Veterans' Administration about its hospitals and clinics around the country. They cited overcrowding, unsanitary conditions, and understaffing as problems throughout the VA's medical system. The VA, in turn, blamed its shortcomings on insufficient funds from Congress. These photos were taken in 1970 by *Life* photographer Co Rentmeester at the Knightsbridge VA Hospital in the Bronx, New York. Rentmeester's photos, when published, provoked an outcry in Congress.

Left. *Lance Corporal Marke Dumpert of the marines, whose neck was broken when a Soviet-made rocket hit his truck near the Demilitarized Zone in South Vietnam, waits helplessly for assistance.*

Right. *Sharing a corner crowded with garbage cans, Frank Stoppiello holds a cigarette for quadraplegic Andrew Kmetz.*

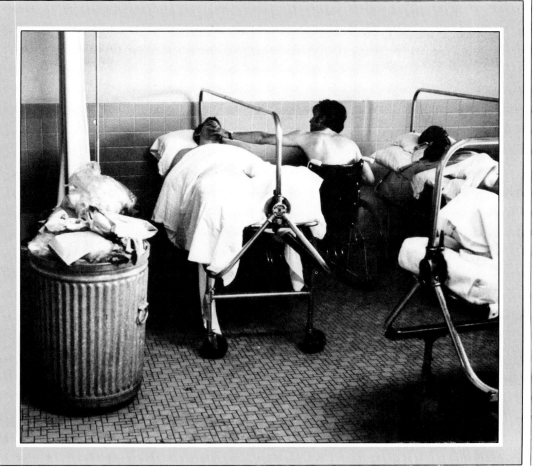

Agency services were long designed for aging World War II and Korean veterans, leaving the VA unprepared for the infusion of young, frequently longhaired and bearded veterans, with their unconventional ailments. Drug programs proved especially cumbersome. "Drug addicts fit into veterans' hospitals about as snugly as a delegation of Black Panthers at an American Legion convention," said a VA official. "One program resembled a hippie camp amid a Marine bivouac." At a Vancouver, Washington, VA hospital the Vietnam veterans drug ward caused havoc. "This is basically a hospital for the elderly—aging World War II veterans—a nursing home," explained VA administrator Dr. Charles Spray. "Then here comes a group of young people, some hardly out of their teens, who are not physically sick. There is very little recreation available for them—sports or energy-consuming activities. So in its place, the young people roam the hospital and its grounds."

Although it instituted new programs and raised the number of Vietnam veterans the agency employed by 25,000, the VA was unable to shed its reputation for unresponsiveness. In 1972 Senator Alan Cranston of California charged that "tens of thousands of veteran addicts on the streets today simply have no faith in the VA drug treatment programs." The U.S. Senate Veterans' Affairs Committee heard testimony in 1977 that "fifty-two percent of veterans who felt that Vietnam had caused psychological problems hold a negative attitude toward seeking help for their problems through VA services."

Incensed by the "payback" they were getting from the government and nation, Vietnam veterans resolved to take care of their own. A U.S. Marines saying popular during the Vietnam War was: "Payback is a motherfucker." One of the first "self-help" projects originated in California. A veterans' organization called the Flower of the Dragon started discussion groups and vocational training programs and began publicizing veteran issues. In 1973 volunteers of the "Veterans Referral Service" in Detroit helped their "unemployed brothers" find jobs. "Operating out of a cubbyhole," as *Newsweek* put it, Veterans Referral Service found more than 800 jobs for Detroit-area vets after October 1973. It also assisted veterans in obtaining housing, records, and college admission. To cut through red tape, the Veterans Referral Service compiled a "good guy list" of government, corporate, and academic bureaucrats willing to help veterans. Only two VA employees made that list.

It was not until 1978 that Vietnam veterans mobilized nationally to promote their cause. Ex-marine Robert Muller, paralyzed from the waist down by VC fire near Con Thien in 1967, founded the Vietnam Veterans of America. The VVA's creed was "no one is going to help us as Vietnam veterans unless we help ourselves." Its appeal for public support stated, "While not ever forgetting Vietnam we need you to join us in putting aside our jungle fatigues,

both literally and symbolically, in order to join us in standing tall, no matter what you thought of the war, proud in our service and of who we are."

In addition to initiating its own counseling and rehabilitation efforts, the VVA's 8,000 members lobbied vigorously among government officials and legislators. "We know," asserted Muller, "that political action sent us to Vietnam and that political action is a vital part of bringing us all back home." Among the VVA's legislative accomplishments were the Emergency Veterans Job Training Act of 1983, which provided on-the-job training for 30,000 Vietnam-era veterans, and Title IVc of the Job Training Partnership Act, which funded community-based veteran job programs. The VVA also worked with Congressman David Bonior of Michigan in 1979 to form the Vietnam Veterans in Congress caucus. "There was no concerned lobby for Vietnam vets up here," said Bonior. "In previous administrations, it just wasn't smart politically to bring up the war again."

The VVA also pushed the Carter administration to upgrade veterans services. In 1978 President Carter ordered improvements in all areas of veterans affairs: employment opportunities, educational opportunities, other veteran services and benefits, and military status. Carter demonstrated his good will toward Vietnam veterans by appointing Max Cleland, a combat officer who had lost both his legs and part of his arm from a grenade explosion at Khe Sanh in 1968, director of the VA. Cleland hired a Vietnam veteran to head the VA's Rehabilitation Medical Service and reorganized veterans' alcohol and drug treatment facilities.

The major victory for the VVA and Cleland was Congressional approval in 1979 of a separate, non-VA counseling program for Vietnam veterans. As part of "Operation Outreach," Congress appropriated $12 million for 90 counseling centers throughout the country and, by 1983, $21 million for as many as 137. Vietnam veterans skilled in counseling, psychology, and medicine manned the centers. They attracted many Vietnam veterans disaffected by past contacts with the VA, handling about 4,000 visits per month. By August 1983 the centers had assisted over 200,000 veterans. The centers provided them with psychological and psychiatric counseling, access to drug and alcohol treatment programs, and information about a variety of government agencies for obtaining veterans benefits, health care, and employment.

For a sizable number of depressed and ailing Vietnam veterans, the outreach centers were a last resort. Steve Cytryszewski of Brooklyn praised them. "Nobody laughs at me," he said. "If I tell them I hit the ground when I hear a sudden noise, they say they do too." An upset veteran told outreach counselor John Caknipe "about a hand-to-hand battle that wiped out his unit. When the dawn came, he found himself surrounded by the grotesquely mutilated bodies of his men and 36 wounded Vietnamese [Commu-

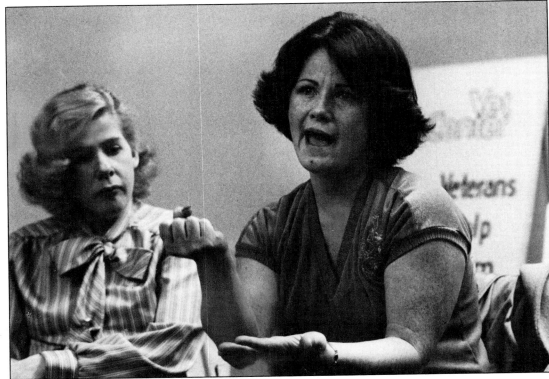

Above. In November 1979 a group of Vietnam veterans attends a counseling session at a California veterans' center. Left. Ann Corsmire, at right, discusses the Vietnam-related problems of her husband, Dick, during a Women's Support Group meeting at a veterans' center in Cincinnati, Ohio, in 1981.

The Forgotten Veterans

For U.S. military nurses, Vietnam meant serving their country and fulfilling their chosen profession. Coming primarily from conservative, traditional backgrounds, many of the 7,000 nurses who served in Vietnam were fresh out of nursing school when they volunteered for duty.

Nursing in military hospitals in Vietnam was far more emotionally draining than stateside assignments. "In U.S. emergency rooms," commented Vietnam nurse Sharon Balsey, "you hardly ever see blast injuries. I just freaked out. ... I never got to the point where the mutilations of bodies didn't bother me."

As nurses witnessed firsthand the loss of men even younger than themselves, some grew depressed by the experience. "People don't want to hear about blood and guts," said Cissy Stellabarger, who assisted in surgery round-the-clock during the 1968 Tet offensive. "But that's all I know about, the grief. It was the first time I've been that frightened."

After the war, most nurses successfully re-entered civilian life. The anguish bred among some veteran nurses, however, hampered their readjustment. These nurses felt isolated among family and friends who were as conservative, as patriotic, and as supportive of the war as they once had been. They often felt confused, on the one hand by the increasingly vitriolic antiwar movement and on the other hand by the fact that others at home were doing so little to understand the horrors of Southeast Asia.

For years these nurses bore their anguish quietly. "I started to shut down my feelings [in Vietnam]," explained Lola McGourty. "It all seemed so useless." But gradually a small number of nurses began reporting symptoms similar to those of male veterans diagnosed as suffering from Post Traumatic Stress Disorder (PTSD): flashbacks and nightmares; anxiety and hypertension; inability to maintain a job or emotional relationships; refuge in drugs or alcohol. Even after fifteen years, nurse Lily Adams rushed out of her house in a frenzy whenever the sound of a helicopter triggered sickening memories of the choppers bringing wounded to the 12th Evacuation Hospital at Cu Chi. Saralee McGoran, who also served at Cu Chi, described her recurring nightmare:

In my dream there was a hospital on one side—and a nightclub on the other. All these beds, just full of bodies, five or six in a bed, and they all had these bleeding eyes. You know how eyes bleed in death? And on the other side, everyone was partying. And that's how it was. Every day there would be broken bodies and pain—and on the other hand the way we coped, not to feel, was to drink beer and have a party.

The Veterans' Administration responded sluggishly to women veterans' requests for psychological counseling, drug and alcohol treatment, as well as medical care for a variety of ailments they claimed were associated with Agent Orange. The VA, already struggling to meet the demands of hundreds of thousands of male Vietnam veterans, was unequipped to deal with the problems of these women.

Women veterans complained that the VA did not adequately publicize the benefits to which they were entitled. The General Accounting Office supported that complaint. In 1982 it charged that the VA had "not effectively informed female veterans of their benefits or assessed their awareness of those benefits."

The VA also tended to ignore women in its efforts to identify the particular needs of Vietnam veterans. A 1981 VA-sponsored study of 1,340 Vietnam veterans did not include a single woman. "Women were forgotten," commented Shad Meshad, a former army psychologist in Vietnam and a pioneer in implementing the VA-supported veterans' outreach program.

It was not until the late 1970s that nurses began organizing to press for improved VA care and recognition of their Vietnam-related maladies. The Women's Project of the Vietnam Veterans of America was initiated in 1978 by Lynda Van Devanter, whose 1983 account of her experiences in Vietnam, *Home Before Morning*, brought attention to her fellow nurses' plight. The Women's Project drew 200 women into a support network and fundraising campaign and assisted women in joining counseling groups and obtaining VA benefits.

As a result of VVA lobbying, the VA in 1983 finally established an Advisory Committee on Women Veterans. At many of its medical centers it also appointed coordinators for women's medical and psychological services. At the same time, the VA sent a questionnaire to 3,000 women veterans that included a survey of the postwar adjustment difficulties of those who had been in Vietnam. In 1984 the VA undertook a study of the potential PTSD cases among women veterans and an analysis, mandated by Congress, of the effects of their exposure to Agent Orange. Both these studies were to be completed in 1987 or 1988. In 1985, therefore, the extent of the impact of Vietnam on women veterans was still uncertain. But women veterans took satisfaction from having gained public acknowledgement of their wartime service and its after-effects upon their lives.

More than anything else, the dedication of the Vietnam Veterans Memorial in 1982 extended recognition of the nurses' personal sacrifices. The names of seven women are etched into the memorial's black granite wall: air force Captain Mary Klinker, First Lieutenant Sharon Lane, Captain Eleanor Alexander, First Lieutenant Hedwig Orlowski, Second Lieutenant Carol Drazba, Second Lieutenant Elizabeth Jones, and Second Lieutenant Pamela Donovan.

At the dedication veteran nurses saw men whose bodies had been patched up and sent along their way years ago. Lily Adams recalls how a male vet held out a flag to her and said, "Doesn't it feel good?" "I started to cry," said Adams. "I was so angry with my country for treating us the way it had. We had been totally rejected. I remember touching that flag and, finally, forgiving."

Many emotional encounters during the dedication brought nurses a sense of a mission accomplished. At the reunion of the 25th Division, Saralee McGoran, once a nurse in Cu Chi, found answers to some of the questions raised by her service. Recognizing her 12th Evac hat, one veteran embraced the nurse who for years had been haunted by the memory of broken bodies. "You saved my life," he told her. "I was there in Cu Chi. Thank the rest of the girls. ... Thanks a lot little lady."

nists], all without hope of medical aid. In despair he shot and killed all 36; his superiors ordered him never to tell what he had done." "When he finally broke," Caknipe said, "he cried for three hours. Then he stood up and said, 'I feel light, I feel light,' and he left."

Not all Vietnam veterans found the centers useful. A disgruntled veteran said, "I stopped going to the center—all there were were a bunch of guys strung out on pot and alcohol and I didn't need that." But to the majority of veterans, Operation Outreach offered a chance to confront problems they would otherwise have carried around for life. John Terzano of the VVA acclaimed it "the one meaningful program for Vietnam veterans." Another veteran enthusiastically concluded, "It is probably the best mental health delivery program in the United States today."

Post-Traumatic Stress Syndrome

Beginning in the late 1960s some veterans, particularly those who saw combat, claimed their social and emotional readjustment difficulties stemmed from a psychological disturbance known as "Post-Traumatic Stress Syndrome." In 1969, a *Military Medicine* article entitled "Combat Plus Twenty Years" contended that "combat experience increases the probability of the presence of emotional illness many years after combat. ... Hopefully," it cautioned, "proper early management of combat precipitated emotional illness can forestall this development. If not, these patients present an almost insurmountable therapeutic problem 15 to 20 years later." Yale psychiatrist Robert Lifton, after hundreds of interviews with veterans, ascribed Post-Traumatic Stress Syndrome to the experience of the war as an "all-encompassing absurdity and moral inversion." Dr. Jeffrey Jay of George Washington University's Center for Family Research blamed it on "the trauma and guilt of the nation. And our failure to deal with our guilt renders the veteran the symptom-carrier for society and increases his emotional burden. This burden isolates the veteran and will freeze him in an attitude of perpetual combat."

For years both the VA and public regarded Post-Traumatic Stress Syndrome skeptically. In October 1969, the VA's chief medical officer told the Senate Veterans' Affairs Committee that "the number of psychiatric casualties [from Vietnam] appears to be smaller than what was incurred in previous conflicts." A Korean War combat veteran voiced the cynicism of much of the public toward the outcry over Vietnam veterans: "I am a little tired of hearing how unique and tough the Vietnam experience was on those who went through it. Any combat veteran in any war who has lived with death for months on end experiences fear, frustration, alienation, and nightmares. The Vietnam experience is not unique."

Nevertheless the evidence began to accumulate, as Dr. Lifton observed, that there was "something different about the Vietnam veterans." Although some Americans had tried to dismiss Vietnam veterans as "whiners," the country could not ignore the emerging consensus among psychiatrists and counselors that Post-Traumatic Stress Syndrome was inextricably bound up with such veterans' problems as drugs, suicide, crime, and violence. In 1980 came a major breakthrough for the 700,000 Vietnam veterans whom the 1981 *Legacies* study estimated to be suffering from the stress syndrome. The American Psychiatric Association officially recognized Post-Traumatic Stress Syndrome as a legitimate and separate category of stress disorder. It defined it as "re-experiencing the trauma by intensive recollections, recurring dreams, or suddenly feeling or acting as if the traumatic event were reoccurring; emotional numbing or withdrawal from the real world; or hyperalertness, sleep disturbance, and survivor guilt."

After much hesitation, the VA in September 1980 accepted PTSD as a diagnosis meriting treatment and benefits. To obtain medical care or compensation for Post-Traumatic Stress Syndrome, a veteran had to be certified a victim by a VA physician. By 1985, 10,000 Vietnam veterans had been awarded disability payments for it. Post-Traumatic Stress Syndrome even attained a legal status in criminal and civil court proceedings. In 1979 a Massachusetts court found John Coughlin "not responsible" for causing a public disturbance because of his "traumatic war diagnosis." In 1981 Charles Heads was acquitted in Louisiana of the shooting death of his brother-in-law by reason of insanity brought on by Post-Traumatic Stress Syndrome. The legal profession hailed it as a landmark decision. In July 1981 a federal appeals court held, in the case of Roger Schwab, that his Post-Traumatic Stress diagnosis was a handicap for which he could not be fired. The Post Office had let Schwab go after he was hospitalized for barricading himself in his home for eleven hours. The time had finally come, wrote journalist Myra MacPherson in *Long Time Passing*, for America "to stop wrangling over what can cause delayed stress, over whether there is a problem—because there is a problem."

Unfinished business

No issues galvanized Vietnam veterans more than MIAs and Agent Orange. Amid the celebration in 1975 for the return of the POWs, thousands of Americans kept solemn vigil for the more than 2,477 U.S. servicemen whose wartime fate remained in doubt. After President Nixon's 1974 State of the Union announcement "that all our troops have returned from Southeast Asia—and they have returned with honor," several wives of MIAs circled the White House in a camper bearing the message "ALL POWs ARE NOT HOME."

The families of MIAs—wives, children, parents, brothers, and sisters—stayed locked in a limbo of uncertainty. Many vowed to accept nothing short of a full accounting of their loved ones' whereabouts and condition. "It has totally suspended my life," said Mrs. Kay Bosiljewic, whose husband was shot down over Vietnam in 1972. "But we won't stop pressing for an answer. It's a matter of honor—one of the basic things this country is all about." The mother of MIA Sergeant Danny Widmer said, "We want Danny accounted for. If he's alive we want him back. If he's dead then we want to know." "We're being told 'Nobody's alive over there. Let's just forget it,'" grumbled Robin Gatwood, whose son Robin was lost in Vietnam on Easter morning in 1972. "I've never known so many ways of alibiing for not taking action."

During World War II, after a review of each case in accord with the Missing Persons Act of 1944, the U.S. had declared 6,056 MIAs "presumed dead" a year and a day after their disappearance. It had done the same to Korea's 5,127 MIAs. The government had sound reasons for applying that procedure in Vietnam. Eighty-two percent of MIAs were members of air crews shot down in dense jungles or other inaccessible areas, making survival unlikely and recovery of bodies nearly impossible. In addition, some air force officers had inflated the MIA count. They frequently reported their men MIA instead of KIA (killed in action) because families would then receive higher benefits. In his 1976 *Nation* article, "Manipulating the MIAs," Robert Musil stated, "Some Air Force squadron commanders used to boast that they never reported one of their men as killed in action, even if the plane was seen to be blown to bits in the air and no parachute opened."

When the government invoked the Missing Persons Act to reclassify Vietnam MIAs as KIAs, however, several families in August 1973 obtained a New York federal court order requiring proof of death. Although it lifted the order six months later, the court stipulated that before issuing a declaration of death the Pentagon must notify next of kin, provide legal counsel, and permit relatives to present evidence against reclassification. This cumbersome process froze the status of many MIAs, except in instances where next of kin requested a change.

Meanwhile, MIA families and friends campaigned to bring their concerns before the public and to prod the president and Congress into getting the Vietnamese government to take action on the MIA problem. The National League of Families of American Prisoners and Missing in Southeast Asia, established in 1970, maintained its headquarters in Washington where it served as a lobbyist and information clearing house for MIA matters. Another organization, Voices in Vital America, raised $3 million selling stainless steel bracelets inscribed with an MIA's name. It used the money to publicize the MIA issue, as well as to supply funds and promotional materials to forty-five other POW/MIA organizations throughout the country. Veterans around the country placed bumper stickers on their cars: "MIAs—We will never forget" or "Bring Home the MIAs." The American Legion and Veterans of Foreign Wars lent their support. And in 1978, the newly formed Vietnam Veterans of America took up the MIA cause.

The absence of diplomatic relations between the U.S. and Vietnam after Saigon's fall in 1975 hampered efforts to resolve the MIA question. Hanoi refused to cooperate on MIAs until Washington agreed to provide reconstruction aid. The U.S., in turn, blocked Vietnam's admission to the U.N. Only after the U.S. and Vietnam moved toward normalizing relations in 1977 did American requests for MIA documentation make any headway. In March 1977 President Carter dispatched a delegation to Hanoi led by Leonard Woodcock, president of the United Auto Workers Union. Hanoi responded by releasing to the delegates the remains of twelve U.S. pilots listed MIA.

Further diplomacy, and private appeals by MIA groups, led to the periodic return of the remains of MIAs discovered by Vietnam's own investigators. On May 30, 1981, for example, Hanoi announced that it had come across the remains of three missing U.S. airmen. By 1984 the Vietnamese had handed over the remains of ninety-six servicemen. Despite the long wait, the chance to bury MIAs brought some comfort to their families. After the funeral for her husband Joe, whose Skyraider had crashed in Laos on April 2, 1965, Mrs. Maerose Evans commented, "I really felt I had to do everything I could to get the answer." Her mother added, "At least we know where he is now."

The task of seeking and identifying MIAs belonged to the Pentagon. It proved a tedious and expensive operation. In just three months of 1977, for example, the Defense Department spent $900,000 hunting for the remains of 375 Vietnam servicemen lost over the sea along the Vietnamese coast. The search netted three unidentifiable bone fragments. At Hawaii's Joint Casualty Resolution Center, Dr. William Annette supervised the processing of MIA remains. "It's detective work," he said. Annette's medical team used every possible clue—fingerprints, dental charts, blood type, bone structure, and even a single hair—to identify the remains of an MIA. "I'm a patient man," Annette explained. "We worked on one case five and a half years and finally, out of the blue, we got him."

The time, expense, and resources consumed in recovering and in certifying MIA remains convinced some observers that it was not worth the effort. After touring the Joint Casualty Resolution Center in 1977, a member of the Woodcock delegation said, "Any country that goes to this much trouble to account for every soldier it loses probably ought not to fight a war." The Pentagon's annual bill for keeping military personnel on the MIA list ran roughly $15 million in additional benefits to their families. MIA families were eligible for more generous benefits ($20,000 to $30,000 per year) than those for widows and children of men killed in action. Savings accounts at 10 percent interest over a period of a decade or more earned up to $200,000 for some MIA families.

Pentagon officials ascribed "mercenary" motives to some MIA relatives. Edward Manly, a Pentagon consultant, cited one woman in Illinois who fought to keep her husband designated MIA to preserve maximum benefits but had him declared legally dead in her state to collect his life insurance. "We are in a comfortable position financially," Mrs. Iris Powers said at a 1975 MIA hearing in Congress. "Some may not be willing to change that. I know that it sounds terrible, but one must be realistic."

By January 1985 only one U.S. serviceman was still officially classified MIA. Remains of some servicemen retrieved from Vietnam, status change requests by families, and military reviews had gradually depleted the MIA rolls. But despite the bureaucratic change in their status, the condition of over 2,300 MIAs remained unknown. Periodic rumors and reported sightings of MIAs in Southeast

effects of exposure to the herbicide known as Agent Orange. From 1967 to 1971 the U.S. military sprayed 96 million pounds of Agent Orange over thickly foliaged regions of Vietnam. Army and navy manuals described Agent Orange as "relatively non-toxic to man and animals." But in 1969 a Bionetics Laboratory study for the National Cancer Institute demonstrated that dioxin, a highly toxic by-product of the manufacturing process of the herbicide, causes deaths and stillbirths among test animals. So the Pentagon began to phase out use of Agent Orange. In 1971 the U.S. Surgeon General prohibited the use of Agent Orange in homes, gardens, and recreational sites.

Most of the soldiers who came in contact with Agent Orange in Vietnam did not know of its possible toxic nature. Agent Orange was sprayed not only from airplanes and helicopters but also from trucks, river boats, and even

Asia fed the belief that some American servicemen were still alive and languishing in Communist prisons. In the years after 1975, Southeast Asian refugees told of seeing or hearing of MIAs "enslaved by Communist authorities" or of remains hidden away by the government. At a January 1980 Senate hearing, for instance, several Vietnamese refugees testified that "the remains of 400 Americans were being stored in Hanoi warehouses." In 1981 former Green Beret Lieutenant Colonel James "Bo" Gritz planned a covert mission into Laos to rescue MIAs supposedly held captive there. Gritz's 1983 foray into Laos, however, obtained no evidence of any U.S. MIAs. This further diminished the hope of many MIA families of seeing their husbands, sons, fathers, and brothers again, dead or alive.

The quest for MIAs was just one of the unsolved mysteries haunting Vietnam veterans and their families. Several hundred thousand Vietnam veterans spent the years since the war seeking answers to the potentially harmful

In Hanoi on August 26, 1978, a U.S. Congressional delegation receives the remains of eleven American fliers for return to the United States.

backpacks. It was often employed to clear camp perimeters. A 1st Air Cavalry veteran recalled, "After the LZ was sprayed, we walked around the perimeter, strung barbed wire all around it. Then we sat down, the helicopters flew in, and this stuff [Agent Orange] was blowing all over the place. Most of us drank out of bomb craters, showered in bomb craters ... and all that water was polluted with Agent Orange." Soldiers sometimes built showers and hibachis out of discarded Agent Orange drums and stored watermelons and potatoes in them.

In Ron DeBoer's 17th Air Cavalry unit in the central highlands the saturation of their patrol sector with Agent Orange afflicted all of them with badly discolored skin, hideous chloracne, and other side effects like nausea and headaches. Thousands of other troops affected by Agent Orange experienced similar symptoms. The men of DeBoer's unit were never told about the hazards of Agent Orange or warned about drinking or bathing in the water of sprayed areas. So they attributed their discomforts to infrequent bathing and the scorching heat.

In November 1967, at a Yale University laboratory, botany Professor Arthur Galston completed some experiments with Agent Orange and similar herbicides to determine if exposure to them posed a danger to human beings or animals. He reached no decisive conclusion but did caution that the use of Agent Orange in Vietnam might have "harmful" and "unpredictable" ramifications. In 1969 Saigon newspapers ran stories about a high incidence of birth defects among Vietnamese children, but the U.S. branded them "Communist propaganda." After their tours in Vietnam, U.S. troops also developed sudden health problems, many of them unusual. Thirty-year-old Jim Albrigsten, for example, suffered constant pain from pus-filled lumps below his skin. Ron DeBoer, thirty-one, lost a testicle to cancer, a rare condition for so young a man. David Spain's face, according to a *Newsweek* report, became "spotted with grayish blisters and pitted scars. . . . He gets nasty headaches once or twice a week . . . and when they are upon him, he flies into raging, roaring furniture-splitting furies so terrifying that his wife and three children go scurrying from the house for cover." Thousands of other Vietnam veterans coped with different forms of cancer and liver damage. Among some of these ailing Vietnam veterans medical tests revealed a high degree of dioxin poisoning. But there was still no well-established proof of a link between their illnesses and Agent Orange.

Then in 1976, an industrial accident in Seveso, Italy, released dioxin into the air, causing a wave of animal deaths and human sickness. The Seveso incident received broad coverage in the United States, where it prompted a renewed interest concerning the level of dioxin in Agent Orange and its potentially adverse effects on veterans. In 1977, for example, WBBM, a CBS affiliate in Chicago, televised an hour-long documentary, "Agent Orange, The Deadly Fog." Veterans, fearful of having suffered or of developing dioxin-related infirmities from Agent Orange in Vietnam—such as chronic skin rashes, respiratory problems, impaired hearing and vision, loss of sex drive, and cancer—besieged the VA with inquiries.

Veterans who claimed they had possibly dioxin-related diseases wanted immediate treatment from the VA; those worried about getting them demanded testing and research. But the VA responded sluggishly to veterans' Agent Orange concerns. A National Veterans Task Force on Agent Orange was formed in 1979, and by 1981 it had persuaded Congress to act. The Congress passed legislation requiring inpatient and outpatient care for "any disability" of a Vietnam veteran who may have been affected by a "toxic substance found in a herbicide" despite "insufficient medical evidence to conclude that such a disability may be associated with exposure." Additional legislation of October 1984 provided "disability and death allowances to veterans and the survivors of veterans who served in Southeast Asia during the Vietnam era and suffered from diseases that may be attributable to the herbicide known as 'Agent Orange.' "

Despite legislation, VA Agent Orange screening and treatment programs continued to draw fire from veterans' groups. Although by 1984 the VA had examined more than 150,000 veterans, many of them complained that their physicals were cursory and incomplete. In 1982 the General Accounting Office leveled similar criticisms at the VA. The VA's position was that the lack of a conclusive scientific connection between Agent Orange and certain Vietnam veteran illnesses placed the burden of proof upon claimants. Two government studies undertaken in 1979, for example, as well as those by a team of Vietnamese doctors and by researchers at the University of Washington, found no definite proof that exposure to Agent Orange could lead to serious illness or death. In 1984 Dr. Barclay Shepard, director of Agent Orange Studies for the VA, maintained, "A lot of veterans are scared because of early news reports of physical damage, while some among any large number of people are going to have health problems as a matter of routine natural incidence. Put that together with disillusionment over the Vietnam War and anger with the government and there is little wonder that many veterans truly believe that they have in some way been hurt. But the evidence has not supported a cause and effect relationship."

To veterans, that "cause and effect relationship" was more than a matter of scientific curiosity. They saw dioxin poisoning from Agent Orange as a delayed killer that could yet put some of them on the KIA list. Worse was the realization that not just their own health and lives but those of their children were at stake. Michael Ryan's story is typical of the thousands of Vietnam veterans who believe their children's birth defects are due to Agent Orange. In 1966 Ryan's unit had operated in an "Agent Orange zone." While there, he lost fifty pounds, broke out in body rashes, and developed lumps in his groin. His symptoms disappeared before he left Vietnam, but his daughter Kerry was later born with a deformed right arm, a hole in her heart, and other birth defects that confined her to a wheelchair. "Kerry is a disabled Vietnam veteran," Ryan declared in 1980. John Woods's son Jeffrey was born with a large tumor of the lymph glands in his face and became badly scarred from six operations. Woods blamed "the defect on damage to his own chromosomes by Agent Orange."

On December 14, 1978, after being denied a disability by the VA, veteran Paul Reutersham declared war in court against the manufacturers of Agent Orange—Dow

Agent Orange

In 1985, ten years after the war, large areas of South Vietnam remained scarred by Agent Orange and other chemical defoliants. Vietnam veterans, and Vietnamese civilians, also charged that Agent Orange permanently scarred their lives by afflicting them with a variety of physical and genetic disorders.

Right. *The parents of these children live in a plantation region of South Vietnam that had been repeatedly hit with herbicides during the war.*

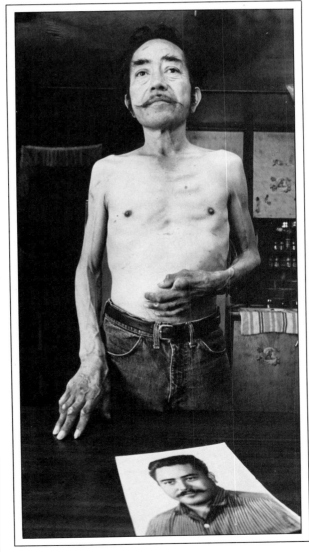

Above. *Former medic John Woods (center) attributes the chronic rashes of his son John, Jr., (left) and the lymphatic tumor of Jeff (right) to his exposure to Agent Orange in Vietnam in 1966–67.*

Left. *Before and after. Air force veteran Daniel Salmon, emaciated by pancreatitis and racked by infections, displays a picture of himself in better days. Salmon was in daily contact with Agent Orange while building runways in South Vietnam in 1967.*

Chemical Company, Monsanto Company, Diamond Shamrock Corporation, Hercules, Inc., and Thompson Hayward Chemical Company. The VA told him that he was not entitled to benefits for his malignant colon cancer because scientific research had not proved conclusively that Agent Orange was responsible. "I got killed in Vietnam," Reutersham once said to his friends, "and didn't know it." Although he died from cancer shortly after filing his suit, Reutersham's legal battle against the chemical companies was joined by 20,000 other veterans as part of a class action suit.

The Agent Orange suit went to trial in a New York City federal court in the spring of 1984. The issue was clear. The veterans' attorney, Victor Yannacone, had argued that "they [the defoliant makers] knew that Agent Orange was contaminated. They should be punished for that." Dow's lawyer, Leonard Rivkin, retorted, "The position of the Dow Chemical Company is that there is no causal relationship between the claimed illnesses and exposure to Agent Orange."

At the beginning of the trial Judge Jack Bernstein advised both sides that a full trial would be long, costly, and probably indecisive. Negotiations ensued between lawyers for the veterans and the chemical manufacturers, and a settlement was eventually reached in May 1984. In return for dropping the suit, the veterans received a $180 million fund. How those funds would be dispensed and for what purpose was not finally determined by the court, veterans, and chemical companies.

Legally and scientifically, therefore, the case against Agent Orange remained unresolved. In the fall of 1984 the U.S. government began an ambitious $100 million study of Agent Orange. The project called for ten years of research and a lengthy report on the study's results. For veterans possibly endangered by Agent Orange, however, time was not on their side.

A time for reconciliation

America's outpouring of sympathy for the Iranian hostages, and the homecoming it gave them, was not only the catalyst for veterans to speak out about their misfortunes. It also evinced the country's evolving attitude toward veterans from indifference to understanding. A Louis Harris poll taken in 1979, for example, showed that "by a 2-to-1 margin, Americans now regard Vietnam veterans as victims of a senseless war rather than perpetrators who share the blame. In 1970, about 50 percent held the latter view." Television reflected it too. Instead of villains and "psychos," Vietnam veterans in shows like "Magnum, P.I.," "Riptide," and "The A Team" began to be portrayed as heroes who made it through a thankless ordeal.

Robert Muller of the Vietnam Veterans of America reported that the attention paid to the returning hostages and the resulting outcry among veterans caused an in-

crease in donations and support for his organization. "The public," he said, "had been given the emotional opportunity to deal with Vietnam for the first time." Former Vietnam infantryman Jan Scruggs saw in the renewed interest in veterans a chance for a national commemoration of their sacrifices and hardships. In April 1979 he started the Vietnam Veterans Memorial Fund.

The fund's goal was to raise $2.5 million to design and construct a memorial in Washington honoring "those who did not come back" from Vietnam. Scruggs made the first donation himself, $2,500 from the sale of some land he owned. In his relentless push for a memorial he gradually gained the sponsorship of such political figures as former President Gerald Ford and First Lady Rosalyn Carter. He persuaded Bob Hope to sign a fund-raising letter sent out to over a million potential donors.

Scruggs also convinced Congress to pass a bill allocating a two-acre parcel of land in Washington for the memorial site. In a bill-signing ceremony in July 1980, President Carter said: "A long and painful process has brought us to this moment. Our nation was divided by this war. For too long, we tried to put that division behind us by forgetting the Vietnam War. In the process we ignored those who bravely answered this nation's call. We are ready at

last to acknowledge more deeply the debt which we can never fully pay to those who served."

To obtain a suitable design for the memorial, Scruggs's Vietnam Fund formed a committee of architectural consultants to oversee a national competition. In May 1981 the committee selected the design of a young Yale University architectural student, Maya Lin. Her design was one of 1,420 submissions. She was awarded a prize of $20,000 for a plan for two 200-foot-long black granite walls on the Washington Mall that would start in a "V" and recede into the ground, one wall pointing west toward the Lincoln Memorial, the other east toward the Washington Monument. Inscribed on each wall in chronological order would be names of the 57,709 Americans listed killed or missing in action in Vietnam. Lin's design included no flags, no statues, no inspiring inscriptions. "I've studied funerary architecture," she said, "the relation of architecture to death."

It was probably inevitable that a memorial to those who fought and died in America's most controversial war would rekindle smoldering passions. Pulitzer Prize-winning architecture critic Paul Gapp of the *Chicago Tribune* called Lin's design "bizarre, neither a building nor sculpture." Veterans wanting a traditional memorial accentuat-

ing the courage and dignity of every soldier who served in Vietnam bridled at Lin's proposal. In the *New York Times* former army officer Tom Carhart wrote, "I believe that the design selected for the memorial in an open competition is pointedly insulting to the sacrifices made for their country by Vietnam veterans. By this will we be remembered: a black gash of shame and sorrow, hacked into the national visage that is the mall." Ex-marine James Webb, Jr., author of the Vietnam novel *Fields of Fire*, resigned from the Memorial Fund Committee to protest the exclusion of the flag. Lin's design, he said, would become "a wailing wall for future anti-draft demonstrators."

Others applauded Lin's memorial plan. Paul Spereiregan, a Washington, D.C., architect, commented, "A great work of art doesn't tell you what to think—it makes you think." A veteran named Larry Cox hailed it as a fitting way "to remind America of what we did." As veterans split over the memorial design, an exasperated Jan Scruggs observed, "They're re-fighting the Vietnam War. It sort of fits the Vietnam experience as a whole."

In 1984 at Cu Chi near Ho Chi Minh City, Bobby Muller (left), the founder of the Vietnam Veterans of America, tours an area defoliated during the war.

In early 1982 Scruggs's committee voted to proceed with the memorial outlined by Lin. "Of all the proposals submitted," it said, "this most clearly meets the spiritual and formal requirement of the program. It is contemplative and reflective." The committee offered a compromise, however, to appease irate veterans. They added a flagpole and commissioned artist Frederick Hart to sculpt a statue of "three combat soldiers gazing searchingly into the distance." Both would be placed on the memorial site after the dedication scheduled for the week of Veterans Day, 1982. The ruckus over, Vietnam veterans eagerly awaited the memorial ceremonies. Said Glen Mundy, who served a tour with the 1st Air Cavalry Division in 1966, "It's time to get it [the war] behind us once and for all."

The week of November 11, 1982, was one the nation's capital will never forget. For several days before Veterans Day, tens of thousands of Vietnam veterans—more than 150,000 in all—streamed into the city. They arrived by plane, car, bus, and train from cities, towns, and farms of every state. Some had hitchhiked. There were veterans in sleek suits and fancy cars who stayed in posh hotels; others came in long hair, beards, old field jackets over plaid shirts and dungarees, and riding motorcycles. Most were what they professed to be: "average" guys with wives and kids, working hard for a living.

Veterans gathered around the city for unit reunions. The marines and navy used one hotel as reunion headquarters, the air force another. The huge Washington Sheraton reserved hospitality rooms for most of the army divisions deployed in Vietnam: the 1st Cavalry, the 101st Airborne, the Americal Division, the 1st, 4th, and 25th Infantry Divisions, as well as the Special Forces. The food, drinks, and beer, and the shouting and laughter of combat buddies getting reacquainted, imparted to the reunion a cathartic effect. "A lot of people here," said ex-paratrooper Russ Lindsey at the Sheraton, "are letting it out for the first time."

Despite the celebrating, the veterans did not stray for long from the purpose that brought them to Washington. Many stopped at the National Cathedral where for three days the roster of Vietnam War dead, about 1,000 names an hour, was read aloud. It was the memorial itself, however, that drew every veteran to its walls. On November 10 Tom Toohey stepped up to the wall, touching the name of Richard Housh. "A real good lieutenant," he said. "I saw him jump up with his pump shotgun one time and blow away four guys coming at us. He was somebody else, one good lieutenant."

"I don't know what it is," said Kenneth Young, who stood staring at the wall for two hours, occasionally stepping up to it to brush his fingers over the names of men he knew. "I don't know what it is," he kept saying. "You have to touch it. There's something about touching it." A National Park Service volunteer, John Bender, flashlight in hand, stayed late each night at the memorial to assist the crowds searching for the names of friends, sons, husbands, fathers, and brothers. "I have a son, John, Jr.," he remarked, "who tried hard to get on this wall. Wounded twice in Vietnam. Thank God he didn't make it up there."

The day of the dedication, November 13, broke raw and windy, but it did not dampen the veterans' spirit. Fifteen thousand of them—outfitted in baggy fatigues, camouflage suits, and jackets and ties—marched proudly down Constitution Avenue toward the memorial. Veteran Tom Yannasone exclaimed, "Can't you feel the camaraderie? Isn't it incredible?" "It's been a long time coming home," said his friend Mark Bloom, once a helicopter pilot in Vietnam. "It's the first time in 12 years that I haven't felt like an alien."

This was no ordinary Veterans Day parade with spit-and-polish high-school bands, middle-aged VFW and American Legion units, and prancing majorettes. Disabled Vietnam veterans, with canes and in wheelchairs, kept pace with the cheering marchers, who strode behind General William Westmoreland, their former commander and the only high officer to appear that day, with an American flag held high. They were the survivors of an army on its last mission: to pay homage to its dead.

At the memorial grounds, almost a quarter of a million people congregated for the afternoon's dedication. Several speakers—Helen J. Stuber of the American Gold Star Mothers, Jan Scruggs, and Al Keller of the American Legion, among others, addressed the massed ranks of veterans and onlookers. The Marine Band played stirring marches, and a color guard presented the flag. "This is the Vietnam veterans day in the sun," observed Jan Scruggs, who had done so much to make it all possible. "It's a little like the hostage situation. When they returned, they got all the hoopla and celebration. That's what we're trying to equal here. This is the big time for the Vietnam veterans."

But it was not the words or rituals that conferred meaning on the occasion. By building the memorial and being present in such numbers at its dedication, Vietnam veterans succeeded in casting off the guilt and shame the war had laid upon them. Max Cleland explained, "Within the soul of each Vietnam veteran there is probably something that says 'Bad war, good soldiers,'" and now they can "separate the war from the warrior." There was a sense of unselfishness too about the veterans' memorial observance. Just as they had borne the brunt of America's suffering in the war, and the ignominy of its defeat, so veterans were taking the lead in the painful struggle for national reconciliation. The memorial, as Jan Scruggs stressed, "was the beginning of the healing process over Vietnam." Said Memorial Fund Chairman Jack Wheeler, "It exposes, and thereby ends, the denial that has characterized the country's reaction to the war." It is probably, he declared, "the single most important step in the process of America's healing and redemption."

Reunion

Until a reunion of the Special Forces during the dedication of the Vietnam Veterans Memorial in November 1984, Green Beret John "Doc" Gallagher had thought Ramon Santiago might be dead. After the Vietcong had overrun their camp at Dak To during the 1968 Tet offensive, Gallagher had patched up a bullet wound in Santiago's throat and sent him out on a medevac helicopter. He did not hear whether Santiago had died or recovered.

When they finally saw each other at the reunion, Gallagher and Santiago rejoiced. Afterward they visited the memorial. Of the twelve men in their unit, Gallagher (shown at left above), Santiago (right above), and a Green Beret named Carter Stevens were the only survivors of the war.

The Salute to Vietnam Veterans

On Veterans Day weekend in November 1982, more than a quarter of a million people gathered in Washington, D.C., for the National Salute to Vietnam Veterans and the dedication of the Vietnam Veterans Memorial. It was an occasion for military unit reunions and a parade. There were also formal dedication ceremonies including speeches, a flag raising, and a color guard. But for the veterans, and the friends and family of the more than 57,000 men and women whose names were inscribed on the memorial wall, the most important moments were private ones. Each day tens of thousands of men, women, and children appeared at the wall, gently touching the name of a loved one or a friend, planting a small flag in the ground, or simply standing in quiet reflection. Remembering the dead and honoring those who returned from Vietnam evoked many emotions but throughout the dedication a sense of dignity and thankfulness prevailed. The national president of the American Gold Star Mothers, Helen J. Stuber, whose only son was killed in Vietnam, expressed the satisfaction of those who were there that "after all these years, our country is pausing to honor the Vietnam veterans."

The Vietnam Veterans Memorial in Washington, D.C.

Top. *Vietnam veterans watch the memorial dedication parade in Washington, D.C., on November 13, 1982. Above. General William C. Westmoreland leads the parade with Medal of Honor recipient Major Robert L. Howard.*

Above. *Vietnam veterans join in the march down Constitution Avenue.*

Opposite. *A member of the Marine Honor Guard stands watch before the Memorial Wall.* Above. *Visitors to the wall are reflected in its polished black granite.* Left. *A veteran's mother stands at the wall with a photograph of her son.*

Left above. One of the many visitors pays tribute to a fallen soldier at the Vietnam Memorial Wall.

Left below. A family grieves for a loved one lost in the Vietnam War.

Above. At the dedication of the memorial, veterans share their emotions and memories of the nation's most controversial war.

Recriminations and Reassessments

In 1973 a group of distinguished military and political leaders convened at Tufts University's Fletcher School of Law and Diplomacy for a colloquium on "The Military Lessons of the Vietnamese War." Representing the military were General William Westmoreland, General S. L. A. Marshall, the military historian Major General Edward Lansdale of counterinsurgency fame, and Colonel Robert Rheault, commander of the Green Berets in Vietnam in 1969. Civilians included former Ambassador to Vietnam Henry Cabot Lodge, senior Pentagon analyst Thomas Thayer, former Ambassador Robert Komer, who served as pacification director in South Vietnam in 1967 and 1968, and Barry Zorthian, head of the Joint U.S. Public Affairs Office in Saigon from 1964 to 1968.

The Tufts colloquium was organized to reconsider the components of American military and political policies in Vietnam—MACV tactics, pacification, the air war, Vietnamization, and

Washington's strategy toward Hanoi. But what engrossed the participants most was the bedeviling question, "What went wrong in South Vietnam?" Air force Colonel Donaldson Frizzell, one of the colloquium coordinators, stated, "If the Vietnam war was a frustrating experience for the United States, it was specially frustrating for those directly involved. Feelings ranged from confusion and chagrin to bitterness and anger. There had been honor in battle and solid technical achievement; there had been heroes and cowards, military succcesses and failures; but overshadowing it all is the terrible fact that the whole effort was for naught."

In his comments on why U.S. policy failed in South Vietnam, General Westmoreland blamed the political restraints on the use of American military ground and air power to cripple the Communists. "From a military standpoint" he said, "it clearly would have been better to have moved much earlier against the enemy's sanctuaries in Laos and Cambodia and possibly even in the southern reaches of North Vietnam. . . . Further, if the military could have employed air and naval power in accord with its best judgment, our strategy could have been accelerated."

Accelerated to victory? "Whether the United States could have won in Vietnam," said Westmoreland, "rested in the long run in the hands of the South Vietnamese." If so, according to Major General George Keegan, U.S. Vietnamization policies could have been the prime cause of failure. "We trained an army and we trained an air force," he asserted. "Wrong equipment, wrong tactics, maybe wrong doctrines. . . . As to equipment, tactics, and doctrines, it was not until 1968 that the Air Force began to think very consciously along the lines of General Abrams' realization: We are going to have to make this fellow self-sustained. But we were very late in providing them with a logistic base on which they would sustain themselves."

Pacification chief Robert Komer asked, Would "another way—pacification—have worked?" "Whether a pacification or counterinsurgency oriented response would have provided a better strategic alternative," he stated, "must remain a historical 'if.'" Komer, however, rightly contended that pacification, rather than the Westmoreland strategy of big-unit search and destroy operations, offered the best opportunity to provide security in the countryside and thus deny the Communists the support of the villagers. In addition, pacification would have avoided the widespread destruction and social dislocation to which U.S. military tactics contributed. "At the least," Komer asserted, "it would probably have resulted in less militarization and Americanization of the conflict. The enormous toll in human life and waste of resources—plus the tragic side effects—might have been far less. And isn't it the very contrast between these horrendous costs and the ambiguous results achieved that helped feed the U.S. disillusionment which foreshortened the long-haul, low cost effort to which we finally retreated?"

The colloquium also evaluated such varied aspects of U.S. involvement in Vietnam as what Americans did and did not learn from the French, cultural relations with the Vietnamese, the cost and technology of U.S. military deployment, and the effect in Washington of the political psychology of Communist strategy. Each participant focused on his own area of expertise and experience, defending the conclusions he had reached while shifting the onus of failure onto the performances and analyses of others. As a result, the colloquium produced few fresh perspectives on the war, just a restatement of well-established views and biases. A comprehensive answer to "What went wrong in Vietnam?" eluded it.

Only one consensus did emerge: America should not and could not ignore the lessons of Vietnam. But for several years after Vietnam those Americans calling for a reexamination of the war were lonely voices. In the national rush to forget Vietnam, few writers and historians were willing to delve into such an unpalatable subject. In military as well as political circles, talk about the lessons of Vietnam was anathema. "Over and over," said Donaldson Frizzell, "one was told in the Pentagon that the war had become a 'non-subject,' and certainly the discussion of it would bring few promotions. 'We have put the war behind us' was a boast that was frequently heard in the centers of national defense after the debacle of spring 1975."

Refighting Vietnam

During the 1960s and early 1970s critics of the war had dominated the discussion and debate over U.S. involvement in Southeast Asia. Prominent among them were George Kahin and John Lewis, authors of *The U.S. in Vietnam* (published in 1967); Bernard Fall, who sharply criticized U.S. strategy in South Vietnam in several books, including *The Two Viet-Nams* (1963) and *Vietnam Witness* (1966); and Frances FitzGerald, whose critique of U.S. intervention, *Fire in the Lake* (1972), was awarded a Pulitzer Prize. But as Americans began to reflect on the war in the late 1970s, new voices began to be heard. Some earnestly searched for answers to the unresolved political and military questions raised by the war as well as lessons for the future. Other commentators, known as revisionists, sought scapegoats, whether political or military, for the failure of U.S. policy in Vietnam. They also tried to counter the prevailing view that U.S. involvement was both misguided and immoral.

Two of the most insistent revisionist voices were Guenter Lewy, a historian at the University of Massachusetts, and Norman Podhoretz, the editor of *Commentary*, who had turned from a liberal critic of the Vietnam War to a posture that came to be called neoconservatism.

It was in 1978 that Lewy's *America in Vietnam* reopened the inquiry into U.S. intervention in South Vietnam. Harvard Professor Michael Walzer called it "the first salvo in the re-fighting of the Vietnam war." Guenter Lewy's main focus—and the central controversy of his book—was the moral ambiguity of the war in Vietnam. "To a large number of Americans," Lewy stated, "the Vietnam war represents not only a political mistake and national defeat but also a moral failure. . . . For many younger people, in particular, America in Vietnam stands as the epitome of evil in the modern world; this view of the American role in Vietnam has contributed significantly to the impairment of national pride and self-confidence that has beset this country since the fall of Vietnam."

America in Vietnam, therefore, challenged the widespread perception of U.S. involvement in Vietnam as immoral. Through internal government and military documents, Lewy tried to show that certain antiwar groups' charges of officially condoned war crimes and wantonly immoral conduct by U.S. troops were not substantiated by the evidence. He emphasized the insistence of U.S. military commanders that American troops follow the official rules of engagement that "sought to strike a balance between the force necessary to accomplish the mission of U.S. forces in Vietnam and the need to reduce to the minimum the casualties and damage inflicted on the civilian population." He also stressed attempts by U.S. troops to obey the rules of engagement despite provocations by the enemy and the dangers these rules posed for themselves and their units. In Lewy's judgment, while violations of the rules of engagement did occur, and frequently, they were contrary to official policy and constituted individual criminal acts.

In addition, Lewy defended controversial U.S. tactics in Vietnam, such as free fire zones, bombing, the relocation of civilians, harassment and interdiction fire, the Phoenix program, and the use of defoliants and napalm, on the grounds that they did not transgress current international standards of war. He rejected the notion of Vietnam critics, like the members of Bertrand Russell's International War Crimes Tribunal, that American forces were engaged in the massive extermination of the people of South Vietnam simply because they were Vietnamese. "Such charges," Lewy argued, "were based on a distorted picture of the actual battlefield situation, on ignorance of existing rules of engagement, and on a tendency to construe every mistake of judgment as a wanton breach of the law of war. Further, many of these critics had only the most rudimentary understanding of international law and freely indulged in fanciful interpretations of conventions and tactics so as to make the American record look as bad as possible."

In *America in Vietnam* Guenter Lewy amassed many official U.S. documents and international legal precedents

Norman Podhoretz (above), author of Why We Were in Vietnam, *and Guenter Lewy (below), author of* America in Vietnam, *sparked controversy with their revisionist attempts to justify U.S. involvement in South Vietnam.*

capable, perhaps, of acquitting the U.S. of systematically committing atrocities in South Vietnam. But though he may have found the U.S. not guilty in a formal legal sense, he did not succeed in exonerating America for conducting a war whose effects, intentional or not, can be judged immoral. Americans disputed the war's morality not because it infringed international legal standards but rather because it violated their perception of what is "just and necessary" in terms of lives, suffering, and destruction.

In his 1981 article, "Vietnam Revised," historian Terry Nardin attacked *America in Vietnam* as a blatant "revisionist" attempt to morally "rehabilitate" the Vietnam War. Former Johnson administration official Paul Kattenberg, whose 1979 history *The Vietnam Trauma in American Foreign Policy* scrutinized America's thirty-year role in South Vietnam, also discounted revisionist efforts like Lewy's to morally redeem the war. "The morality of the U.S. involvement must further be judged in terms of its ultimate results," he stated. "Did the United States by intervening mitigate more pain and suffering than it caused by intervening, or than would have resulted if it had not intervened? By this test, the morality of U.S. intervention is extremely difficult to justify. Even if one judges that U.S. engagement was not intrinsically immoral it would be hard to assess as not having resulted ultimately in more pain and suffering than if it [the U.S.] had not intervened at all."

A noble cause?

If *America in Vietnam* unsettled Vietnam War critics, Norman Podhoretz's *Why We Were in Vietnam*, published in 1982, provoked them to outrage. Podhoretz questioned the moral and political reasoning of those whose denunciation of the war begat the Vietnam Syndrome. "By April 30, 1975," he stated, "the debate over Vietnam had been settled in favor of the moral and political positions of the antiwar movement. At best Vietnam had been a blunder; at worst, it had been a crime. . . . That the United States was defeated in Vietnam is certain. But did that defeat mean what the antiwar movement seems to have persuaded everyone it meant? Do the policies that led the United States into Vietnam deserve the discredit that has been attached to them? Does the United States deserve the moral contumely that Vietnam has brought upon it in the eyes of so many people both at home and abroad?"

Podhoretz's answer to this was a resounding "no." The United States, he posited, entered Vietnam for one purpose: to preserve the South from communism. While allowing for the misperceptions, political futility, and excesses of U.S. tactics in South Vietnam, Podhoretz excoriated the characterization of Americans as evil and their policies immoral. "Imprudent though it may have been to try and save South Vietnam from Communism," he pronounced, "it was also an attempt born of noble ideals and impulses." America's only immoral act, in his view, was its

158

Reflections of War

In its war of attrition to grind down the Communists, the U.S. military resorted to controversial tactics whose success was measured by the grim statistics of the "body count." MACV Commander Gen. William Westmoreland defended the tactics as the best means available to defeat an elusive enemy. Critics contended that they were excessively destructive. As Americans began reexamining the war in the late 1970s, once again policymakers, military strategists, and members of the antiwar movement debated the effectiveness and morality of the American way of war in Vietnam.

Far left. *The body count. Communist soldiers killed in a March 1967 battle with the U.S. 4th Division are buried in a mass grave. Left. Search and destroy. Soldiers of the 173d Airborne Brigade charge VC positions in War Zone D, 1967. Top. During a civilian relocation operation VC suspects are interrogated in Binh Dinh, 1967.*

abandonment of that country to the North Vietnamese in 1975.

In his review of *Why We Were in Vietnam* in the *New York Times*, James Fallows chastised Podhoretz for political naiveté. "Mr. Podhoretz seems to think that this closes the question: If American presidents meant well at the beginning the ensuing chain of consequences is legitimized by their good intent. He seems to recognize no difference between morality of intention and morality of effect. He will not grant that certain courses of action, appropriate at one level of effort, may at other levels demand sacrifices out of proportion to what can possibly be gained, and can become 'immoral' in that sense." Robert Harris, editor of the *Saturday Review*, called Podhoretz the "high-brow hit man for the neoconservative movement." Certainly *Why We Were in Vietnam* was a continuation of the revisionist strategy, pioneered by Guenter Lewy, to remove the moral guilt associated with Vietnam and therefore the political constraints some conservatives felt that it imposed upon Washington.

As they scrambled to counter revisionism, steadfast war critics in turn faced a barrage of charges that they and the antiwar positions they espoused had morally and politically undercut the U.S. war effort in South Vietnam. In 1975 President Ford had exhorted Americans not to repeat the recriminations and purges that followed the "loss of China" in the 1950s. But in 1978 Guenter Lewy fanned the embers by suggesting the antiwar movement was exploited by the North Vietnamese, especially during the 1968 Tet offensive. "North Vietnam," he wrote, "sought to make the most of the anti-war movement in America. . . . Communist propaganda regularly reported peace demonstrations as proof that the American people were weakening in their resolve." Former Vietcong official Truong Nhu Tang supported Lewy's contention that the Communists tried to take advantage of the antiwar movement. In *A Viet Cong Memoir*, published in 1985, Tang wrote that the North Vietnamese and Vietcong leadership planned their military and political strategy so as to exert maximum pressure on public opinion and increase dissent in the U.S.

Norman Podhoretz escalated the attack on Vietnam dissenters, impugning them, at least in part, for the aggression and upheaval resulting from the Communist victory in Southeast Asia. Opponents of the war have vigorously resisted being blamed for the U.S. defeat in South Vietnam. "Those of us who opposed American intervention yet did not want a Communist victory," Irving Howe and Michael Walzer rejoined, "were in the difficult position of having no happy ending to offer—for the sad reason that no happy ending was possible any longer, if ever it had been. And we were in the difficult position of urging a relatively complex argument at a moment when most Americans . . . wanted blinding simplicities." Harvard Professor Stanley Hoffmann advised "those who condemned the

war . . . to resist all attempts to make them feel guilty for the stand they took against the war."

In effect, the attempts of Lewy, Podhoretz, and other conservatives to shift responsibility to the antiwar movement for failure in Vietnam and what has happened since were groundless. In *Vietnam Reconsidered*, for instance, University of Berkeley Professor Todd Gitlin noted that such postwar attacks on Vietnam "doves" were pointless and irrelevant. "There's no evidence that the movement directly affected public opinion," he declared. Furthermore, the conservatives ignored the fact that throughout the war the antiwar protesters were regarded with hostility and even contempt by most Americans. Public support for the war, therefore, depended primarily on the confidence of Americans that U.S. policy would succeed. Americans began turning against the war in large numbers only when they came to the same realization: U.S. policy was not working.

Amid the swirl of political and moral recriminations, military historians began rethinking the strategic and tactical facets of U.S. intervention in South Vietnam. In 1973 Colonel Donaldson Frizzell reviewed America's strategy of attrition in Vietnam. "Something obviously went wrong in the Vietnamese application," he stated. "Military force failed to yield satisfactory results as a political instrument. America adopted a traditional military strategy based on . . . attrition of the enemy. . . . Moreover, success in a battle of attrition depends on the ability to inflict unacceptable losses on the enemy. The problem in Vietnam lay in finding a satisfactory definition of 'unacceptable losses.'"

In his memoir, *A Soldier Reports*, published in 1976, Westmoreland defended his Vietnam tactics as the best means available to him for achieving U.S. goals in Vietnam. He also dared his critics to propose a viable alternative. "In any case," he said, "what alternative was there to a war of attrition? A ground invasion of North Vietnam was out . . . and President Johnson had stated publicly that he would not broaden the war. . . . I had to get on with meeting the crisis within South Vietnam, and only by seeking, fighting, and destroying the enemy could that be done."

Westmoreland's position on strategy did not fare well among historians. In 1978, for example, even Guenter Lewy chided the general for his search and destroy tactics, which "badly underestimated the ability of the other side to escalate in response to the American buildup." In a 1977 article in *Parameters*, John Collins, a military tactician and former army colonel who served in Vietnam from 1967 to 1968, called Westmoreland's direction of the ground war "a senseless strategy" that launched "a series of spectacular sweeps that boosted casualties on both sides, but also convinced the common [Vietnamese] people that neither American nor South Vietnamese troops would stay to protect them."

The most ambitious reappraisal of Vietnam strategy

appeared in 1981. It was *On Strategy: The Vietnam War in Context* by Colonel Harry Summers of the U.S. Army War College. Summers argued that in fact the U.S. had no rational strategy in Vietnam. He reprehended both civilian policymakers and the military for this strategic vacuum. One of the principal civilian errors, according to Summers, resulted from President Johnson's aversion to mobilizing the national will because he did not want to cut back on his Great Society domestic social programs. "The North Vietnamese," Summers said, "after their experience with the French, had every reason to believe that American morale could be our weak strategic link. Knowing they did not have the military means to defeat us, they concentrated on this weakness." What Summers failed adequately to consider were the important reasons, beyond the Great Society, that kept Johnson from fully mobilizing the national will. On the one hand, the president worried about the impact of putting the nation on a war footing and the possibility that the Vietnam conflict might escalate to unmanageable proportions, bringing the U.S. into conflict with China and perhaps even the Soviet Union. On the other hand, President Johnson also felt that Americans would not be willing to pay the price of mobilization.

Summers also—with good reason—castigated the military for its reluctance to forewarn the president of the disastrous consequences of his policy. For example, some American commanders, most prominently General William Westmoreland, had complained that the president, abetted by the civilian officials in the Pentagon, denied the military the leeway for achieving victory. But should not those commanders have resigned their positions? Summers believed so: "There are some who have yielded to the temptation to blame everything on the commander-in-chief, President Johnson. But ... it was the duty and responsibility of his military advisers to warn him of the likely consequences of his actions, to recommend alternatives, and, as Napoleon put it, to tender their resignations rather than be the instrument of the army's downfall."

Without an overall political and military strategy, Summers stated, the U.S. tactical approach in Vietnam—a hybrid of counterinsurgency and conventional warfare—was doomed. "To have understood the true nature of the Vietnamese War required not only a strict definition of the enemy," he wrote, "it also required a knowledge of the nature of war itself. [But] our understanding was clouded by confusion over preparation for war and the conduct of the war, by fears of nuclear war, by fears of Chinese intervention." In the final analysis, according to Summers, by waging "two wars," counterinsurgency and search and destroy, the U.S. ceded the strategic initiative to the enemy. The North Vietnamese were free to use guerrilla warfare as a blind to cover their long-term conventional attack on South Vietnam.

As an alternative strategy, Summers believed American forces should have been deployed for a "tactical offensive" against the North Vietnamese, isolating the battlefield in South Vietnam through a series of land, naval, and air operations designed to deny North Vietnam "the physical capability to move men and supplies through the Lao corridor, down the coastline, across the DMZ, and through Cambodia."

As time passed, the need to reassess America's involvement in South Vietnam produced numerous other historical analyses of a wide variety of issues. In *America's Longest War*, Professor George Herring of the University of Kentucky concluded that "the ultimate failure in Vietnam revealed the inherent flaws in a policy of global containment." General Bruce Palmer, Jr., in *The 25-Year War*, believed pacification rather than overemploying massive firepower and conventional warfare might have led to success. One of the most intriguing Vietnam reappraisals was that of Leslie Gelb, a senior fellow at the Brookings Institute, in *The Irony of Vietnam: The System Worked*. U.S. presidential administrations from Eisenhower to Nixon, Gelb argued, had no intention "to win" in Vietnam at all. In *The Irony of Vietnam* he described "the reality that those making decisions to increase U.S. involvement were aware that victory would probably not be the result." Their objective, Gelb concluded, was not military victory but what was minimally necessary to prevent the fall of South Vietnam to communism. Gelb's analysis did not receive the attention it merited for its exploration of the continuity of America's Vietnam policy spanning three decades and several presidential administrations. It convincingly countered the long-prevalent opinion that U.S. decision making regarding Vietnam was the result of a totally inconsistent, irrational response to events in Southeast Asia.

Despite the passage of time and the renewed interest in America's role in Southeast Asia, in the decade after the war historians have reached no general agreement about what went awry in Vietnam, much less about what the U.S. could have done to change the war's outcome. The lament of Robert Shaplen, the *New Yorker*'s Southeast Asian correspondent, in 1970 still applied in 1985. "Vietnam, Vietnam," he wrote, "there are no sure answers."

The "television war"

It seemed appropriate that America's first "television war" be reexamined not just in print, but by the medium that had daily brought it into millions of living rooms throughout the country. Television's coverage of the war in Vietnam had been a source of much political contention. Presidents, policymakers, congressmen, and generals had accused it of bias, distortion, oversimplification, and sensationalism. Stung by such assaults on its integrity and competence, television quietly acquiesced in the country's postwar desire to forget Vietnam. Except for an occasional documentary, like the December 1977 ABC program about the war's effect on members of the class of 1964 at a New Jersey high school, or journalistic updates on events in Southeast Asia, such as the Public Broadcasting Service's April 1978 look at "Vietnam and Its Life After the War," discussion about Vietnam was noticeably missing from the nation's airwaves during most of the 1970s.

In 1979 the Public Broadcasting Service began production of a thirteen-hour documentary series, "Vietnam: A Television History," developed under the direction of former *Time* magazine and *Washington Post* journalist Stanley Karnow and Richard Ellison, who previously headed overseas production for Time-Life Films. It was shown in the fall of 1983 over 200 PBS stations. PBS's thirteen programs were comprehensive in scope, beginning with French colonial Vietnam, continuing through America's two-decade presence there, and concluding with the war's repercussions in Southeast Asia and the United States. "Vietnam: A Television History" tried to satisfy America's need for an objective historical account, as *Time* observed, "of why the U.S. went to Vietnam, how it lost a sense of purpose in being there, and how and why it left."

The series was a joint venture with British Central Independent Television and French Antenne-2 broadcasting company. As a result, the series lacked a consistent perspective on the events of the war, particularly American actions. The British- and French-produced programs of the series tended to be far more critical of U.S. policy in South Vietnam than those made by the Americans. The documentary also exhibited the limitations of television. It tended to favor chronological narrative and visual presentation over analysis and discussion.

The PBS series aired with minimal controversy but a program presented by CBS Reports in early 1982 aroused a storm. In the second week of January CBS began publicizing an edition of CBS Reports entitled "The Uncounted Enemy: A Vietnam Deception," to be shown at 9:30 on the evening of January 23. In addition to televised promotion, the network took full-page advertisements in the *Washington Post* and the *New York Times* on the day before broadcast. The ads showed a drawing of U.S. military commanders seated around a conference table. Superimposed on it was the word "Conspiracy."

The text of the ads promised startling revelations about "decisions made at the highest level of military intelligence to suppress and alter critical information on the number and placement of enemy troops in Vietnam. A deliberate plot to fool the American public, the Congress, and perhaps even the White House into believing we were winning a war that in fact we were losing. Who lied to us? Why did they do it? What did they hope to gain? How did they succeed so long? And what were the tragic consequences of their deception? Tomorrow night the incredible answer to these questions. At last."

A principal figure behind CBS's charges was a former CIA analyst named Samuel Adams. Beginning in 1966 Adams, who had served as a CIA intelligence specialist on enemy activity in South Vietnam, became convinced that enemy forces, both Vietcong and North Vietnamese, numbered approximately 600,000, an estimate spectacularly higher than the military's official count of 270,000. Moreover, he believed the U.S. military was deliberately keeping the enemy order of battle artificially low.

In May 1975, after leaving the CIA, Adams published his allegations about the manipulation of enemy troop figures in *Harper's Magazine*. In September he also repeated them before the House Select Committee on Intelligence. In 1980 a CBS producer, George Crile, who was a *Harper's* editor when Adams's article appeared, visited Adams at his Virginia farm. Adams told Crile of his recent research and conclusion that the military had not only illegitimately held down order of battle estimates, but had intentionally underreported the number of enemy troops infiltrating South Vietnam via the Ho Chi Minh Trail.

In November 1980 Crile informed his superior at CBS, Howard Springer, about his proposal to document "how the U.S. military command in South Vietnam entered into an elaborate conspiracy to deceive Washington and the American public as to the nature and size of the enemy we were fighting." In April 1981 CBS gave Crile its final approval for "The Uncounted Enemy: A Vietnam Deception." Sam Adams was boldly taking his decade-long obsession with the order of battle issue to a new forum, national television.

At 9:30 P.M. on January 27, 1982, 9 million prime-time viewers tuned in CBS's Vietnam exposé. While battle scenes flashed across the screen, veteran CBS reporter Mike Wallace laid out Adams's conspiracy theory. "The fact is," Wallace stated, "that we Americans were misinformed about the nature and size of the enemy we were facing, and tonight we're going to present evidence of what we have come to believe was a conscious effort—indeed a conspiracy at the highest levels of American military intelligence—to suppress and alter critical intelligence on the enemy in the year leading up to the Tet offensive."

CBS presented the substance of its case in a few key interviews involving General Westmoreland, Adams, and two of Westmoreland's former aides, Colonel Gains Hawkins and retired Major General Joseph McChristian. When Wallace asked a visibly nervous Westmoreland about Adams's order of battle contentions, the general denied them. The camera then switched to Gains Hawkins and George Crile. Hawkins said that he and General McChristian had briefed General Westmoreland jointly about the discrepancy between the high numbers of enemy troops in the field and the lower figures in the order of battle. Hawkins recalled Westmoreland saying, "What am I going to tell the press? What am I going to tell the Congress? What am I going to tell the President?"

General McChristian recollected that "by the time I left his [Westmoreland's] office, I had the definite impression that he felt if he sent those figures back to Washington at that time, it would create a political bombshell."

The camera immediately zoomed in on Westmoreland. Asked why he rejected the higher enemy troop figures reported by McChristian, Westmoreland replied, "I did not accept his [McChristian's] recommendation. I did not accept it. And I didn't accept it because of political reasons." The political reason? Wallace asked. Westmoreland answered, "Because the people in Washington were not . . . sophisticated enough to understand and evaluate this thing, and neither were the media."

Mike Wallace intoned: "We underscore what General Westmoreland just said about his decision. He chose not to inform the Congress, the President, not even the Joint Chiefs of Staff, of the evidence collected by his intelligence chief, evidence which indicated a far larger enemy." Westmoreland's responses, therefore, as CBS interpreted them for millions of viewers, suggested that he tampered with the order of battle for political reasons.

General Westmoreland quickly responded, accusing CBS of a "vicious, scurrilous, and premeditated attack on my character and personal integrity" and demanding that Mike Wallace "apologize to the American people for the cruel hoax he and his associates tried to perpetuate upon the American people." CBS would not retract, so on September 13, 1982, an indignant General Westmoreland filed a $120 million libel suit against the network, Mike Wallace, George Crile, and Sam Adams.

The legal battle that ensued involved far more than the issue of libel. It was rooted in the broader national attempt to reassess the Vietnam War, to understand why so huge an expenditure of lives, effort, and money had come to naught. In the war's aftermath Americans were asking why, despite so many optimistic pronouncements from Washington, Communist forces had continued to struggle successfully against superior American and South Viet-

Members of a British television crew shoot footage in Vietnam for the Public Broadcasting Service's documentary "Vietnam: A Television History."

namese forces and firepower. They also wanted to know who and what was responsible for America's frustration and ultimate failure. The White House? The military? Once again, the credibility of the men and institutions responsible for the government's Vietnam policy were coming under fire.

"The Uncounted Enemy: A Vietnam Deception" was seen by many as an attempt to place the blame on the U.S. commander in South Vietnam, General Westmoreland, and by implication the military. General Westmoreland himself felt that CBS's charges were directed not just at him but at the entire military establishment and its conduct of the war. Throughout the Vietnam conflict U.S. military leaders, especially General Westmoreland, maintained that the American press had misreported U.S. military actions and thereby turned the American public against the war with negative newspaper and television accounts. For Westmoreland and his supporters, there-

National Security Affairs Walt Rostow, as well as Richard Helms, former director of the Central Intelligence Agency, and General Westmoreland himself, the MACV commander from 1965 to 1968 and later army chief of staff.

The trial pitted Westmoreland and the high civilian policymakers who testified on his behalf against Sam Adams and several lower-ranking military officers who supported CBS's case. Rostow and McNamara, who agreed to appear only after being subpoenaed, testified that President Johnson was fully aware of the order of battle contention between MACV and the CIA. Rostow stated that the "home forces of the Viet Cong had been dropped from the order-of-battle in November 1967, not to minimize the strength of the enemy, as the CBS documentary asserted, but because their numbers were uncertain and they were not a major offensive threat." McNamara said that the dispute had represented "an honest disagreement between people putting forth their best figures."

General William Westmoreland, Ret., (left) and CBS reporter Mike Wallace flank the opening picture of the controversial TV special "The Uncounted Enemy: A Vietnam Deception."

fore, his legal action sought not only vindication of himself and the military but the exposure of the consistently biased journalism that he felt had contributed to America's demoralization on the homefront and defeat on the battlefield in South Vietnam. He and those who supported him were equally determined that the military not be made a scapegoat for America's failure.

When Westmoreland's suit against CBS opened in October 1984 at the New York Federal Court in Manhattan, it captured national attention. Two issues were before the court: Did CBS falsely accuse Westmoreland of conspiracy, and did it do so knowingly and with malice? Some trial observers expected it to be "the libel case of the century."

The witness list read like a "Who's Who" of U.S. political and military leaders during the Vietnam War, including such Kennedy and Johnson administration luminaries as former Secretary of Defense Robert McNamara, ex-Secretary of State Dean Rusk, former Special Assistant for

In testimony for CBS several ex-military officers formerly under Westmoreland's command contended that the enemy strength figures were deliberately distorted. Lieutenant Richard McArthur said that his figures on VC guerrilla forces had been "massacred by his superiors—falsified, faked, whatever terminology you would like me to use." Former intelligence officer Lieutenant Colonel George Hamscher said that he was told at the headquarters of the army Pacific Command in Honolulu that General Westmoreland "could not live with a higher figure for enemy strength than 300,000: That was the message we got."

The pivotal CBS witnesses against Westmoreland were his former MACV intelligence specialists Major General Joseph McChristian and Colonel Gains Hawkins. On February 6, 1985, McChristian testified that "Westmoreland acted improperly in 1967 by delaying a cable to Washington reporting higher enemy strength because it would be a 'political bombshell.'" When asked if "at any time prior to this time in your military service had you ever had a superior officer discuss with you the political implications of any enemy strength estimate," McChristian answered crisply, "No, sir."

On February 13 Gains Hawkins contradicted Westmoreland's denial that he had arbitrarily placed a "ceiling" on enemy strength totals. He recounted a 1967 briefing at which Westmoreland complained about his enemy strength estimates being "politically unacceptable." He repeated substantially what he had said in the documentary about Westmoreland's concern of how the president, the Congress, and the press would react to the high figures. "We'd better take another look at these figures," Hawkins quoted Westmoreland as saying. McChristian and Hawkins's testimony was highly detrimental to Westmoreland's case. How detrimental became apparent when the general on February 18, just one week before the case was to go to the jury, reached an agreement with CBS and dropped his suit. The agreement stipulated no payment of damages by CBS, and the network promised not to sue Westmoreland for court costs, which were estimated to exceed a total of $8 million for both sides. A joint statement was issued: "CBS respects General Westmoreland's long and faithful service to his country and never intended to assert, and does not believe, that General Westmoreland was unpatriotic or disloyal in performing his duties as he saw them. General Westmoreland respects the long and distinguished journalistic tradition of CBS and the rights of journalists to examine the complex issues of Vietnam and to present perspectives contrary to his own."

Westmoreland and CBS each claimed victory. "I consider that I won," the general asserted. "We came here to clear the name of a general," Westmoreland's counsel Dan Burt told reporters. "That's what I, in my heart, believe we have done." CBS attorney David Boies declared the joint statement was not an apology: "I said in my opening statement to the jury that we will not challenge General Westmoreland's motive for engaging in the deception. I said that when General Westmoreland engaged in the deception it might very well be that he felt it was in the interests of the country."

Some retired military leaders and other Westmoreland backers, who had helped raise some of his $3.3 million defense fund, expressed disappointment with the settlement. "They [CBS] didn't really apologize," remarked Admiral Thomas Moorer, former chairman of the Joint Chiefs of Staff. "Knowing very little about the legal aspect, I wouldn't have quit at that point." According to a poll of the jurors by the *New York Times*, the majority of the jury was leaning toward CBS and was unpersuaded that the network had been negligent in producing the program. A *Washington Post* editorial stated that although CBS acknowledged General Westmoreland's patriotism and loyalty, they were never at issue in the case. "What was at issue was," it stated, "whether he, and behind him the military enterprise, fudged intelligence estimates for political reasons. The testimony of General McChristian and Colonel Hawkins—or at least the bitter disappointment

that General Westmoreland expressed in their testimony—pretty much undermined him on this score."

Trial judge Pierre Leval told jurors while discharging them, "I think it is safe to say that no verdict or judgment that either you or I would have been able to render in this case could have escaped widespread disagreement. So I suggest to you that it may be for the best that the verdict will be left to history."

While a conclusive historical verdict on the issues raised by the Westmoreland suit awaited a careful examination by scholars of the thousands of documents that had been gathered for evidence, some judgments could be reached from the testimony. Statements by Westmoreland and his former intelligence aides indicated that the general, as CBS alleged, had placed an arbitrary ceiling on enemy troop strength estimates and had allowed political considerations to unduly influence his decision. What of CBS's allegations of a conspiracy led by Westmoreland to deceive the president? Former policymakers and presidential advisers like Rostow and McNamara, who would have also been victims of such a deception, repeatedly emphasized that neither they nor the president were misinformed about the order of battle debate or about its potential military ramifications. What is more, testimony by witnesses on both sides showed that the White House and MACV in late 1967 were both expecting a major enemy Tet offensive. CBS's charge, therefore, that Westmoreland's handling of the order of battle left Washington and U.S. military forces totally unprepared for attack during Tet proved baseless.

The Vietnam War in books and movies

In the spring of 1971, at Firebase Rendezvous on the edge of the A Shau Valley, John DelVecchio and another soldier of the 101st Airborne Division sat talking about Vietnam, the war, and what it meant for the men who had to fight it. Finally, DelVecchio's friend coaxed him to write a book about their experiences. "You can do it, man," he said. "You write about this place. You been here a long time. People gotta know what it was really like." Most of the novels and personal accounts about "what it was really like" in Vietnam, however, were not published until years after the United States withdrew from the war.

There were exceptions. Robin Moore's *The Green Berets*, published in 1965, was the first American novel about the Vietnam War. It adopted the war book convention of "good guy" American versus "bad guy" enemy, in this case, the Vietnamese Communists. A saga about the courageous efforts of U.S. Special Forces and Vietnamese units to hold an outpost against VC guerrillas, *The Green Berets* justified the involvement of American soldiers in Vietnam in the heroic terms of duty, honor, and defense of one's country. When a Frenchman asks a Green Beret named Scharne why he is fighting "for these people [Vietnamese] who steal most of what you give them and are afraid to fight for this," Scharne answers, "First, I am a professional soldier and I take orders and do what I am told. Second, I don't want my children fighting the Communists at home."

The Green Berets proved so popular in 1965 that it hit the *New York Times* bestseller list. It was the only Vietnam novel or personal narrative to become a bestseller between 1965 and 1982.

In the middle and late 1970s writers, many of them veterans, pressed publishers with Vietnam manuscripts. Slowly, publishers took gambles on their work. In 1976 Viking Press came out with Charles Durden's *No Bugles, No Drums*. In 1977 Farrar, Strauss, Giroux issued Larry Heinemann's *Close Quarters*. Beginning in 1978 a rising interest in Vietnam war literature brought a surge of new novels. They included Tim O'Brien's *Going After Cacciato*, Winston Groom's *Better Times Than These*, James Webb's *Fields of Fire*, Gustav Hasford's *The Short-Timers*, John Cassidy's *A Station in the Delta*, and John DelVecchio's *The Thirteenth Valley*—all by men who had fought in Vietnam. After 1975 collections of first-person accounts and memoirs also proliferated; these included C. D. B. Bryan's *Friendly Fire*, Ron Kovic's *Born on the Fourth of July*, Philip Caputo's *A Rumor of War*, Al Santoli's *Everything We Had*, Mark Baker's *Nam*, and Wallace Terry's narratives of black soldiers in *Bloods*. In 1985 there were nearly 100 Vietnam novels and personal accounts in print, most of them published after the end of the war.

Driving these writers was their determination not to let the sacrifices of the men who fought and died in Vietnam go unremembered. Philip Caputo, for example, dedicated *A Rumor of War* to the memory of a fallen comrade and all the other nearly forgotten Vietnam veterans: "As I write this, eleven years after your death, the country for which you died wished to forget the war in which you died." In *Nam* Mark Baker wished to commemorate the generation of Americans "wasted" in Vietnam. And "when they returned home," he said, "they were wasted again, like greasy paper plates after the picnic."

Vietnam fiction and personal accounts reflected two different perspectives of the war. Some stressed the need to document what fighting the war was actually like for the American soldiers. Others emphasized the chaotic nature of the war and the impossibility of recounting the soldiers' experiences in realistic terms. A third theme, common to most novels and personal accounts, was the soldiers' disillusionment at having been asked to risk their lives for a cause that neither the government nor the American people would allow them to win.

Novels like *Fields of Fire*, *Better Times Than These*, and *The Thirteenth Valley* set out to recreate realistically, in great detail, the combat world of the "grunts" in South Vietnam. Each of them focuses on members of a single infantry unit and involves soldiers with nicknames like "Chief," "Cherry," "Snake," "Wild Man," and "Doc."

There are no major battles, only a series of deadly cat-and-mouse games with the VC or NVA. The soldiers, unlike their counterparts in World War II novels, do not fight for God and country nor do they spout uplifting, patriotic ideals. They have one overriding goal: to help each other survive a war none understands.

This theme of struggling to survive a senseless war is especially emphasized in personal accounts. *Nam* contains an account by one soldier who says,

My friends over there gave me a medal for digging a hole with my bare hands and walking across water. I was known as a definite survivor. I didn't chase Charlie that far after I left the helicopter. I didn't. I'm sorry, but I have to tell you the truth. One of the first things you realized when you got to Nam was that you weren't going to win this war. There was no way we could win doing what we were doing. After the first month, me and everybody else over there said, 'I'm going to put in my twelve months and then I'm getting the fuck out of here. It's not worth it.' "

Philip Caputo writes in *A Rumor of War*, "At times, the comradeship that was the war's only redeeming quality caused some of its worst crimes—acts of retribution for friends who had been killed. Some men could not withstand the stress of guerrilla fighting." "Others," he observed, "were made pitiless by an overpowering greed for survival. Self-preservation, the most basic and tyrannical of all instincts, can turn a man into a coward or, as was more often the case in Vietnam, into a creature who destroys without hesitation or remorse whatever poses even a potential threat to his life. A sergeant in my platoon, ordinarily a pleasant-going man, told me once, 'Lieutenant, I've got a wife and two kids at home and I'm going to see 'em again and don't care who I've got to kill or how many of 'em to do it.' "

In his review of *A Rumor of War*, Peter Prescott of *Newsweek* wrote, "This book was long overdue. . . . For years we have needed an account by a veteran, not a journalist, of what it was like to fight America's war in Vietnam." Other veteran-writers, either of novels or personal narratives, found the war in Vietnam too absurd, too chaotic, to be recounted with realistic characters, plots, and settings. Instead they wrote bizarre treatments of Vietnam that stressed the incomprehensibility of the fighting and suffering. Among them are Charles Durden's *No Bugles, No Drums* and Tim O'Brien's *Going After Cacciato*. In *Vietnam in Prose and Film*, James Wilson explained, "literary responses that retreat into 'rock 'n' roll madness' imply the impossibility of social, political, and historical understanding. . . . Therefore the Vietnamese landscape and culture are forever mysterious and unknowable." The inspiration for such a "rock 'n' roll madness" approach was perhaps Michael Herr's journalistic reports that appeared in *Esquire* magazine and in 1977 were published in a book entitled *Dispatches*. *Dispatches* was a fast-paced, almost stream-of-consciousness account of Herr's experiences in Vietnam during the late 1960s and early 1970s. "You could be in the most protected place in Vietnam," he wrote, "and still know that your safety was provisional, that early death, blindness, loss of legs, arms, or balls could come in on the freaky fluky. . . . Saigon and Cholon and Danang held such hostile vibes that you felt you were being dry-sniped."

Tim O'Brien's *Going After Cacciato* tells the story of a combat soldier who deserts his unit near the Cambodian border. The deserter, Cacciato, embarks on a journey across Southeast Asia, Asia, the Middle East, and Europe to reach Paris, his fantasy haven from the terrors and carnage of the Vietnam War. The men in his platoon follow to bring him back, an adventure that takes them through strange and eerie times and places. Along the way they fall into a dark labyrinth of VC tunnels where an enemy cadre exposes their ignorance of the people and country in which they were fighting. When a GI asks him "why was the land so scary—the criss-crossed paddies, the tunnels and burial mounds, thick hedges and poverty and fear," the cadre answers, "The soldier is but the representative of the land. The land is your true enemy."

During their travels to Paris, Cacciato's pursuers never catch him. Meanwhile, they gradually lose their illusions about the war and their role within it. Ultimately the reader discovers the search has never actually happened. Cacciato has deserted, but the rest is just a dream of Private First Class Paul Berlin, standing night watch for his unit.

In Charles Durden's *No Bugles, No Drums* the Vietnamese landscape and the American soldiers moving across it represent a world gone mad with violence, insanity, and topsy-turvy values. Deserters live in luxury. U.S. soldiers guard a pig farm where villagers grow rice, use it for animal feed, and then sell the animals to purchase rice for themselves. American soldier Angelo Bruno Cocuzza, known as "Crazy Dago," hits the big time with a numbers game involving bets on the total of South Vietnamese killed each day. Private Jamie Hawkins describes the whole business of the war as "some fuckin' far-out reality."

A consistent theme of Vietnam novels and personal accounts is the veterans' feeling of having been betrayed: by the military which fought a war it did not believe it could win, by the government which prevented it from winning,

John Wayne in the 1968 movie, The Green Berets, based on Robin Moore's 1965 bestseller.

and by the antiwar movement which seemed to mock them. In *The Thirteenth Valley* by John DelVecchio soldiers of the 101st Airborne in 1970 are relentlessly pushed through the jungles by their commander, the "Green Man," who flies overhead in a helicopter, remote from their fear and suffering. The objective: destroying an NVA base complex to show progress in a war that the soldiers and America, but not the military brass, have given up on.

In *Fields of Fire* by James Webb, Harvard dropout Will Goodrich enlists to join the marine band, ends up a grunt, and is spurned by his unit because of his college background and antiwar ideas. Goodrich's reluctance to fight indirectly causes the death of several members of his platoon. And when he returns home after being wounded, Goodrich, guilt-ridden, has a change of heart. At a Harvard antiwar rally he blasts the protesters for "copping out" on the war. "Look at yourselves," he cries. "How many of you are going to get hurt in Vietnam? I didn't see any of you in Vietnam. I saw dudes, man, dudes. And truck drivers and coal miners and farmers. I didn't see you. Where were you? Flunking your draft physicals? What do you care if it ends? You won't get hurt."

For Ron Kovic, betrayal meant being "sucked in" by American traditions of duty, honor, and courage that Vietnam proved empty myths. "Every Saturday afternoon," Kovic recalls in his memoirs, *Born on the Fourth of July*, "we'd all go down to the movies in the shopping center and watch . . . war movies with John Wayne and Audie Murphy. . . . I'll never forget Audie Murphy in *To Hell and Back*. At the end he jumps on top of a flaming tank that's just about to explode and grabs the machine gun, blasting it into the German lines. He was so brave I had chills running up and down my back, wishing it was me up there. . . . It was the greatest movie I ever saw in my life."

But then Kovic's tour as a marine in Vietnam—the endless patrols, the random death, the aimlessness of the fighting—vitiated his ideals of war. And the indifference both of the military and the public to men like him who came back physically broken exploded his dreams of glory and appreciation. "It was the end," he wrote, "of whatever belief I'd still had in what I'd done in Vietnam. Now I wanted to know what I'd lost my legs for, why I and the others had gone at all."

The passing of years did not bring to the Vietnam War the patina of sentimentality or glorification that time has bestowed on other wars, particularly World War II. Robert Gottlieb, editor-in-chief of Alfred A. Knopf, noted that all of the torrent of manuscripts that came across his desk were "steeped in disenchanted honor." It is not surprising, therefore, that Hollywood filmmakers proved to be chary of Vietnam as a movie subject. During the 1960s the war was featured in only one major motion picture, John Wayne's *The Green Berets*, based on Robin Moore's 1965 bestseller. Wayne thought it was "extremely important that not only the people of the United States but those all over the world should know why it is necessary for us to be in Vietnam." He told President Johnson he would make "the kind of picture that will help our cause throughout the world." Wayne's production of *The Green Berets* incorporated the hawkish, gung-ho attitude of Moore's novel. His World War II-type plot and heroic dialogue were incongruous next to the real nature of the war and men fighting it, and his attempt to whip up support for U.S. policy in Southeast Asia was more pathetic than stirring.

The first postwar films to grapple with Vietnam, such as *Rolling Thunder* and *Heroes*, in 1977, dealt not with the war itself but the scarred veterans' return to peacetime America.

Coming Home (1978) gave a more sophisticated treat-ment of the problems of returning veterans. About a love affair between Jon Voigt as a paraplegic and Jane Fonda playing the wife of a soldier still in Vietnam, *Coming Home* took an antiwar position, as did most Vietnam films released in the late 1970s.

Later, movies focusing on actual Vietnam combat began appearing in theaters. *The Deer Hunter* released in 1978 relates the experiences of three Pennsylvanian steelworkers who leave their mill jobs for the rice paddies of South Vietnam. The main character, played by Robert De-Niro, survives physically intact but emotionally wounded. The war leaves one of his two buddies confined to a wheelchair, the other dead in Saigon from a game of Russian roulette, a game that was actually played infrequently, if at all, in Vietnam but was used by the filmmaker as a symbol for the seemingly random killing in the war.

Max Youngstein, the producer of *The Boys in Company C*, felt that by 1978 "America was ready to look back at what happened in Vietnam, warts and all." His movie shows the "warts"—the cynicism, alienation, and unrest among U.S. troops—through the actions of a unit of young marines disaffected by the war. It took Wendell Mayes seven years to find a producer for his script, *Go Tell the Spartans*. About a group of U.S. advisers during the early days of U.S. involvement in South Vietnam, the film

spotlights the cultural and political barriers separating Vietnamese from Americans that should have been, but were not, seriously considered by U.S. policymakers.

The most expansive, and costly ($30 million), seventies film about the Vietnam War was Francis Ford Coppola's *Apocalypse Now*. After three years in production, *Apocalypse Now* premiered in the fall of 1978. Coppola had grand expectations for his Vietnam panorama despite the reservations of his Hollywood colleagues. "When I started," he said, "basically people said 'Are you crazy? You can't make a movie on Vietnam, the American public does not want it.' ... The movie doesn't make you feel guilty, but it attempts to be cathartic. You have to be able to look the war straight in the eyes in order to be able to accept it, finally, for what it was."

Apocalypse Now is an account of an American intelligence officer, played by Martin Sheen, ordered to "terminate" a renegade colonel (Marlon Brando), who had taken command of tribesmen in the mountains along the Cambodian border. The officer's trip toward Brando's hideout becomes a deep descent into the inferno of war, inhabited by drugged-out soldiers, a crazed commander who wipes out a coastal village and chats about surfing amid its charred remains, mutinous soldiers in a river fort, and the mad colonel who has set himself up as a demigod among primitive tribesmen. *Apocalypse Now* was a long,

long way from the World War II rouser *Sands of Iwo Jima*. From the military's standpoint it was way too far from the realities of the Vietnam War, much less World War II. The army denigrated the film as "simply a series of some of the worst things, real and imagined, that happened or could have happened during the Vietnam War."

Apocalypse Now irritated many Vietnam veterans, as well, because of its grotesque depiction of the war, the American military, and even the enemy. In fact, however, veterans and film reviewers have voiced similar complaints about the lack of realism in most war movies, whether about World War I, World War II, Korea, or Vietnam. Filmmakers, seeking mass appeal, have not apologized for, or disguised, their use of any war, including Vietnam, as a vehicle for adventure, melodrama, and romance. United Artists, for example, promoted *Apocalypse Now* as a "high epic adventure," and *Coming Home* as "one of the most beautiful love stories you'll ever see." Hollywood had finally brought the Vietnam War to cinema audiences across the country. But those who wanted to see the Vietnam War realistically depicted found Hollywood's versions far more fancy than fact.

Left. *In this scene from* Apocalypse Now *U.S. helicopters attack a Vietcong village.* Right. *Robert DeNiro (left) and John Savage as POWs in the film* The Deer Hunter.

The Legacy of Vietnam

After 1975 the leading characters in the real-life drama of Vietnam, the policymakers who conceived, engineered, and managed the U.S. war effort, for the most part left the stage of national politics. A standard refrain of resentful veterans was that the leaders who sent them to fight in Vietnam retired comfortably to academia to write books about it. Many of the principal political figures of the Kennedy, Johnson, and Nixon administrations indeed either resumed or began careers in teaching and scholarship. Most, too, wrote about the war. Ten years after the fall of South Vietnam abruptly ended America's involvement there, some were still defending it; others were admitting to misgivings.

Dean Rusk typified the intellectuals of the Kennedy administration whom journalist David Halberstam called the "best and the brightest." A former Rhodes scholar, Rusk advanced in the State Department to become assistant secretary of state for Far Eastern affairs in 1950. In 1961 President

Kennedy appointed him secretary of state, a post he held until 1968. In 1970 Rusk went to the University of Georgia to teach international law.

Throughout his eight years as secretary of state, Rusk consistently advocated the use of American military power in Southeast Asia. Years of reflection did not change his mind. In January 1985 he told the *Wall Street Journal,* "The doctrine of collective security had mandated America's SEATO commitment to South Vietnam as a demonstration to allies and enemies that it would also uphold its commitment to the Atlantic Alliance." Former National Security Adviser Zbigniew Brzezinski had remarked that the "Old Guard" of Vietnam foreign policy had succumbed to "self-searching, agonizing, and apologizing." Rusk called that "manure. . . . If you stand back and look at it, the U.S. went halfway around the world, lost 50,000 dead and 300,000 casualties, to make good on the promise of the SEATO treaty. Because of that, people still have to bear in mind, even in Moscow, that possibility that those damn fool Americans might do it again."

Though unapologetic about his staunch support for President Kennedy's and President Johnson's Vietnam policy, Rusk did say, "I made two mistakes in judgment. I underestimated the tenacity of the North Vietnamese Army. They took incredible casualties. And I overestimated the patience of the American people." What would he do differently if the same situation should reoccur? Rusk speculated, "Were we right in deliberately deciding not to create a war fever in the U.S.? We decided that in a nuclear age, it would be just too dangerous. We were trying to do it in cold blood at home while our fellows had to do it in hot blood in Vietnam. . . . Vietnam," he added, "was the first war fought on TV every day. We can only speculate what would have happened if Anzio and Guadalcanal had been on TV. In our next war Congress will have to decide what to do about censorship from the very beginning."

Like Rusk, Walt Whitman Rostow, who served as Kennedy's deputy special assistant for national security affairs and Johnson's special assistant, felt no remorse for his stance on Vietnam. In his 1972 study *The Diffusion of Power,* he affirmed his belief that U.S. military intervention in South Vietnam was necessary and appropriate. Regarding Johnson's April 1967 decision to limit the U.S. troop increase in South Vietnam to 45,000, he wrote, "fears of enlarging the war played a large role in his refusal to expand forces beyond that level or to use them outside South Vietnam. I believed then—and believe now—that those fears were exaggerated." Asked recently about what could or should have been done differently in Vietnam, Rostow replied, "We should have blocked the Ho

Chi Minh trail on the ground. I took that view at the time. Put a couple of U.S. divisions across the Ho Chi Minh trail in Laos, and I think we could have won the thing."

McGeorge Bundy, Rostow's predecessor as Johnson's special assistant for national security, once thought the same. After jumping from dean of arts and sciences at Harvard University to Washington in 1961, Bundy had enthusiastically supported Kennedy's and then Johnson's military escalation in South Vietnam. When he left the administration in 1966, however, Bundy was not so sanguine, and in 1968 he joined the "wise men" who counseled Johnson to de-escalate the war. After leaving government, Bundy became a history professor at New York University.

Bundy's close friend, Yale President Kingman Brewster, once quipped, "Mac is going to spend the rest of his life trying to justify his mistakes on Vietnam." Bundy later dismissed Brewster's comment as "baloney," but he did dwell on the positive aspects of America's Vietnam enterprise. "The case of Vietnam, with all its excesses," he stated in 1978, "may have been a force for enlightenment. There we learned, in a very hard way, that it was not enough to be right about the purpose of our opponent; we had to understand also our own limitations and those of our friends, and above all we had to distinguish more sharply an interest that was real but limited from an interest that was vital. . . . And we also know that the internal divisions which seemed so shocking at the time turned out to be endurable. . . . If Vietnam is a demonstration of our capacity for many kinds of error, it is also, even more than Watergate, a demonstration of our internal strength."

In 1985, nearly twenty years after his retirement from public office and the Vietnam War, McGeorge Bundy said this about the "single greatest lesson" he had learned: "Ask yourself ahead of time about any adventure. How much is this game worth?"

McGeorge Bundy's brother William, until 1967 Johnson's assistant secretary of state for East Asian and Pacific affairs, reexamined Vietnam first as a research associate at the Massachusetts Institute of Technology's Center for International Studies and then as editor of *Foreign Affairs,* the magazine of the prestigious Council on Foreign Relations. He later went to work on a history of U.S. foreign policy between 1972 and 1985.

In a 1979 article, "Who Lost Patagonia?" Bundy expressed relief that Americans had not turned against each other in an "inquisition" as to "who lost Vietnam. . . . Candidates at all levels," he wrote, "who had supported the war at times of decision were able to proclaim their disillusionment in varying degrees . . . and to join in a tacit consensus that decisions over a long period of time, under administrations of both parties, were inextricably intertwined, and that any partisan advantage was simply not possible over a matter the nation professed to put behind it." Moreover, Bundy saw a bipartisan consensus over the lessons of Vietnam. "I can share," he told an interviewer in

March 1985, "what I believe to be the general judgment that it [the Vietnam War] has tended to make public opinion and officials both more cautious in approaching third world situations of instability or conflict, and that it has had some impact on the general willingness of the public and the government to look at the use of force or forceful measures in such situations."

Henry Cabot Lodge epitomized the bipartisanship William Bundy attributed to America's Vietnam policy. A stalwart Massachusetts Republican, Lodge served two terms as U.S. ambassador to Vietnam under the Kennedy and Johnson Democratic administrations. In 1969 Republican President Nixon made him head of the U.S. delegation to the Vietnam peace talks in Paris.

Lodge expressed no qualms about his Vietnam service on behalf of two administrations, three presidents, and two political parties. "I believed," he stated in his memoirs, "that many mistakes had been made since 1945 and that if, in that period, the Indochina question had been wisely handled, the United States need never have gone there. In that sense the American presence there was a mistake. In 1963, however, these were all speculations. The reality was that, regardless of how we got there, Americans were in Vietnam and in combat. To accept, therefore, was a duty." After his death on February 27, 1985, the *Boston Globe* extolled Lodge's devotion to duty throughout his country's Vietnam tribulations. He was, the *Globe* said, "a

granite hard symbol of bipartisanship."

Of all the members of President Kennedy's and President Johnson's cabinet none became more closely associated with the Vietnam War than former Secretary of Defense Robert McNamara. In 1966 Congressional critics began referring to it as "McNamara's War." After leaving the government in 1968, however, McNamara stoutly resisted pressure from colleagues, historians, and the press to write or speak about his Vietnam years for the historical record. It took a court subpoena during the 1984 Westmoreland libel suit against CBS to elicit his observations about his role in directing America's most divisive war. In his trial deposition McNamara emphasized that his answers were being "extracted against his will."

Although in his testimony McNamara was reticent about offering sweeping judgments of the Johnson administration's Vietnam policy, he did comment, for the first time since leaving the Pentagon, on his own role in conducting the war. He testified that, unlike General Westmoreland, the Joint Chiefs of Staff, and the White House, he had reached the conclusion as early as 1965 or 1966 that the war could "not be won militarily." He also described his gradual shift from hawk to dove and his attempt to convince President Johnson that political initiatives, not troop increases, constituted the only solution to the expanding conflict in South Vietnam. His doubts had culminated in the compiling of the history of American in-

After leaving the Pentagon in 1968, Secretary of Defense Robert McNamara (below) directed the World Bank. Following his eight years as secretary of state, Dean Rusk (left) began teaching international law at the University of Georgia.

McGeorge Bundy (below), who was President Lyndon Johnson's special assistant for national security until 1966, teaches history at New York University.

173

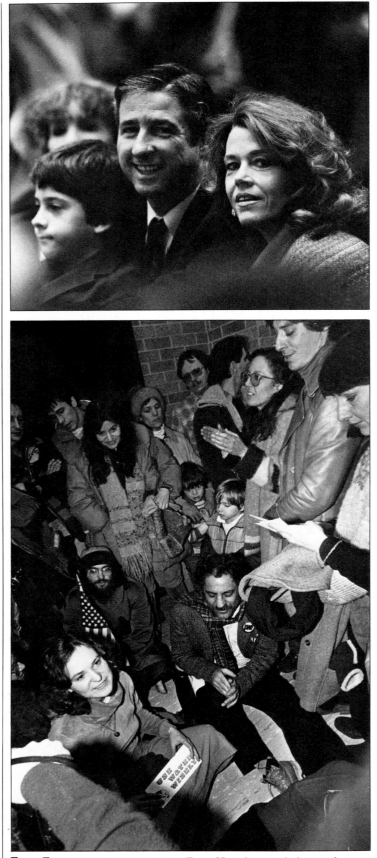

Top. *Former antiwar activist Tom Hayden with his wife, actress Jane Fonda, after his swearing-in as a California state legislator, 1982.* Bottom. *Former Yippie Abbie Hoffman (right center, seated) leads a sit-in in Doylestown, Pennsylvania.*

volvement in Vietnam known as *The Pentagon Papers.*

To the disappointment of many observers, what McNamara did not reveal was why he continued to support the war publicly after 1965 even though he harbored severe reservations about the prospects for military success. Nor did he explain adequately why he remained adamant, as a major participant, about not reassessing America's handling of Vietnam. Frustrated journalists and historians suspected the former defense secretary's traumatic disillusionment with the Vietnam conflict, and guilt for his part in directing it, were chiefly responsible. During his short time on the stand, however, McNamara gave no sign that he would ever again break his silence on the war.

In contrast to McNamara, former National Security Adviser and Secretary of State Henry Kissinger became effusive in his commentary, analysis, and justifications of a war that, from 1969 onward, became known as "Nixon's War." After joining the faculty of Georgetown University in 1977, he published three books that, in part, strive to illuminate the impact of Vietnam, past, present, and future: *White House Years* (1979), *For the Record* (1981), and *Years of Upheaval* (1982).

Kissinger took the hindsight view of many U.S. policymakers that Vietnam did not merit the strategic importance accorded it. But he differed from most in his conviction that, once committed, the U.S. should have persevered, not cut and run. "Whether the strategic stakes justified a massive American involvement," he wrote in 1982, "must be doubted in retrospect." The lesson? In 1985 Kissinger told the *Wall Street Journal,* "We are to be blamed for not doing in 1969 what we did in 1972 [increased military pressure by bombing North Vietnam and mining Haiphong Harbor]. That's the lesson I'm learning from it. . . . Once American forces are committed," he has concluded, "you do not have the choice to lose with moderation. If you use power, you must prevail."

Kissinger was doleful about the reverberations of the Vietnam era: "Vietnam put in motion such a weakening of America and created so many frustrations that a reaction to the right was inevitable." In Kissinger's view, the morality of America's role in Vietnam is being decided by the unfolding events in Southeast Asia: "The horrible fate of the peoples of Indochina since 1975—the mass murders, the concentration camps, the political oppression, the boat people—is now rendering a final verdict on whether it was our resistance to totalitarianism, or our abandonment of our friends, that was the true immorality of the Indochina conflict."

What of Richard Nixon, whose handling of Vietnam induced such deep turbulence in America? After resigning from office in August 1974 under the threat of impeachment, Nixon at first sought the seclusion of his San Clemente, California, compound. But as he had done so often in his stormy career, Richard Nixon confounded his friends and enemies alike by reentering public life, by writing, and making speeches and personal appearances. Between 1974 and 1984 he wrote several books on foreign policy: *RN*, a memoir (1978); *The Real War* (1980); *Leaders* (1982); and *Real Peace* (1984).

Nixon's 1985 book, *No More Vietnams*, was the capstone of his reflection about a war he called the most "misunderstood" event in American history, one he said was "misreported" then and is "misremembered now." As the former commander in chief saw it, the United States "won the war in Vietnam but we lost the peace. All that we had achieved in twelve years of fighting was thrown away in a spasm of congressional irresponsibility." Nixon was unremitting in his criticism of Congress for having "snatched defeat from the jaws of victory." "Once our troops were out of Vietnam," he wrote in *No More Vietnams*, "Congress initiated a total retreat from our commitments to the South Vietnamese people. First, it destroyed our ability to enforce the peace agreement, through legislation prohibiting the use of American military power in Indochina. Then it undercut South Vietnam's ability to defend itself, by drastically reducing our military aid. Within two years the balance of power swung decisively in Hanoi's favor." Nixon ignored Congressional and public concern, however, about what winning in South Vietnam would have entailed in lives, commitment, and money and whether victory in the long term would have been possible at any price.

Nixon considered the Vietnam conflict not a unique phenomenon but one the U.S. may encounter again, especially in Third World countries: "Nobody wants another Vietnam," he has stated. "Because they fear that any U.S. intervention in Third World countries might lead to another Vietnam, the new isolationists contend that the United States has no strategic interests in the Third World that would justify the use of our military power, and that we should limit our role to foreign aid programs and diplomatic initiatives. They are wrong."

The man who coined the term the "Vietnam Syndrome" has prescribed this cure: "Getting over the Vietnam syndrome means more than standing ready to use American military forces. It means being willing to provide military aid to friends who need it; being united, with each other and with our Western allies, in our responses to Soviet-backed aggression around the world; and, above all, having the wisdom and the vision to support non-military programs to address the poverty, injustice, and political instability that plague so many Third World countries. . . . No more Vietnams," he has concluded, "can mean we will not try again. It should mean that we will not fail again."

Where are they now?

In 1985, the tenth anniversary of South Vietnam's collapse, newspaper articles and magazine stories began asking, "Where are they now?"—the antiwar leaders and youthful dissenters who made domestic war against the Vietnam War and the policymakers who directed it. Two of the most "notorious" spokesmen for the 1960s "revolution" that opposed the war and the political and economic system behind it were Abbie Hoffman and Jerry Rubin. Hoffman, the self-styled resistance leader and author of the "Yippie" manifesto, *Woodstock Nation*, had a few years earlier emerged from a long period "underground," where he had tried to escape trial for possessing cocaine. He proved to be as defiant as when he led the Yippie assault on the American "establishment." "Because of the risks we took, America is better off," he claimed. "Because we applied ourselves as free, authentic human beings, we saved democracy. Democracy is people, not just the people in *People* magazine."

1960s radical-turned-stockbroker Jerry Rubin at work on Wall Street, 1980.

Time changed Jerry Rubin, as it did many of the "Sixties Generation." At thirty-nine he had opted for a set of "non-radical" values and become a prosperous stockbroker. "I led thousands of students in the streets, presidents would quiver when they heard my name, and I was the subject of many arguments at dinner tables all over America," he recalled, "but that was the past. . . . We do not carry picket signs now. . . . We want to carry our values into the corporate room." Rennie Davis, who helped devise tactics for disrupting the 1968 Democratic convention in Chicago, found himself by 1985 to be a salesman for the John Hancock Insurance Company, living what he called, "A sweet, useful life."

Tom Hayden, one of the founders of Students for a Democratic Society, also traded the student revolutionary symbols of long hair, jeans, and leftist slogans for the more conventional mode of clean-cut politician in jacket and tie. After running unsuccessfully for the U.S. Senate in 1976, Hayden won election to the California State Assembly in 1982. He still credits the striving of the young sixties rebels with substantial political and social achievements: "We ended a war, toppled two presidents, desegregated the South, and broke other barriers of discrimination." In an interview in 1985, Hayden even called for a monument to those who demonstrated against the war. "While we should celebrate and respect the sense of honor and patriotism that led men to fight in Vietnam," he stated, "there was no less a sense of honor or patriotism among those of us who opposed the war."

There were many celebrities on the rosters of antiwar protesters, among them "Baby Doctor" Benjamin Spock; folk singer Joan Baez; actress Jane Fonda, who married Tom Hayden; comedian Dick Gregory; and a host of politicians, teachers, and community leaders. The rank and file of the antiwar movement, however, were the committed, unpublicized men and women who gave it the momentum and numbers it needed. For them, looking back on the Vietnam War years later evoked a mixture of pride, nostalgia, and, in some instances, self-reproach. Stephen Cohen worked tirelessly for Eugene McCarthy's 1968 presidential campaign. From 1966 to 1972, while a student at Amherst College and at Yale Law School, he became an antiwar activist. "I cared so deeply about Vietnam," he confided to journalist Myra MacPherson, "because I am Jewish and I cannot forget the Holocaust. . . . I couldn't understand the lack of protest. The lesson I derived was: If your country is doing something wrong, you've got to try to change it. . . . Vietnam, of course, was not the equivalent of the Holocaust, but we were killing a helluva lot of people."

Molly Ivins, a columnist for the *Dallas Times Herald* who was an antiwar activist in the 1960s, recalled, "I was for civil rights and against the war, and people told me I was a liberal. Some told me I was a Communist." Protesting the war took most of her time and energy, but Ivins did not regret her commitment to the movement. "The movement was an all-absorbing thing," she remarked. "I didn't stop to think over what plans I should have. . . . There wasn't much time for yourself." Looking back, however, there was a wistfulness to Ivins's recollection of the years she devoted to opposing the Vietnam War. "I feel I gave a whole bunch of the best years of my life to that. Now I do not think of myself as an activist or an organizer. Now I have to put my life together."

As time passed, most antiwar protesters and political activists moved on to the more traditional pursuits of career, marriage, and raising families. But some, like Stephen Cohen, transferred their zeal to antinuclear and civil rights issues, social work, and teaching. "For some," Cohen says, "Vietnam did create a political conscience. They're still at it. They're just not all that visible." In 1985 former Black Panther Bobby Seale was attending Temple

University and directing a youth training program. "I want to contribute to social change by being the last word behind a nonprofit organization," he said. Mark Rudd, founder of Students for a Democratic Society, spent years as a fugitive from the law for conspiracy to riot in Chicago. After surrendering to police in 1977, Rudd received a sentence of two years probation and was fined $2,000. In 1984 Rudd was teaching at a vocational school in Albuquerque, New Mexico.

Some members of the Vietnam generation who evaded more than protested the war became critical of their behavior. In Myra MacPherson's *Long Time Passing*, a look at the impact of Vietnam on those who came of age during the war, a man who would give only his first name confessed to having pulled a scam to beat the draft. "I decided I'm going to get out by being crazy," he recalled. "I get this fancy note from this Boston shrink. His name has gotten around to everyone. For sixty bucks, I got the note. It says, in essence, that if you send this guy, you should have surrendered six months ago." But, he went on, "my guilt is that I see these guys walking around who went. I didn't go. . . . I apologize every day of my life to them." In a May 1981 *New York Times* editorial, Michael Blumenthal wrote that he evaded the draft in 1969 by inhaling "canvas dust from the sewing tables at a tent factory in upstate New York. I was merely another college graduate student evading the draft. . . . I was attempting to revive a childhood history of bronchial asthma that I hoped would keep me safely at home, morally and physically untainted."

The decisions of thousands of men to avoid Vietnam did more than leave them morally ill at ease twenty years later. The lives of the estimated 17,500 draft evaders and 10,000 deserters, and their families, were indelibly marked by their refusal to serve. Many fled to Canada or Sweden. Others eked out shadowy existences as fugitives from prosecution in the United States. Kevin Brieze, after refusing induction in Texas, crossed with his wife into Canada. When news of his draft evasion got around his small Texas town, Brieze recalled, "The KKK broke my mother-in-law's windows, slashed her tires, crank-called, and broke into her house. They literally ran her out of town." Jack Calhoun was an army deserter who stayed in Toronto, Canada. As an ROTC candidate at the University of Wisconsin, he became afraid he would "either get sent to Vietnam or used to put down antiwar demonstrations or ghetto riots. I couldn't do any of those things." In the spring of 1970, he said, "it really just came to me—Canada. Which I didn't want to do. I had been brought up as an American patriot. The last thing that came to my mind was Canada, but I saw there was no way at all to resolve my problem without going to jail, and I was afraid I couldn't take it in jail. . . . And I couldn't do anything to end the war in jail. . . . So I came to Canada."

In August 1974, as part of his effort to bind the wounds of Vietnam, President Gerald Ford proposed amnesty for draft evaders and deserters. Evaders would have to present themselves to a United States attorney before January 31, 1975, then pledge allegiance to the country and fulfill a two-year period of alternate service. "Deserters," the president stipulated, "could escape punishment once they pledged allegiance to the United States and agree to spend two years in the branch of the military to which they had once belonged." "All, in a sense, are casualties," Ford told the nation, "still abroad and absent without leave from the real America. I want them to come home if they want to work their way back." In addition, 250,000 men who had failed to register for the draft and 200,000 veterans with "undesirable, bad conduct, and dishonorable discharges" could request an upgrading of their status.

President Ford's clemency program, as his Clemency Board chairman, Charles Goodell, conceded, was "a partial success at best." Pro-amnesty groups deemed it a "dangerous trap," a "cynical smokescreen," and "shamnesty." Red tape, and what some considered the onerous conditions of clemency, discouraged some eligible men from applying. One draft resister remarked, "They want me to shuffle and scrape and mumble, 'I'm sorry folks, I shouldn't of done it—please forgive me,' all so Ford can feel good about letting Nixon off the hook. They can cram it." When the program expired at the end of 1975, only 8,000 had received formal clemency. President Ford later said, "It was tragic that so few participated."

In 1976 President Jimmy Carter gave high-priority to pardoning Vietnam draft and military offenders. "I do not favor blanket amnesty," Carter stated in February. "I do favor a blanket pardon. There is a difference. Amnesty means what you did was right; pardon means what you did is forgiven. I cannot equate the actions of those who went to Vietnam thinking it was wrong—many of whom lost their lives—with those who thought it was wrong and defected. But exile for this long a period of time is adequate punishment."

Carter's pardon extended to several categories of Vietnam exiles. Draft violators could have their records erased. Thousands of evaders could return without prosecution. Also covered were the 250,000 who never registered. Nearly 100,000 men who entered and then deserted the armed forces were, however, not eligible. Inevitably the president's pardon stirred controversy. Senator Barry Goldwater called it "the most disgraceful thing a president has ever done." Veterans organizations warned that it would corrode military discipline. Bernard Slaughter, a Vietnam combat veteran, said, "I think Carter has sold out every American veteran living and dead." Another veteran applauded the pardon: "Bravo! Bravo! to the man who rejected the Vietnam draft—and to the President for his timely pardon. I am a veteran of combat in Vietnam, and I feel no bitterness toward those who resisted. I feel it is I who should be pardoned for having continued to participate."

Carter's pardon program fell short of its objective. It attracted just 9 percent of the 432,000 men covered by it. For those who took advantage of it, pardon meant a chance to come home. In Ottawa, Canada, Kevin Brieze, who was twenty-nine by then, "jumped around and knocked over chairs" upon hearing of the pardon. Still, he was nervous about the reception he might get at home. He planned "to test the atmosphere with friends before seeing his parents." After several weeks in the States, Brieze decided to go back to Canada. Not all exiles wanted to return to the U.S. permanently. In January 1979 Joe Nichell of Toronto said, "My home is here now." Said Jeff Egner, an army deserter, "Quite a few of us have found Canada in many ways good to us and good for us."

Ten years after

Amnesty, pardons, and the recognition of veterans' needs helped to reduce the blight the Vietnam War had imposed on the lives of the individuals it affected most. To President Ronald Reagan in 1981, however, Vietnam remained a blight on U.S. foreign policy and the country's standing in the world, which he was determined to remove. Reagan interpreted his impressive victory over Jimmy Carter as a mandate to restore America's power and prestige in international affairs. His foreign policy agenda included the rebuilding of America's defense capabilities, which he charged, had been drained by the Vietnam War and neglected in its aftermath. He also favored a readiness to intervene abroad, politically and militarily, to protect U.S. allies or strategic interests. Reagan insisted in 1981 that "Vietnam was a necessary war, necessary to check the expansionist designs of the Soviet Union and its client states and to uphold the global position of the United States. . . . America failed not because it was defeated but because the military was denied permission to win."

President Reagan's stated resolve to reverse what he considered to be America's post-Vietnam decline translated into a major arms build-up. After taking office he more than doubled the 5 percent per year budget increase for defense proposed by President Carter, raising the total defense budget from $133.9 billion in 1980 to $227 billion in 1984. Besides beefing up U.S. conventional forces and equipment with more navy surface vessels and submarines, bombers and fighter planes, and army tanks and attack helicopters, Reagan added to the U.S. nuclear arsenal new cruise and Trident missiles and in March 1985 obtained limited Congressional approval for another missile program, a plan to build new ICBMs called MX (for Missile Experimental).

Reagan's most ambitious and controversial defense proposal involved the development of an orbiting space antiballistic weapons system. In the spring of 1985 Congress approved funds for the initial research on this so-called star wars project, which was expected to cost $30 billion over the next six years. But there was criticism both in the House and Senate that the president's MX and space weapons projects were restarting the arms race. Reagan discounted that: "We're already in an arms race, but only the Soviets are racing. They are outspending us in the military field by 50 percent, and more than double, sometimes triple on their strategic forces. Our best hope of persuading them to live in peace is to convince them they cannot win a war."

Although by electing Reagan in 1980 and reelecting him four years later a majority of Americans showed their support for his overall goal of strengthening U.S. defense, they also shared Congress's uneasiness about the high cost and its effect on the $200 billion budget deficit facing the government in 1985. This concern over military spending was reminiscent of the "guns vs. butter" debate during the Vietnam War. Just as opponents of President Johnson's Vietnam escalation in 1965 decried the economic damage it inflicted on the Great Society programs, so twenty years later critics of Reagan's arms build-up opposed vast military expenditures that threatened the existence of New Deal and Great Society programs in welfare, social security, health, and education.

Reagan's rhetoric about buttressing America's defense and reasserting U.S. military power to counter Soviet "expansion" recalled the global containment foreign policy doctrine originated in the 1940s. Historian George Herring, in a 1981 article "The Vietnam Syndrome and American Foreign Policy," observed that the president's attempt to exorcise the Vietnam Syndrome from America's vocabulary was a prelude to a more confrontational foreign policy. "The Reagan administration," he has stated, "seems to favor a return to the days of global containment, relying on a massive military buildup and intervention in the world's trouble spots to check Soviet expansion and regain the position we have lost."

To garner support for its refurbished containment policy the Reagan administration reintroduced the so-called domino theory embraced by America's "cold warriors" in the 1950s. Despite the fact that the domino theory as originally enunciated was proven wrong in Southeast Asia—the Philippines, Indonesia, Thailand, and Singapore continue to survive as non-Communist states—it has gained new currency in the debate over Soviet involvement in such troubled areas as the Middle East and Central America. Early in his first term President Reagan said, "The Soviet Union underlies all the unrest that is going on. If they weren't engaged in this game of dominoes, there wouldn't be any hot spots in the world."

Reagan and other U.S. policymakers perceived Angola, Iran, and Afghanistan as dominoes that fell to communism because of U.S. weakness and indecisiveness resulting from defeat in Vietnam. Former Secretary of State Henry Kissinger, for example, called the failure of the U.S. policy toward those countries "the indirect consequence of Viet-

nam." The domino theory has been cited particularly with regard to the instability in Central America. When he was secretary of state, Alexander Haig asserted that the problem in El Salvador was "external intervention in the internal affairs of a sovereign nation in this hemisphere—nothing more, nothing less." Assistant Secretary of State Thomas Enders ominously forecast in 1982, "If after Nicaragua, El Salvador is captured by a violent minority, who in Central America would not live in fear? How long would it be before major strategic interests—the Panama Canal, sea lanes, oil supplies—were at risk?" To the Reagan administration, the dominoes had reached our neighborhood.

Reagan officials consistently maintained that Nicaragua, ruled by the pro-Communist Sandinista party, and the leftist insurgents in El Salvador were spearheading Soviet-inspired and -supplied subversion in Central America. In February 1981, for instance, the White House published a white paper entitled "Communist Interference in El Salvador." On its first page were seven arrows, each indicating the shipment route of Soviet weapons from Nicaragua to El Salvador. "The Reagan administration's strategic vision," as political scientist Morris Blachman aptly stated, "emphasizes that the conflict in El Salvador is part and parcel of the East-West conflict."

In raising the specter of toppling dominoes in Central America and placing the turmoil there in a cold war context, the Reagan administration was, as had previous administrations with regard to Southeast Asia, assuming too much. Although the Sandinista government had received tens of millions of dollars of Soviet aid since 1979, it was not clear whether Nicaragua's arms build-up presaged aggression against its neighbors or was the result of the Sandinistas overreacting to fears of U.S. military interference. White House support for anti-Communist Nicaraguan guerrillas, called the "contras," did little to allay Sandinista anxiety. Moreover, while U.S. intelligence reported that the Sandinista regime smuggled weapons to the El Salvadoran leftists trying to overthrow the government of José Napoleon Duarte, there was no substantial evidence that this was part of a monolithic Soviet offensive to take over Central America. Furthermore, gloomy reports from Washington about external assistance to El Salvadoran leftist guerrillas obscured the local factors behind their insurgency. Applying the domino theory to Central America, therefore, did more to distort than clarify the strategic ramifications of events in Nicaragua and El Salvador.

President Reagan's cold war rhetoric sharply contrasted with the human rights-oriented foreign policies of

Bruce Jones leads a group of CIA-backed Nicaraguan contras—rebels seeking to overthrow the Marxist-led Sandinista government—across the Sardina River into no man's land on the border between Costa Rica and Nicaragua.

his predecessor, Jimmy Carter, in the 1970s. His tough talk was accompanied by a stated willingness to use military power to assert U.S. interests abroad. Beginning in 1973, for example, U.S. relations with Colonel Muammar Qaddafi's Libyan government became strained. Washington loudly criticized his close ties to the Soviet Union, his sponsorship of international terrorism, and his belligerence in the Middle East and Mediterranean. Libya's "incorporation" of the strategic Gulf of Sidra into its territorial waters further incensed the United States, which refused to recognize Qaddafi's claims. During a two–day military exercise in August 1981, when U.S. naval vessels ventured into the Gulf of Sidra, two Libyan Soviet–built SU–22 jets approached, firing upon the two American F–14 "Tomcat" fighter planes sent to intercept them. After a brief dogfight, the U.S. aircraft, unhit, shot down both Libyan planes with Sidewinder missiles.

The Reagan administration did not hesitate to deploy U.S. troops to back its foreign policy. After the Israeli sweep into Lebanon in June 1982, the United States arranged for a peace keeping force of American, French, and Italian troops to supervise the evacuation of Palestine Liberation Organization units trapped in Beirut. On August 25, 800 U.S. Marines came ashore in Beirut, armed with M16 rifles and antitank weapons. By September 10, the evacuation was completed and the marines withdrew. But in October Washington ordered the marines back into Beirut after fighting broke out among Christian Phalangists, Syrians, and remaining bands of Palestinian guerrillas. Twelve hundred U.S. Marines conducted peace keeping operations in Beirut for the next two years. On September 30, 1983, Congress invoked the War Powers Act for the first time since Vietnam, enabling the White House to continue the marines' deployment in Lebanon for only eighteen more months.

About three weeks later, on the morning of October 23, 1983, a two–and–one–half–ton truck sped down the main highway toward the U.S. Marine headquarters at Beirut airport. It maneuvered past a series of steel fences, sandbag barricades, and security guards, hurtling into the center of the headquarters. The truck's "suicide driver," an unidentified terrorist, then detonated his truckload of explosives. The explosion collapsed

the four-story building, killing 240 marines and sailors billeted inside. "I haven't seen carnage like that since Vietnam," marine spokesman Major Robert Jordan commented.

Reagan's deployment of U.S. troops in Lebanon was an embarrassing failure. Not only did U.S. troops fail to achieve the president's foreign policy aim of stabilizing the situation in Lebanon, they also suffered major casualties in a frustrating, defensive battle against a variety of Lebanese terrorists and warring factions. In effect, what happened to U.S. troops in Lebanon was a disturbing reminder to the American people of the limitations imposed upon involving U.S. military power abroad.

The Lebanon fiasco, however, did not deter President Reagan from using American military power again. In 1979, in the tiny Caribbean nation of Grenada, leftist leader Maurice Bishop had overthrown Grenada's anti-Communist Prime Minister Eric Gairy. Within three days of Bishop's coup, a Cuban ship bearing Soviet armaments steamed into Grenada's port. In November 1979 Bishop announced that Cuba's Fidel Castro would help Grenada

construct an international airport to increase tourism. Almost immediately, a contingent of Cubans arrived to begin work on a 10,000-foot runway, suitable for jumbo jets—and long-range military aircraft. Then in May 1980 Grenada signed a treaty with Moscow giving the Soviets permission to land TU-95s (long-range reconnaissance aircraft) in Grenada when the runway was finished. Reagan became irate. "It isn't nutmeg that's at stake in the Caribbean," he said, "it's U.S. national security."

In June 1983 Bishop, for reasons not yet explained, made friendly overtures to the U.S. As a result, his Cuban advisers plotted with his subordinates to push him aside. On October 13 Grenadan Deputy Prime Minister Bernard Coard arrested Bishop. A crowd of Grenadans trying to free Bishop on October 19 were attacked by troops inside Soviet-made armored personnel carriers. Moments later, General Hudson Austin, a former prison guard, executed Bishop with a pistol shot to the head. Austin then imposed a twenty-four-hour curfew. Violators would be shot on sight, said Grenada radio.

Apprised of developments in Grenada, President Reagan convened a Special Situation Group meeting. According to Secretary of State George Schultz, the group's top priority was insuring the safety of the 1,000 Americans in Grenada, including 600 students at St. George's Medical College. As a precaution, the president dispatched a naval task force to Grenadan waters. Meanwhile, the leaders of the six nations of the Organization of the Eastern Caribbean States (Antigua, Dominica, Saint Lucia, Saint Kitts-Nevis, Montserrat, and Saint Vincent) requested that the U.S. intervene "to bring normalcy back" to Grenada. On Saturday, October 22, President Reagan approved a military operation, code-named Urgent Fury, to rescue the Americans caught in Grenada. It involved more than 5,000 troops from all four branches of the military.

No American combat troops had gone into offensive action on foreign shores since the *Mayaguez* incident in 1975. The assault on Grenada took place on Tuesday, October 25. U.S. attack forces, against moderate resistance, secured the island by Wednesday night and liberated the Americans there. In Washington President Reagan commented, "We got there just in time." Vice President George Bush stated, "If the United States is not willing to help a small democratic country, who will?"

Reagan's revival of a containment-oriented foreign policy met opposition in the press and Congress. Critics have likened U.S. intervention in Lebanon, El Salvador, Nicaragua, and Grenada to Vietnam. Some members of Congress disparaged the deployment of U.S. Marines in Lebanon as a "mission impossible" that disregarded the lessons of Vietnam. "Some say that Lebanon is not Vietnam," said Senator Edward Kennedy in 1983. "But I reply, we must not give the President the power to turn it into one." In February 1982 former Senator George McGovern deprecated the president's policy toward El Salvador. "Once again," he declared, "the United States assumes that insurgents are actually fighting a proxy war for the Soviets. We're re-

Rescuers search for victims in the rubble of the U.S. Marine headquarters in Beirut, demolished by a terrorist truck bomb, October 23, 1983. Two hundred and forty men were killed.

An American military helicopter patrols Grenada near the town of Carricon.

Grenada

On October 25, 1983, 6,000 U.S. soldiers invaded the tiny Caribbean nation of Grenada, whose government had been thrown into chaos by a bloody left-wing coup against Prime Minister Maurice Bishop. The U.S. had acted, said President Ronald Reagan, to prevent Cuba and the Soviet Union, Bishop's erstwhile sponsors, from establishing another beachhead in the Western Hemisphere and also to protect the lives of some 600 American medical students trapped on the island. The success of the invasion helped serve notice that the United States stood prepared to use military force to defend its strategic interests.

An American marine guards a captured Grenadan citizen.

Right. U.S. troops with the 82d Airborne Division await their flight back to Fort Bragg from Grenada's Point Salines Airport.

peating the mistake of supporting an unpopular government." Central American affairs specialist Richard Newfarmer, a fellow at the Overseas Development Council in Washington, D.C., said of U.S. attitudes toward Nicaragua, "The administration believes the Sandinistas enjoy no popular legitimacy and are dominated by the Cubans and the Soviets, and so negotiations must include the make-up of the Nicaraguan government itself, something the Sandinistas, having just fought a revolution to obtain power, were not about to negotiate." After the U.S. invasion of Grenada, House Speaker Tip O'Neill remarked, "We can't go the way of gunboat diplomacy. Reagan's policy is wrong. His policy is frightening."

The majority of Americans suggested by their widespread support for Reagan at the polls in 1980 and 1984 that they shared his concern about Soviet activities in Third World countries, about strengthening America's defenses, and about making U.S. military power a credible instrument of U.S. foreign policy. Most Americans, for example, approved the downing of the two attacking Libyan jets in 1981. In a *Newsweek* poll at the time of Reagan's election in 1980, 68 percent of those polled thought "the U.S. has been falling behind the Soviet Union in power and influence." After Washington sent U.S. troops to Lebanon, a CBS News/*New York Times* survey in September 1983 found that "the public believes by more than 2 to 1 that the outcome of the struggle there [Lebanon] is important to the defense interests of the United States." Following the U.S. Grenada operation, a November 1983 *Newsweek* poll showed that more than 58 percent of Americans sanctioned "the participation of U.S. military forces in the invasion of Grenada."

But despite President Reagan's claim that popular support for his decisions to send troops to Lebanon and Grenada marked the end of the Vietnam Syndrome, Americans had not discarded the principal lesson they drew from the war: prudence about committing U.S. military power abroad. Americans backed the sending of troops to Lebanon only as a peace keeping force, not as combat forces. And the Grenada invasion indicated only that Americans might tolerate quick, decisive, and low-cost military intervention, not necessarily longer term, more complex involvements like Vietnam had been. In 1983, for instance, a *New York Times* poll showed that 77 percent of Americans still thought the U.S. "should have stayed out of Vietnam."

Over the years polls by the *New York Times*, *Newsweek*, and *Time* also revealed strong public misgivings about deploying U.S. troops in Central America or other Third World trouble spots. Even the upper echelons of the U.S. Army were reluctant to do so. In June 1983, for example, several U.S. Army generals, including John Vessey, chairman of the Joint Chiefs of Staff, told the *New York Times* that the JCS opposed "any American intervention in Central America without the unequivocal support of Congress and the people." After five years in office, President Reagan had not succeeded in forming a consensus for waging the kind of limited "containment" war against Communist-inspired insurgencies that he believed the U.S. should have won in Vietnam and should be prepared to fight in the future.

More than a decade after U.S. combat troops withdrew from South Vietnam, therefore, the Vietnam experience continued to cause broad disagreement about the use of American military power abroad. Retrospective analyses by foreign policymakers in April 1985, the tenth anniversary of the fall of Saigon, demonstrated the extent to which a common assessment of Vietnam had eluded them. Former hawks and doves remained divided over how and why the U.S. got involved in South Vietnam, whether or not such involvement was politically and morally justified, and what the war has come to mean for America.

Still the argument over Vietnam had changed in one important respect—a more pragmatic, more reasonable tone had replaced the rancorous, bitter disputes of the 1960s and early 1970s. As journalist Stanley Karnow, author of *Vietnam: A History*, observed, "The animosities and the passions have been replaced by a quest to find out what went wrong and to avoid future disasters."

The anguish, of course, had not entirely abated. Hard-pressed refugees from Communist rule in Southeast Asia struggled to reach the U.S. and other havens where they could seek new lives. For veterans and their families the unresolved MIA and Agent Orange issues made the war a continuing, and disturbing, presence. The government's medical verdict on Agent Orange, for example, awaited ten years of study and research begun in 1984. Occasionally, too, newspaper reports of violence between pro- and anti-Communist refugees in many communities of the U.S. presented grim reminders of how much enmity the Vietnam War had sown among the Vietnamese people. Thus, in 1985, twenty years after the U.S. Marines landed on the beaches at Da Nang, some of the painful effects of the nation's Vietnam experience lingered on, the legacy of the most divisive, traumatic conflict in American history since the Civil War.

★ ★ ★

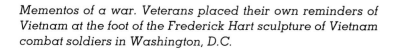

Mementos of a war. Veterans placed their own reminders of Vietnam at the foot of the Frederick Hart sculpture of Vietnam combat soldiers in Washington, D.C.

Bibliography

I. Books and Articles

Ablin, David, and Marlow Hood. "The Lesser Evil, an Interview with Norodom Sihanouk." *New York Review of Books*, March 14, 1985.

Adams, Anthony. "A Study of Veterans' Viewpoints on TV Coverage of the Vietnam War." *Journalism Quarterly* 59 1977.

Adams, Sam. "Vietnam Cover-Up." *Harper's*, May 1975.

Alley, Rewi. *Refugees from Viet Nam in China*. New World Pr., 1980.

Andelman, David A. "Laos After the Takeover." *New York Times Magazine*, October 24, 1976.

Apple, R. W. "New Stirrings of Patriotism." *New York Times Magazine*, December 11, 1983.

Auster, Al, and Leonard Quart. "Hollywood and Vietnam." *Cineaste*, Spring 1979.

Baker, Mark. *Nam*. Berkley Bks., 1981.

Barnett, Anthony, and John Pilger. *Aftermath*. New Statesman, Report 5, 1982.

Barron, John, and Anthony Paul. *Murder of a Gentle Land*. Reader's Digest Pr., 1977.

Beidler, Philip. *American Literature and the Experience of Vietnam*. University of Georgia Pr., 1982.

Bennett, Philip. "Students Help Refugees Adjust to Boston." *The Harvard Independent*, April 10, 1980.

Berger, Peter. "Indochina and the American Conscience." *Commentary*, February 1980.

Biewin, R. "TV's Newest Villain: The Vietnam Veteran." *TV Guide*, July 19, 1975.

Boland, John C. "Enterprise Gadfly: Lawyer Dan Burt Has Washington Abuzz." *Barron's*, June 1982.

Boua, Chantou, and Ben Kiernan. "Bureaucracy of Death." *New Statesman*, May 2, 1980.

Braestrup, Peter. "The Uncounted Enemy." *Washington Journalism Review*, April 1982.

Brandon, Donald. "Carter and Asia." *Asian Affairs*, May/June 1978.

Breslin, John. "Vietnam Legacy." *America*, September 1976.

Brown, MacAlister. "Laos." *Current History*, April 1983.

Brown, MacAlister, and Joseph J. Zasloff. "New Stages of Revolution in Laos." *Current History*, December 1976.

Broyles, William, Jr. "The Road to Hill 10." *The Atlantic*, April 1985.

Bryan, C. D. B. "Barely Suppressed Screams." *Harper's*, June 1984.

_____ . *Friendly Fire*. Putnam, 1976.

Brzezinski, Zbigniew. *Power and Principle*. Farrar, Strauss & Giroux, 1983.

Buckley, Kevin. "Vietnam: The Defense's Case." *New York Review of Books*, December 7, 1978.

Bundy, William P. "Who Lost Patagonia?" *Foreign Affairs*, Fall 1979.

Burchett, Wilfred. *Grasshoppers & Elephants*. Urizen, 1977.

Caputo, Philip. *A Rumor of War*. Ballantine Bks., 1977.

Card, Josephina J. *Lives After Vietnam*. Lexington Bks., 1983.

Carter, Jimmy. *Keeping Faith*. Bantam, 1982.

Cassidy, John. *A Station in the Delta*. Scribner, 1979.

CBS News. "CBS Reports: The Uncounted Enemy: A Vietnam Deception" Broadcast January 23, 1982. Transcript.

Chace, James. "Is a Foreign Policy Consensus Possible?" *Foreign Affairs*, Fall 1978.

Chandler, David P. "Revising the Past in Democratic Kampuchea." *Pacific Affairs*, Summer 1983.

Chandler, David P., and Ben Kiernan, eds. *Revolution and its Aftermath in Kampuchea: Eight Essays*. Yale University Southeast Asia Studies, 1983.

Chandler, Jerome. "A Funny Thing Happened on the Way to Washington." *Saturday Evening Post*, January/February 1982.

Charney, Joel, and John Spragens, Jr. *Obstacles to Recovery in Vietnam and Kampuchea*. Impact Audit 3, Oxfam America, 1984.

The Chinese Rulers' Crimes Against Kampuchea. Ministry of Foreign Affairs, People's Republic of Kampuchea, April 1984.

Chomsky, Noam. "The Secular Priesthood." *Working Papers for a New Society*, May–June 1970.

Chomsky, Noam, and Edward S. Herman. "Distortions at Fourth Hand." *The Nation*, June 25, 1977.

Clarke, Capt. Douglas L. *The Missing Man, Politics and the MIA*. National Defense University, 1979.

Collins, John. "Vietnam Postmortem." *Parameters*, March 1978.

Corson, William. *Consequences of Failure*. Norton, 1974.

Dawson, Alan. *55 Days*. Prentice-Hall, 1977.

Del Vecchio, John. *The Thirteenth Valley*. Bantam, 1982.

Draper, Theodore. "Ghosts of Vietnam." *Dissent*, Winter 1979.

Drew, Elizabeth. *American Journal: The Events of 1976*. Random, 1977.

_____ . *Campaign Journal*. Macmillan, 1985.

_____ . *Portrait of an Election*. Simon & Schuster, 1981.

Duiker, William J. *Vietnam Since the Fall of Saigon*. Center for International Studies, 1980.

Dunn, Joe. "In Search of Lessons." *Parameters*, December 1979.

Durden, Charles. *No Bugles, No Drums*. Viking Pr., 1976.

Eastlake, William. *The Bamboo Bed*. Simon & Schuster, 1969.

Egendorf, Arthur. "Postwar Healing of Vietnam Veterans." *Hospital and Community Psychiatry*, November 1982.

Elliott, David W. P., ed. *The Third Indochina Conflict*. Westview Pr., 1981.

Erlich, Reese, and Evaristo Garza. "Blood-Brothers." *Mother Jones*, November 1983.

"Exchange on Cambodia." *New York Review of Books*, September 27, 1984.

Fallows, James. "In Defense of an Indefensible War." *New York Times Book Review*, March 28, 1982.

_____ . *National Defense*. Random, 1981.

Feeney, William R. "U.S. Strategic Interests in the Pacific." *Current History*, April 1982.

Figley, Charles R., and Seymour Leventman. *Strangers at Home*. Praeger, 1980.

FitzGerald, Frances. *Fire in the Lake*. Vintage Bks., 1972.

Ford, Daniel. *Incident at Muc Wa*. Doubleday, 1967.

Ford, Gerald. *A Time to Heal*. Harper & Row/Reader's Digest, 1979.

Franjola, Matt. "Indochina—Recollections and Projections." 1976.

Gallup Organization. *Gallup Opinion Index*, June 1965–January 1981.

Garner, John W. "Sino-Vietnamese Conflict and the Sino-American Rapprochement." *Political Science Quarterly*, Fall 1981.

Garrett, Banning N., and Bonnie S. Glaser. *War and Peace*. Institute of International Studies, 1984.

Gelb, Leslie, and Richard Betts. *The Irony of Vietnam: The System Worked*. The Brookings Institution, 1979.

Germard, Jack W., and Jules Witcover. *Blue Smoke and Mirrors*. Viking Pr., 1981.

Gigot, Paul A. "Lost or Merely Forgotten?" *National Review*, August 17, 1979.

Grant, Bruce. *The Boat People*. Penguin, 1979.

Groom, Winston. *Better Times Than These*. Summit Bks., 1978.

"Gunboats to Grenada." *The New Republic*, November 14, 1983.

Hagerty, Elizabeth Ann. "Vietnamese in Southern California." Ph.D. diss., United States International University, 1980.

Halberstam, David. *The Best and the Brightest*. Random, 1972.

_____ . *The Powers that Be*. Knopf, 1979.

Hartmann, Robert. *Palace Politics*. McGraw-Hill, 1980.

Hasford, Gustav. *The Short-Timers*. Harper & Row, 1979.

Hawthorne, Lesleyanne, ed. *Refugee: The Vietnamese Experience*. Oxford Univ. Pr., 1982.

Hazen, Sebbat Merse. "Kampuchea." Ph.D. diss., University of Southern California, 1983.

Heineman, Larry. *Close Quarters*. Farrar, Straus & Giroux, 1974.

Hendin, Herbert, and Ann Pollinger Haas. *Wounds of War*. Basic Bks. 1984.

Herring, George C. "The 'Vietnam Syndrome' and American Foreign Policy." *The Virginia Quarterly Review*, Autumn 1981.

Herrington, Stuart A. *Peace With Honor*. Presidio Pr., 1983.

Hersh, Seymour M. *The Price of Power*. Summit Bks., 1984.

Hildebrand, George, and Gareth Porter. *Cambodia: Starvation and Revolution*. Monthly Review Pr., 1976.

Hoffman, Stanley. "The Sulking Giant." *The New Republic*, May 3, 1975.

Holeindre, Roger, and Marcel Marsal. *Hanoi: Combats Pour Un Empire*. Jacques Grancher, 1979.

Horner, Charles. "America Five Years After Defeat." *Commentary*, April 1980.

Hosti, Ole R., and James N. Rosenau. *American Leadership in World Affairs*. Allen & Unwin, 1984.

Hsiung, James C., and Winberg Chai, eds. *Asia and U.S. Foreign Policy*. Praeger, 1981.

Indochina Issues, nos. 1–58. Center for International Policy, March 1979–June 1985.

Isaacs, Arnold R. *Without Honor: Defeat in Vietnam and Cambodia*. Johns Hopkins Univ. Pr., 1983.

Jackson, Karl D., and Jacqueline Desbarats. "Woe Unto the Defeated: Political Executions in Vietnam." 1984.

Jencks, Harlan W. "China's 'Punitive' War in Vietnam: A Military Assessment." *Asian Survey*, August 1979.

"J'etais a Phnom Penh." *L'Express*, May 12–18, 1975.

Jordan, Hamilton. *Crisis*. Putnam, 1982.
"Just Take Our Word For It." *Columbia Journalism Review*, January/February 1984.

Kane, Christine L. "Inside the Death Factory." *New Boston Review*, May/June 1981.
Karnow, Stanley. *Vietnam: A History*. Viking Pr., 1983.
Kattenburg, Paul. *The Vietnam Trauma in American Foreign Policy, 1945–75*. Transaction Bks., 1980.
Kiernan, Ben. "Conflict in the Kampuchean Communist Movement." *Journal of Contemporary Asia*, 10, no. 1/2 (1980).
Kissinger, Henry. *White House Years*. Little, Brown, 1979.
—————. *Years of Upheaval*. Little, Brown, 1982.
Klein, Joe. *Payback*. Knopf, 1984.
Klein, Robert. *Wounded Men, Broken Promises*. Macmillan, 1981.
Kolpacoff, Victor. *The Prisoner of Quai Dong*. NAL, 1967.
Kopit, Arthur. *Indians*. Hill & Wang, 1969.
Kovic, Ron. *Born on the Fourth of July*. Pocket Bks., 1976.
Kowet, Don, and Sally Bedell. "Anatomy of a Smear." *TV Guide*, May 29, 1982.

Lacouture, Jean. "The Bloodiest Revolution." *New York Review of Books*, March 31, 1977.
Ledeen, Michael, and William Lewis. *Debacle*. Knopf, 1981.
Lelyveld, Joseph. "The Enduring Legacy." *New York Times Magazine*, March 31, 1985.
"Let Them Rest in Peace." *The Nation*, March 12, 1977.
Le Thi Anh. "The New Vietnam." *National Review*, April 29, 1977.
Lewy, Guenter. *America in Vietnam*. Oxford Univ. Pr., 1978.
—————. "Vietnam: New Light on the Question of American Guilt." *Commentary*, February 1978.
Lifton, Robert Jay. *Home from the War*. Simon & Schuster, 1973.
Lodge, Henry Cabot. *The Storm Has Many Eyes*. Norton, 1973.

"Machismo Diplomacy." *The Nation*, May 31, 1975.
MacPherson, Myra. *Long Time Passing*. Doubleday, 1984.
Mamet, David. "Conventional Warfare." *Esquire*, March 1985.
Marchino, Michael, and Robert K. Musil. "The American Mercenaries." *The Nation*, April 10, 1976.
Martin, Earl S. *Reaching the Other Side*. Crown, 1978.
Mason, Linda, and Roger Brown. *Rice, Rivalry, and Politics*. Univ. of Notre Dame Pr., 1983.
May, Edgar. "Inmate Veterans." *Corrections Magazine*, March 1979.
"MIA: The Heartless Ploy." *The Nation*, September 25, 1976.
Moore, Robin. *The Green Berets*. Crown, 1965.
Morris, Roger. "What to Make of Mayaguez." *The New Republic*, June 14, 1975.
Morris, Stephen J. "Vietnam's Vietnam." *The Atlantic*, January 1985.
Murray, Charles. "The Domino That Didn't Fall." *The Atlantic*, November 1984.
Musil, Robert K. "Manipulating the MIAs." *The Nation*, October 9, 1976.

Naipaul, V. S. "An Island Betrayed." *Harper's*, March 1984.
Nardin, Terry, and Jerome Slater. "Vietnam Revised." *World Politics*, April 1981.
National Veterans' Law Center. *Self-Help Guide on Agent Orange*. Veterans Education Project, Inc., 1983.
NBC News. "Meet the Press." Broadcast November 19, 1967. Transcript.
Newfarmer, Richard, ed. *From Gunboats to Diplomacy*. Johns Hopkins Univ. Pr., 1984.
Ngo Vinh Long. "Rewriting Vietnamese History." *Journal of Contemporary Asia* 10, no. 3 (1980).
Nguyen Lan, and Lynell Burmark-Parasuraman. *The Process of Americanization: Problems of the Vietnamese Refugees*. Alameda County Superintendent of Schools Office, 1981.
Nguyen Long, with Harry Kendall. *After Saigon Fell*. Institute of East Asian Studies, 1981.
Nguyen Ngoc Ngan, with E. E. Richey. *The Will of Heaven*. Dutton, 1982.
Nguyen Van Canh, with Earle Cooper. *Vietnam Under Communism, 1975–1982*. Hoover Inst. Pr., 1983.
Nixon, Richard M. *No More Vietnams*. Arbor House, 1985.

O'Ballance, Edgar. *The Wars in Vietnam 1954–1980*. Hippocrene Books, 1981.
O'Brien, Tim. *Going After Cacciato*. Dell, 1975.
—————. "The Violent Vet." *Esquire*, December 1979.
O'Daniel, Larry J. *Missing in Action*. Arlington House, 1979.
Osborne, John. *White House Watch: The Ford Years*. New Republic Bks., 1977.
—————. "White House Watch: Mayaguez Questions." *The New Republic*, June 7, 1975.

Palmer, Gen. Bruce, Jr. *The 25-Year War*. Univ. of Kentucky Pr., 1984.
Pao-min Chang. *Beijing, Hanoi, and the Overseas Chinese*. Institute of East Asian Studies, University of California, Berkeley, 1983.
Pate, James L. "CMA in Central America." *Soldier of Fortune*, January 1985.
Pike, Douglas. "Inside Vietnam." *Strategic Review*, Summer 1978.
—————. "Southeast Asia and the Superpowers: The Dust Settles." *Current History*, April 1983.
—————. "The USSR and Vietnam." *Asian Survey*, December 1979.
Pilisuk, Marc. "The Legacy of the Vietnam Veteran." *Journal of Social Issues* 31, no. 4 (1975).
Podhoretz, Norman. "The Present Danger." *Commentary*, March 1980.
—————. *Why We Were in Vietnam*. Simon & Schuster, 1982.
"Pol Pot's Interview with Yugoslav Journalists." *Journal of Contemporary Asia* 8, no. 3 (1978).
Ponchaud, François. *Cambodia Year Zero*. Penguin/Holt, Rinehart & Winston, 1978.
"Prisoners of Conscience." *The Progressive*, October 12, 1982.

Rabe, David. *The Basic Training of Pavlo Hummel*. Viking Pr., 1969.

Ranney, Austin, ed. *The American Elections of 1980*. American Enterprise Institute for Public Policy Research, 1981.
Ravenal, Earl. "Consequences of the End Game in Vietnam." *Foreign Affairs*, July 1975.
"Resisters Without a Draft." *The New Republic*, December 13, 1982.
Robinson, Michael J., and Margaret Sheehan. *Over the Wire and on TV*. Russell Sage Foundation, 1983.
Rostow, W. W. *The Diffusion of Power*. Macmillan, 1972.
Rubin, Barry. *Paved With Good Intentions*. Oxford Univ. Pr., 1980.
Ruscio, Alain. *Vivre au Vietnam*. Editions Sociales, 1981.

Sack, John. M. NAL, 1966.
Sagan, Ginetta, and Stephen Denney. *Violations of Human Rights in the Socialist Republic of Vietnam*. Aurora Foundation, 1983.
Saikal, Amin. *The Rise and Fall of the Shah*. Princeton Univ. Pr., 1980.
St. Cartmail, Keith. *Exodus Indochina*. Heinemann, 1983.
Sanders, Clinton. "The Portrayal of War and the Fighting Man in Novels of the Vietnam War." *The Journal of Popular Culture*, Winter 1969.
Sanders, Sol, and William Henderson. "The Consequences of Vietnam." *Orbis*, Spring 1977.
Shaplen, Robert. "Return to Vietnam (Part One)." *New Yorker*, April 22, 1985.
—————. "Return to Vietnam (Part Two)." *New Yorker*, April 29, 1985.
—————. *The Road From War*. Harper & Row, 1970.
Shawcross, William. "The Burial of Cambodia." *New York Review of Books*, May 10, 1984.
—————. *The Quality of Mercy*. Simon & Schuster, 1984.
—————. *Sideshow*. Simon & Schuster, 1979.
Snepp, Frank. *Decent Interval*. Random, 1977.
Starr, Paul. *The Discarded Army*. Charterhouse, 1973.
Steel, Ronald. *Walter Lippmann and the American Century*. Atlantic–Little, Brown, 1980.
Steele, Jonathan. *Soviet Power*. Simon & Schuster, 1983.
Suid, Lawrence. *Guts and Glory*. Addison-Wesley, 1978.
Summers, Harry G. *On Strategy: The Vietnam War in Context*. Presidio Pr., 1982.
—————. "What Did You Do in Vietnam, Grandpa?" *Army*, November 1978.
Swain, Jon. "Diary of a Doomed City." *Sunday Times* (London), May 11, 1975.

Taylor, Maxwell D. *Swords and Plowshares*. Norton, 1972.
Thayer, Carlyle A. "Vietnam's New Pragmatism." *Current History*, April 1983.
Thompson, Margaret, ed. *President Carter 1980*. Congressional Quarterly, Inc., 1981.
Thompson, W. Scott, and Donaldson D. Frizzell, eds. *The Lessons of Vietnam*. Crane, Russak & Co., 1977.
Those Who Leave (The "problem of Vietnamese refugees"). Vietnam Courier, 1979.
Todd, Olivier. "Comment Hanoi nous a trahis." *L'Express*, June 14, 1980.
"Triple Ripples from the Mayaguez." *National Review Bulletin*, June 13, 1975.
Truong Nhu Tang. "The Myth of a Liberation." *New York Review of Books*, October 21, 1982.
Truong Nhu Tang, with David Chanoff and Doan Van Toai. *A Vietcong Memoir*. Harcourt Brace Jovanovich, 1985.
Tucker, Robert W. "Oil and American Power—Three Years Later." *Commentary*, January 1977.
—————. "The Purposes of American Power." *Foreign Affairs*, Summer 1980.
Turley, William S., and Jeffrey Race. "The Third Indochina War. *Foreign Policy*, Spring 1980.
Twentieth Century Fund Task Force on Policies Toward Veterans. *Those Who Served*. Twentieth Century Fund, 1975.

U.S. Committee for Refugees. *Vietnamese Boat People*. American Council for Nationalities Service, February 1984.

Vance, Cyrus. *Hard Choices*. Simon & Schuster, 1983.
Van Devanter, Lynda, with Christopher Morgan. *Home Before Morning*. Warner Bks., 1983.
Van Tien Dung, Sr. Gen. *Our Great Spring Victory*. Translated by John Spragens, Jr. Monthly Review Pr., 1977.
Vickery, Michael. *Cambodia 1975–1982*. South End Pr., 1984.
—————. "Democratic Kampuchea—CIA to the Rescue." *Bulletin of Concerned Asian Scholars* 14, no. 4 (1982).
Vietnam 1975–1979. Etudes Vietnamiennes, no. 58 (1980).

Wain, Barry. *The Refused*. Simon & Schuster, 1981.
WGBH-TV. *Vietnam: A Television History*. Part 7, Tet. Transcript. 1983.
White, Peter T. "Kampuchea Awakens from a Nightmare." *National Geographic*, May 1982.
Wilcox, Fred A. *Waiting for an Army to Die*. Vintage Bks., 1983.
Wilson, James. *Vietnam in Prose and Film*. McFarland & Co., 1982.
Woodley, Richard. "Killing Time with the War Dreamers." *Esquire*, August 1976.

Yi Jun. "The Sino-Vietnamese War." *Wide Angle*, March 16, 1979.

Zegovia, Donald S., ed. *Soviet Policy in East Asia*. Yale Univ. Pr., 1983.

II. Government and Government-Sponsored Published Reports

Foreign Broadcast Information Service. *Yellow Book*. December 1978–March 1979.
Hammond, Richard. *National Survey of Veterans Summary Report*. Office of Controller, Reports and Statistics Service, Veterans' Administration, 1980.
Hawk, David. *Statement Before the Subcommittee on Human Rights and International Organizations of the Committee on Foreign Affairs, United States House of Representatives, November 16 and 17, 1983*. GPO, 1983.

Hosmer, Stephen T. *Viet Cong Repression And Its Implications for the Future*. Rand Corporation, 1970.

Le Gro, Col. William E. *Vietnam from Cease-Fire to Capitulation*. Indochina Monographs, U.S. Army Center of Military History, 1981.

Turley, William S. "Vietnam Since Reunification." *Problems of Communism*, March–April 1977.

U.S. Department of Commerce, Bureau of the Census. *Statistical Abstract of the United States 1985*. GPO, 1984.

Veterans' Administration. *Data on Vietnam-Era Veterans*. Office of Controller, Reports and Statistics Service, Veterans' Administration, September 1977.

_____ . *Legacies of Vietnam: Comparative Adjustment of Veterans and their Peers*. GPO, 1981 .

III. Newspapers and Periodicals

The authors consulted the following newspapers and periodicals: *Boston Globe, Congressional Record, Department of State Bulletin, Far Eastern Economic Review, Newsweek, New York Times, Soldier of Fortune, Time, Wall Street Journal,* and *Washington Post* (1975–1985 inclusive).

IV. Interviews

Elizabeth Becker, *Washington Post* correspondent.
Vincente "Ben" Blaz, Representative, U.S. Congress.
Geoffrey M. Boehm, former Warrant Officer and helicopter pilot, 1st Air Cavalry.
John M. Boyle, Ph.D., Harris & Associates.
William Bundy, former Assistant Secretary of State.
Dale Dye, Executive Editor, *Soldier of Fortune*.
Matt Franjola, Associated Press correspondent.
Roger Hilsman, former Assistant Secretary of State.
Roy Innis, National Director, Congress of Racial Equality.
Karl D. Jackson, Professor of Political Science, University of California at Berkeley.
Le Thanh Dau, Vietnamese refugee.
Robert Reynolds, Massachusetts Vietnam-Era Veterans' Coordinator.
Al Rockoff, free-lance photographer.
Walt Whitman Rostow, former Special Assistant to the President.
Sichan Siv, Minister Counsellor, Khmer People's National Liberation Front.
Clark Smith, Winter Soldier Archives.
Mary Stout, former nurse, 2d Surgical Hospital, Cu Chi and National Membership Director, Vietnam Veterans of America.
Tran Trong Khanh, Press Secretary, Permanent Mission of the Socialist Republic of Vietnam to the United Nations.

Map Credits

All maps prepared by Diane McCaffery. Sources are as follows:
p. 65—Chanda, Nayan, "Cambodia: Fifteen days that shook Asia," *Far Eastern Economic Review*, January 19, 1979, p. 11.
p. 122—Carter, Jimmy, *Keeping Faith*, Bantam, 1982, p. 508.

Photography Credits

Cover Photograph
John Ficara—Woodfin Camp & Associates

The New Vietnam
pp. 7–9, Photoreporters. p. 11, Colin Campbell. p. 13, John Spragens, Jr., Collection. p. 15, Courtesy Harcourt Brace Jovanovich, Publishers. p. 16, top, Roger Pic/Gamma-Liaison; bottom, Marc Riboud—Magnum. p. 17, Thomas Billhardt, Berlin, GDR. pp. 21–22, Marc Riboud—Magnum. p. 23, Abbas—Magnum. p. 25, Marc Riboud—Magnum.

Exodus Vietnam
p. 27, Jacques Pavlovsky—SYGMA. pp. 29–31, Bryan Grigsby. p. 33, K. Caugler—U.N.H.C.R. pp. 34–35, Jacques Pavlovsky—SYGMA. pp. 39–41, Alain Dejean—SYGMA. p. 42, Herman J. Kokojan—Black Star.

Khmer Rouge Takeover
p. 44, Ennio Iacobucci, Rome. pp. 46–47, © Al Rockoff. p. 48, top, AP/Wide World; bottom, Agence Vietnamienne d'Information. p. 49, Borel/Gamma-Liaison.

Revolution Against Revolution
p. 51, Fritz Sitte, Villach, Austria. pp. 52–53, SYGMA. p. 55, Courtesy of Cornell University Libraries. p. 57, Alain Taieb Collection—SYGMA. p. 59, SYGMA. pp. 60–61, David Hawk Collection. pp. 63–66, Japan Press Photos. p. 70, top, James Adamson—SYGMA; bottom, UPI/Bettmann Newsphotos. p. 71, James Adamson—SYGMA. p. 72, top, Japan Press Photos; bottom, Eastfoto.

Cambodia Aftermath
pp. 74–77, Philip Jones Griffiths—Magnum. p. 79, © Marcia Weinstein. p. 81, © 1985 Daniel Burstein—Contact.

The Shape of Indochina
p. 83, Marc Riboud. p. 84, Robin Moyer—Black Star. p. 85, © Robin Moyer. p. 87, Gian Micalessin—Albatross Press Agency, Trieste. p. 88, Nihon Denpa News, Ltd. p. 89, © Alexander Bowie. p. 92, top, © Tim Page. pp. 92, bottom, 93, Thomas Billhardt, Berlin, GDR. pp. 94–95, © Alexander Bowie.

Vietnam Ten Years After
pp. 97–103, © Tim Page.

Vietnam and the American Spirit
p. 105, UPI/Bettmann Newsphotos. p. 107, By permission of Bill Mauldin and Will-Jo Associates, Inc. p. 108, U.S. Navy. p. 109, David Hume Kennerly, courtesy of Gerald R. Ford Library. p. 110, Cilo/Gamma-Liaison. p. 111, J. P. Laffont—SYGMA. p. 112, Henri Bureau—SYGMA. p. 113, *Boston Globe*. p. 116, UPI/Bettmann Newsphotos. p. 119, François Lochon/Gamma-Liaison. pp. 120–21, top, © 1985 David Burnett—Contact. p. 121, bottom, AP/Wide World. p. 123, Heikki Kotilaineu—Photoreporters.

"When Johnny Comes Marching Home"
p. 125, *U.S. News and World Report*, courtesy of the Library of Congress. p. 126, AP/Wide World. p. 127, Alain Keler—SYGMA. p. 129, Robin Hood. pp. 132–33, Co Rentmeester—LIFE Magazine, © 1970, Time Inc. p. 135, top, James D. Wilson—*Newsweek;* bottom, Gordon Baer, courtesy of Black Star. p. 139, UPI/Bettmann Newsphotos. p. 141, top, Mike Goldwater—NETWORK; bottom, Wendy Watriss. p. 143, © David Munro. p. 145, Sal Lopes.

The Salute to Vietnam Veterans
p. 147, Everett C. Johnson—Folio Inc. p. 148, top, © 1985 David Burnett—Contact; bottom, Diana Walker/Gamma-Liaison. p. 149, Dane Penland— © Smithsonian Institution. p. 150, © 1985 Louie Psihoyos—Contact. p. 151, top, John Ficara—Woodfin Camp & Associates; bottom, Jeff Tinsley— © Smithsonian Institution. p. 152, © 1985 Louie Psihoyos—Contact. p. 153, © Al Rockoff.

Recriminations and Reassessments
p. 155, George W. Gardner. p. 157, top, Jim Kalett, courtesy of Simon and Schuster; bottom, courtesy of University of Massachusetts, Amherst. p. 158, AP/Wide World. p. 159, top, Philip Jones Griffiths—Magnum; bottom, U.S. Army. p. 163, WGBH, Boston. p. 164, Bernard Gotfryd—Woodfin Camp & Associates. p. 167, The Museum of Modern Art/Film Stills Archive. p. 168, © Nancy Moran. p. 169, Philip Jones Griffiths—Magnum.

The Legacy of Vietnam
pp. 171–73, left, AP/Wide World. p. 173, center, courtesy of University of Georgia. p. 173, right, 174–75, UPI/Bettmann Newsphotos. p. 179, © Harry Benson. p. 180, Eli Reed—Magnum. p. 182, top, Abbas—Magnum; bottom, Wally McNamee—Woodfin Camp & Associates. p. 183, © 1985 David Burnett—Contact. p. 185, Janice Rogovin.

Acknowledgments

Boston Publishing Company would like to acknowledge the kind assistance of the following people: Dorothy Bacon, Time-Life Bureau, London; Dick Berry, Tokyo; Dr. Arthur Blank, national director, VA Readjustment Counseling Service, Washington, D.C.; Charles W. Dunn, professor and chairman, Department of Celtic Languages, Harvard University; David Hawk, director, Cambodian Documentation Commission; Elisabeth Kraemer-Singh, Time-Life Bureau, Bonn; Ann Natanson, Time-Life Bureau, Rome; Sophie Quinn-Judge, Bangkok; John Spragens, Jr.; Rick Weidman, government liaison, Vietnam Veterans of America, Washington, D.C.

Index

Names, Acronyms, Terms

Agent Orange—a chemical defoliant widely used in Vietnam to deny jungle cover to the enemy. Named after the color-coded stripe painted around the barrels in which it was stored.

Angka—"the Organization." The generic name used by the Communist party of Kampuchea to refer to itself.

ARVN—Army of the Republic of Vietnam (South Vietnam).

ASEAN—Association of Southeast Asian Nations (Thailand, Singapore, Malaysia, Indonesia, the Philippines, and Brunei), formed in 1967.

CGDK—Coalition Government of Democratic Kampuchea, the 1982 anti-Vietnam coalition joining the Khmer Rouge, KPNLF, and Sihanoukist forces.

Charlie—GI slang from "Victor Charlie," the U.S. military term for Vietcong.

CIA—Central Intelligence Agency.

COMECON—Council for Mutual Economic Assistance; the Soviet bloc joined by Vietnam in 1978.

containment—U.S. political and military strategy first proposed by State Department analyst George F. Kennan in 1947 as a means of containing Soviet communism.

COSVN—Central Office for South Vietnam. Communist military and political headquarters for southern South Vietnam.

CPK—Communist party of Kampuchea.

CPT—Communist party of Thailand.

Cultural Revolution—collective name for series of purges of Chinese individuals and institutions begun in 1965 with Mao Tse-tung's approval.

Democratic Kampuchea—name given Cambodia by the victorious Khmer Rouge.

DRV—Democratic Republic of Vietnam. The government of Ho Chi Minh, provisionally confined to North Vietnam by the Geneva accords of 1954.

free fire zone—territory designated by the government of South Vietnam to be completely under enemy control, thus permitting unlimited use of firepower against anyone in the zone. Such zones did not usually include populated areas.

Ho Chi Minh City—name given Saigon following its takeover by the Vietnamese Communists.

Ho Chi Minh Trail—the main North Vietnamese logistical and supply pipeline into South Vietnam during the war.

ICBM—intercontinental ballistic missile.

Khmer Rouge—orginally members of the Pracheachon, the Cambodian leftist party. Named "Khmers Rouges" by Sihanouk to distinguish them from the right-wing "blues." Later the insurgents of the CPK.

KNUFNS—Kampuchea National United Front for National Salvation, a "front" of Cambodian rebels formed by Vietnam in December 1978 to oppose the Pol Pot government.

KPNLF—Khmer People's National Liberation Front, anti-Vietnam Cambodians under the leadership of former Prime Minister Son Sann.

Lao Dong party—Vietnam Worker's party (Marxist-Leninist party of North Vietnam). Founded by Ho Chi Minh in May 1951. Absorbed the Vietminh and was the ruling party of the DRV.

LZ—landing zone.

MACV—Military Assistance Command, Vietnam. U.S. command over all U.S. military activities in Vietnam, originated in 1962.

MIA—missing in action.

Military Management Committee—supervisory group established by Hanoi after the victory in 1975 to take charge of the Saigon region.

MX—missile-experimental. Missile program, part of Reagan administration's plans for "strategic modernization" of U.S. military forces.

NCO—noncommissioned officer.

New Economic Zones—agricultural areas and jungle lands that Vietnam hoped to recover and cultivate.

NLF—Communist National Liberation Front in South Vietnam.

OPEC—Organization of Petroleum Exporting Countries.

Operation Outreach—a counseling program for Vietnam veterans established by the U.S. Congress in 1979.

order of battle—the arrangement and disposition of military units deployed for battle.

pacification—unofficial term given to various programs of the South Vietnamese and U.S. governments to destroy enemy influence in the villages and gain support for the government of South Vietnam.

Pathet Lao—Laotian Communist insurgents who came to power in 1974.

PAVN—People's Army of Vietnam. Originally North Vietnam's army. Later the army of Vietnam.

Pentagon Papers—a secret U.S. government history of the Vietnam War commissioned by Secretary of Defense McNamara in 1967 and leaked to the press by Daniel Ellsberg in 1971.

Phoenix program (Phung Hoang)—a South Vietnamese intelligence program advised by the U.S. military, the Phoenix program was designed to neutralize the Vietcong infrastructure through identification and arrest or assassination of key party cadres.

PLA—People's Liberation Army (of China).

PRG—Provisional Revolutionary Government. Established by the NLF in 1969.

PRK—People's Republic of Kampuchea. Vietnam-sponsored government of Cambodia, under President Heng Samrin.

PTSD—Post-Traumatic Stress Disorder, experienced by some American veterans of the Vietnam War.

RGNUC—Royal Government of National Union of Cambodia, nominally headed by Prince Sihanouk. The front organization for the Khmer Rouge during the civil war.

RVNAF—Republic of Vietnam Armed Forces.

SAM—surface-to-air missile.

SEATO—Southeast Asia Treaty Organization. Organized in 1954 between Thailand, Pakistan, and the Philippines and the U.S., Britain, France, Australia, and New Zealand to form an alliance against Communist subversion, especially in Indochina.

Socialist Republic of Vietnam—name given to reunified Vietnam by the National Assembly in 1976.

Tet offensive—a major NLF offensive of January 1968 against cities and military installations throughout South Vietnam; launched during Tet, the Vietnamese New Year.

Urgent Fury—code name for U.S. invasion of Grenada in 1983.

VC—Vietcong. Originally derogatory slang for the NLF; a contraction of Vietnam Cong San (Vietnamese Communist).

VCP—Vietnam Communist party. Name Ho Chi Minh gave his party in 1930. It was reassumed by the Lao Dong party at the 1976 Fourth Party Congress.

Vietnam Syndrome—term coined by Richard Nixon to describe what he considered to be the global retrenchment of U.S. foreign policy in the wake of the Vietnam War.